W9-BTD-123

THE
LAST WARLORD

The Life and Legend of Dostum,
the Afghan Warrior Who Led US Special Forces
to Topple the Taliban Regime

BRIAN GLYN WILLIAMS, PhD

CHICAGO
REVIEW
PRESS

NEW HANOVER COUNTY
PUBLIC LIBRARY
201 CHESTNUT STREET
WILMINGTON, NC 28401

Copyright © 2013 by Brian Glyn Williams
All rights reserved
Published by Chicago Review Press, Incorporated
814 North Franklin Street
Chicago, Illinois 60610
ISBN 978-1-61374-800-8

Interior design: PerfecType, Nashville, TN

Library of Congress Cataloging-in-Publication Data

Williams, Brian Glyn.
  The last warlord : the life and legend of Dostum, the Afghan warrior who led US
special forces to topple the Taliban regime / Brian Glyn Williams, PhD.
    pages cm
  Summary: "In The Last Warlord, scholar Brian Glyn Williams takes Westerners
inside the world of general Abdul Rashid Dostum, one of the most powerful of
the Afghan warlords who have dominated the country since the Soviet invasion.
Based on lengthy interviews with Dostum and his family and subcommanders, as
well as local chieftains, mullahs, elders, Taliban enemies and prisoners of war, and
women's rights activists, The Last Warlord tells the story of Dostum's rise to power
from peasant villager to the man who fought a long and bitter war against the
Taliban and Al Qaeda fanatics who sought to repress his people. The book details
how, after 9/11, the CIA contacted the mysterious Mongol warrior to help US Special Forces wage a covert, horse-mounted war in the mountains of Afghanistan
that ended in a stunning victory; how Dostum was later marginalized by US and
Afghan leaders; and how sensational media accounts have made him the object of
rampant mythologizing. With the United States drawing down troops in 2014 and
Dostum poised to re-enter the world stage to fight a resurgent Taliban, The Last
Warlord provides important historical context to the controversy swirling around
Afghanistan's warlord culture and is an essential contribution to the debate on
Afghanistan's future"-- Provided by publisher.
  ISBN 978-1-61374-800-8 (hardback)
  1. Dustum, 'Abd al-Rashid, 1954– 2. Afghanistan—Politics and govern-
ment—1989-2001. 3. Afghanistan—Politics and government—2001– 4. Warlord-
ism—Afghanistan—History 5. Taliban. I. Title.

  DS371.33.D8W55 2013
  958.104'742092--dc23
  [B]

                               2013008742

Printed in the United States of America
5 4 3 2 1

For my friends from Indiana, Wisconsin, and London:

Forbes McIntosh, Chuk Starett, Dominique Lawrenz, Sean Buckman,
Ed Lee, Mike Waterfield, Ray Szylko, Mikol Forth,
Shane and Ben Soldinger, Chee McCardle, Jake Blavat, Mike McCue,
Anton Garcia, Colleen Kanzora, and Carrie Jacob.

"It's time for a new generation who don't have blood on their hands to build our nation. Perhaps it is fitting that I am my people's last warlord."

—General Abdul Rashid Dostum

CONTENTS

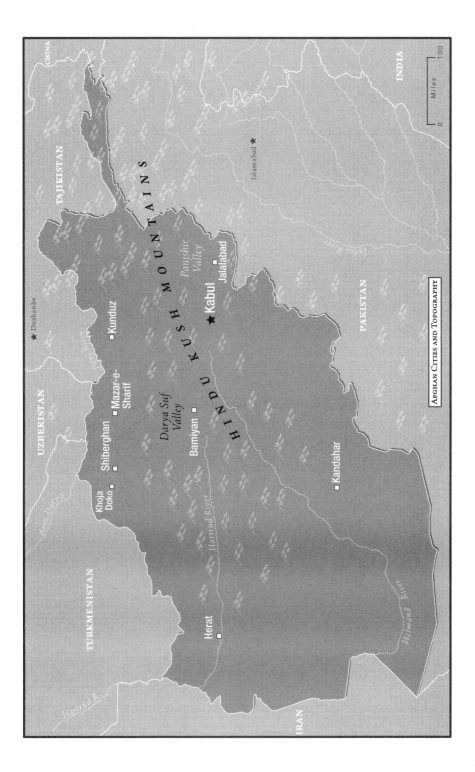

AFGHAN CITIES AND TOPOGRAPHY

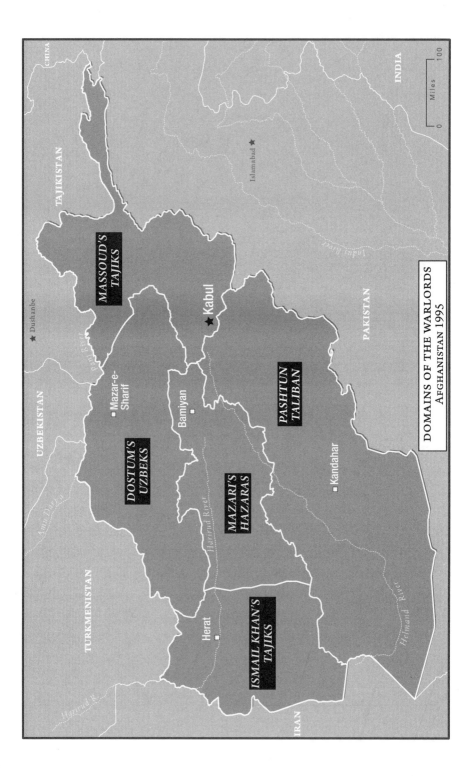

DOMAINS OF THE WARLORDS
Afghanistan 1995

PREFACE

RESEARCHING THIS BOOK on General Abdul Rashid Dostum (pronounced Doe-STUM), one of Afghanistan's most powerful and controversial warlords, was the greatest challenge of my life. To collect Dostum's story I traveled to Afghanistan four times and crossed fifteen of its war-torn provinces. There I interviewed Taliban prisoners of war, anti-Taliban field commanders, newly liberated Afghan women, US soldiers, village elders, and General Dostum himself.

The most difficult task I faced was getting my subject to open up and tell me his story. Some of the difficulties came from Dostum's reluctance to share his account of hidden intrigues, bygone legends, and past betrayals with an outsider like me. In Afghan-Uzbek warrior culture, victories and personal triumphs are celebrated; personal tragedies, dark secrets, and defeats are not.

Other difficulties stemmed from Dostum's background as an Afghan fighting man. His mind was focused on the logistics and immediacy of warfare, not his role in the greater flow of history. While Dostum might remember the effects of a B-52 bomber clearing Taliban from the path of an Uzbek cavalry charge, he typically forgot the number of horsemen riding alongside him.

The very specifics that are the lifeblood of a historian are of little consequence to those focused on staying alive in battle. While Afghans I spoke with were wonderful storytellers, they rarely offered the linear, fact-filled history Westerners expect. For these reasons the story of Dostum's rise to power, love of a woman, betrayal, and phoenixlike resurrection to free his people from the Taliban doubtless contains stories that are half legend. But for all their flaws, these accounts are a unique historical record and provide the bones for this story. I should also point out that I am a historian by training, not an investigative journalist, so I was not able to fully investigate all of the mysteries concerning Dostum's remarkable life. Considering the difficult conditions I was working in, there are bound to be questions about Dostum that I have not been able to answer here.

I was not drawn to General Dostum because he is a romanticized hero or demonized villain. When I first met the fierce general, I was reminded of the words of the great Sufi mystic poet Jalaluddin Rumi: "Show me the good wherein no evil is contained, or the evil where there is no good. Good and evil are indivisible. Good cannot exist without evil."

While we Americans are prone to simplistically dividing the world between good and bad, I was drawn to Dostum precisely because he is something in between. His story is neither black nor white; it is a story of gray. It is a story of the real world.

This perhaps is the most suitable color for a story about one man's role in a murky "war on terror" whose seeds were planted in Afghanistan long before the tragic events of 9/11.

CHRONOLOGY

1206   Genghis Khan unites the Mongol nomads for world conquest.

1300s   The Mongol rulers of Russia gradually convert from paganism to a moderate version of Sufi mystical Islam under the ruler Uzbek Khan.

1502   The Mongol Golden Horde, which rules Russia, is overthrown.

1512   After winning the battle of Kul-i-Malik, the Uzbeks, a migrating splinter group from the Golden Horde, conquer the heart of Central Asia, Turkistan. Uzbek tribes settle in what would eventually become known as Uzbekistan and northern Afghanistan.

1864   The Uzbeks living north of the Amu Darya River are conquered by the Russian Empire.

1881   The Uzbeks to the south of the Amu Darya are definitively conquered by the Afghan Pashtuns and brought into the state of Afghanistan with great brutality.

1924   The Uzbeks of the former Russian Empire are given their own Soviet republic known as Uzbekistan by the new Communist government.

1954   Abdul Rashid, the boy who will later become known as Dostum, is born.

1968   Abdul Rashid leaves school to work in the oil and gas refineries of Shiberghan.

1974–76   Abdul Rashid completes his two-year national service in the Afghan Army. He joins the elite 444 Commando Unit based in Jalalabad.

1976–78   Dostum works in the gas and oil refineries of Shiberghan.

**April
1978**   President Mohammad Daoud Khan is overthrown by the Afghan Communist party.

**Fall of
1978**   Abdul Rashid joins the Afghan Communist Army in the place of his brother and, during his subsequent time of service, earns the nom de guerre "Dostum."

**September
1979**   Haifzullah Amin, the head of the radical Khalqi branch of the Afghan Communist Party, is declared president. The Khalqis inaugurate unpopular reforms leading to further rebellion from insurgents known as the mujahideen or *ashrars*.

**December 25,
1979**   The Soviet Union invades Afghanistan to prevent the Islamist mujahideen rebels from overthrowing the Communist government. Soon thereafter the moderate Parchami Communist faction comes to power and promotes ethnic leaders, including Dostum.

1987   Dostum's tribal militia is upgraded to the Fifty-Third Division, and he is given the Hero of Afghanistan award by the Afghan government for his anti-insurgent activities.

February 15,

1989   The Soviet Union withdraws from Afghanistan in defeat after losing more than fourteen thousand troops. Many expect a swift mujahideen victory.

Spring

1989   Dostum and his men play a key role in the Afghan government's defeat of the mujahideen in the eastern city of Jalalabad. This victory leads to a three-year stalemate between the former Communist government and the mujahideen rebels.

December 25,

1991   The Soviet Union falls. The Afghan government of President Mohammad Najibullah is shortly thereafter cut off from Soviet funds and becomes unable to pay its troops.

April

1992   Dostum and Massoud jointly overthrow the Najibullah government, which has begun to disarm non-Pashtun militias.

Fall of

1992   Dostum is excluded from the new mujahideen government. In response he establishes a de facto sub-state on the plains of northern Afghanistan.

January

1994   Dostum and Hekmatyar try to overthrow Rabbani's Tajik-dominated mujahideen government.

Summer
1994   The militant Pashtun movement known as the Taliban is formed in southern Afghanistan.

1995   The Taliban conquer Ismail Khan's sub-state based in the western town of Herat.

1996   The Taliban conquer Kabul and give sanctuary to Osama bin Laden's terrorist organization.

Spring
1996   Dostum and Massoud unite to create the Northern Alliance opposition, a group of moderate northern fighters of the Taliban.

Spring
1997   Malik betrays Dostum and allows the Taliban to briefly take Mazar-e-Sharif.

August
1998   Dostum is beaten a second time by the Taliban and forced into exile in Turkey. Soon thereafter the Hazara lands fall to the Taliban, leaving just Massoud's enclave in the northeast free of Taliban rule.

Spring
1999   Massoud's capital of Taloqan falls to the Taliban.

April
2001   Massoud warns the Americans, "If President Bush doesn't help us, then these terrorists will damage the United States and Europe very soon—and it will be too late." The United States does not arm Massoud or supply him with funds.

April

2001 Dostum returns from exile to fight the Taliban from the mountains around the Darya Suf Valley.

Summer

2001 Dostum seizes the Zhari District from the Taliban. They respond by diverting thousands of troops from the front to fight against Massoud and put down his insurgency.

September 9,

2001 Massoud, the mastermind behind the Northern Alliance opposition to the Taliban, is killed by al-Qaeda terrorists.

September 11,

2001 The US mainland is attacked by al-Qaeda terrorists.

October

2001 A CIA Special Activities team infiltrates Dostum's mountain base to arrange joint operations against the Taliban.

October 19,

2001 Green Beret A-Team ODA 595 infiltrates Dostum's rebel zone.

November 5,

2001 Dostum's horsemen launch the decisive cavalry charge of Bai Beche, leading to the fall of the Taliban.

November 9–10,

2001 Dostum and his allies break out of the mountains and seize the city of Mazar-e-Sharif. This leads to the fall of the Taliban army in the north.

November 13,

2001 Kabul falls to Fahim Khan's Tajik forces.

November 23,

2001   The last Taliban holdouts in the north surrender at Kunduz.

December 22,

2001   Hamid Karzai, a Pashtun, is sworn in as interim president of post-Taliban Afghanistan.

2002   Dostum is marginalized by the Karzai government and its US backers, since he is a warlord.

2013   Dostum and other Northern Alliance warlords begin preparing their armed networks to fight the Taliban in anticipation of the US withdrawal from Afghanistan in 2014.

THE
LAST WARLORD

1

THE WARLORD OF MAZAR

"When we heard about the terrorists' attacks on your
country's towers, there was this strange silence.
At that moment we all sensed everything was about
to change. . . . We sensed that the Americans
would be coming to Afghanistan."

—General Abdul Rashid Dostum,
anti-Taliban commander of the
Northern Alliance opposition

**MAZAR-E-SHARIF, THE PLAINS OF NORTHERN AFGHANISTAN.
SUMMER 2003.**

As our Russian-made jeep pushed its way through the crowds that thronged
the streets of this dusty Afghan city, I sneaked a peek at the Uzbek gunmen
sitting on either side of me. The soldier on my right seemed to be staring
out the window at the usual backdrop of dirty children, bicycling townsmen,
burqa-clad women, and camels, so he became the target of my furtive glances.

3

Watching him out of the corner of my eye, I tried hard not to focus on the AK-47 assault rifle sitting on his lap with its barrel pointing in my direction.

Then I noticed the most intriguing feature of the gun. There, underneath the gunman's dirty hand, I spied a sticker that he had affixed to the wooden stock of his rifle. It was a decal of a scantily clad Indian dancer or perhaps a Bollywood actress. Staring at the sticker, I asked myself, *Is that a talisman of protection? Representation of forbidden fruit? Or simply a way to blunt the lethality of an instrument designed to kill?*

The incongruity of the sticker and the weapon brought to my mind the Taliban soldiers, whose favorite means of conveyance had been Toyota Hilux Surf pickup trucks. Never before had there been a less apt brand name for a "technical" military vehicle. The average Toyota Hilux Surf came decorated with standard-issue pastel colors more suited for Miami's South Beach than the deserts of Afghanistan. The images of turbaned Taliban troopers, wearing amulets to ward off the evil eye and riding in the back of these brightly colored Japanese pickup trucks, would have been laughable had the Talibs not brought so much misery to the Afghan people.

But as I had come to discover during my brief time in this land, such bizarre blending of things Western-modern and Afghan-traditional did not seem to bother the Afghans; on the contrary, it defined them.

I realized at that moment that, if I was to truly understand the Afghans, I would have to accept such seeming contradictions with the same shrug of the shoulders that they did. This was how things were done in this country, which seemed to be trapped somewhere between the Middle Ages and the twenty-first century.

I sensed that for all my initial frustration with the Afghan way of doing things, I was gradually coming to enjoy their easy accommodation of things both Western and Afghan. If you judged the Afghans solely by their strange admixtures or their outward appearance, you missed the chance to probe beneath the surface and enter their world.

I realized that this rule of thumb certainly applied to the *jang salars*, the warlords of whom so much has been written in the press. While the warlords had been described in frightening abstract terms, I felt the urge to probe deeper to see who they were as three-dimensional human beings. I suspected that the warlords, who were as fundamental a part of life in Afghanistan as the video stores and beauty salons that had sprung up since the overthrow of the Taliban, had stories of their own to tell.

My quest to understand one warlord in particular had driven me from my safe home in Boston to a shrine town located in Afghanistan's frontier on the vast plains of Inner Asia. As a scholar of Central Asia, I was drawn to General Abdul Rashid Dostum, a Northern Alliance Uzbek commander whose exploits eerily mimicked those of his Turkic and Mongol ancestors. As I read over the ancient texts telling of the nomadic battles for control of the shrine of Mazar-e-Sharif from the Middle Ages to the nineteenth century, I was stunned by their similarity to Dostum's 2001 defeat of the Taliban. While the locals told me this was no coincidence but the fulfillment of an ancient prophecy, I was skeptical. And this scholarly skepticism had driven me across the planet to uncover the real reasons for the locals' belief that the Talibans' overthrow had been foretold in the sixteenth century.

Lost in the jumbled recollections of my long journey from Boston to the capital, Kabul, and over the Hindu Kush mountains to Mazar-e-Sharif, I was startled when my driver announced in Uzbek, "Prepare yourself, *khoja* [teacher], we've arrived. The general is waiting to see you."

With those words I understood that perhaps the most dangerous stage of my journey to understand Afghanistan and its mysteries was about to begin. It was now time to meet a man who had been described as "one of the best equipped and armed warlords, ever."[1]

Breathing deeply, I dispelled from my mind the images of war correspondents who had been killed for probing too deeply into Afghanistan's secrets, and stepped out of the truck and into the blazing sun. A cloud of fine sand instantly enveloped me as I followed my gun-toting companions across a dusty street to the general's headquarters. As usual, my Uzbek guards seemed to be completely unfazed by the heat, wind, and sand. But I

was an American scholar, not a hardened Afghan fighter, and these annoy-
ances were beginning to get to me. Blinking as I cleared a mixture of sweat
and sand from my eyes, I hid my envy of my travel companions as I took in
the sight of General Dostum's nondescript compound.

At first glance it appeared to be like any other faceless edifice in the
sprawling maze of Mazar-e-Sharif, but for one menacing detail. Unlike
the neighboring bullet-pocked mansions, this one had dozens of soldiers
planted before its entrance. As we drew near the compound, several of them
stared at me curiously while I tried to make out what they were saying about
me in their Turkic-Mongol Uzbek tongue.

To them I was obviously a *kelgindi*, a foreigner, one of that strange
breed of scruffy-bearded Westerners who had descended on their land to
help them fight their Taliban oppressors after 9/11. Or perhaps I was an aid
worker or a war correspondent from some exotic country they could never
imagine.

For me the Uzbek soldiers were yet another example of the strange
contradictions that had come to define Afghanistan. They were all armed
with Russian weaponry—AK-47s, a couple of heavy PK machine guns, and
enough rocket-propelled grenades (RPGs) to start a small war—but clad in
what appeared to be standard-issue US Army uniforms.

The soldiers' Russian weaponry was not what struck me as odd. As a
professor specializing in terrorism and ethnic violence in Central Eurasia,
I had encountered similarly armed gunmen from Kosovo to Kazakhstan.
The ubiquitous Automatic Kalashnikov 47 in particular seemed to be de
rigueur for the insurgents, thugs, paramilitaries, and child soldiers I had
run into in other war zones in the region. But Turko-Mongol militiamen
dressed like camouflaged GI Joes? That was something one didn't see
every day.

The US military had airlifted thousands of uniforms to the Northern
Alliance Uzbek fighters in the opening days of 2001's Operation Enduring Freedom. Central Command's aim had been to provide these poorly
clothed anti-Taliban tribal warriors with uniforms that would instill in

them a sense of esprit de corps. The Pentagon hoped that the green-and-black fatigues would help the Uzbeks feel and act like a bona fide army.

And not just any army—the Americans wanted the Northern Alliance Uzbeks to know that they were part of the US-led coalition to eradicate the terrorists who had just attacked the US mainland on 9/11. The uniforms proclaimed that the Uzbeks, who had a score of their own to settle with the Taliban, had the full backing of the US government in prosecuting their proxy war.

While some skeptics had ridiculed what they considered the Pentagon's unrealistic hopes for a group of ragtag Northern Alliance opposition fighters against the Taliban, others felt they had real potential. After years of neglect and isolation by the West, Dostum's Uzbek rebels were chomping at the bit to go after their hereditary enemies, the Pashtun Taliban. Now they had the full support of a vengeful global superpower that had just awoken to the terrorist threat emanating from Afghanistan.

According to the US Special Forces Green Berets who subsequently fought alongside them, the Uzbeks' camouflage uniforms seemed to have done the trick. Proudly wearing their green camos (which, incidentally, were of zero value in blending into Afghanistan's uniformly brown terrain), they had ridden off to war much as their nomadic ancestors had, vowing to avenge themselves on their Taliban enemies.

But as the Uzbek cavalry charged into battle, many predicted catastrophe. Fighters on horseback had no place on the modern battlefield, some argued. The brave Uzbek riders would be massacred by the Talibans' modern firepower just as the Polish lancers had been in World War II when they had foolishly charged the Nazis' tanks.[2] Despite all the romanticism associated with horse-mounted warfare, the era of equestrian warriors had come to an inglorious end with the advent of machine guns and mechanized armor.

But in what has to be one of the greatest upsets in modern military history, the Uzbek descendants of Genghis Khan proved the doubters wrong. In one of the most decisive campaigns of the entire war on terror, the hardy Uzbeks cut their way through one Taliban defensive line after another. Galloping through the smoke of supporting American satellite-guided bombs delivered by B-52s, they charged the Taliban's tanks, firing armor-piercing RPGs and Kalashnikovs from the hip.[3] It was said to have been pure Hollywood: Uzbek riders swerving to avoid incoming tank rounds, blowing up tanks with RPGs, and clambering onto Taliban armor to place explosive charges.

Once they had gathered their momentum, they were unstoppable—and Dostum's Uzbeks had not relented until they had liberated the holy city of Mazar-e-Sharif and brought the Taliban house of cards crashing down in a matter of weeks.[4] The US "invasion" of Afghanistan was over before Christmas and long before most US troops could be mobilized. That minor miracle begged one question: how had no more than two thousand lightly armed horsemen and a few dozen US troops defeated a Taliban force of as many as ten thousand men armed and equipped with better weapons and bolstered by fanatical al-Qaeda fighters?

The Uzbeks offered a simple answer that was classic Afghan in its self-obviousness and mixture of ancient and new. In addition to US close air support, they claimed that they had received the divine protection of *malaks* (angels) sent from the shrine of Mazar-e-Sharif to fight alongside them. Their seemingly suicidal charge had been prophesized centuries earlier by Sufi mystics. Their actions were part of a grand design that had been set in place long ago at a legendary battle between good and evil known as Kul-i-Malik (The Lake of the King).

More grounded (or perhaps more cynical) voices pointed out that the Uzbeks also had the support of a twelve-man US Special Forces A-Team code-named Tiger 02. This American Green Beret team and several US Air Force close air support combat controllers had called the fury of joint-direct-attack-ammunition bombs down from bombers and onto the Taliban as the Uzbeks charged them. If there were any heavenly beings operating in the Afghan theater of operation, they came in the form of lumbering B-52 bombers, not sword-bearing angels.[5]

Regardless of who protected them, angels or US bombers, one thing was clear. The Uzbeks' assault was the most historic cavalry action since the fateful charge of Queen Victoria's nineteenth-century Light Brigade. But far from being gunned down like their doomed British counterparts, Dostum's Uzbek horsemen had emerged victorious and changed the course of history. In so doing, they had turned military doctrine on its head.

It should also be noted that the Uzbeks and their Special Forces comrades-in-arms delivered a much-needed victory to millions of grieving Americans. In light of the dejected mood in post-9/11 America, the Battle of Mazar became an instant sensation back home in the United States. When the classified photographs of a horse-mounted American Special Forces combat controller named Bart Decker and allied Uzbeks were beamed back to Washington, one stateside analyst forwarded them to Secretary of Defense Donald Rumsfeld. Rumsfeld promptly declassified them and displayed them to the US press corps.[6]

Not to be outdone by his boss, Deputy Secretary of Defense Paul Wolfowitz publicly read a declassified after-action report from a Green Beret Tiger 02 Special Forces commander named Mark Nutsch, who rode with the Uzbeks. This colorful report was to become the most memorable eyewitness account of the entire proxy war in Afghanistan.[7] It read as follows:

> I am advising a man on how to best employ light infantry and horse cavalry in the attack against Taliban T-55s (tanks) and mortars, artillery, personnel carriers and machine guns—a tactic which I think became outdated with the introduction of the Gatling (machine) gun. (The Mujahadeen) have done this every day we have been on the ground. They have attacked with 10-round AKs per man, with PK gunners having less than 100 rounds, little water and less food. I have observed a PK gunner who walked 10-plus miles to get to the fight, who was proud to show me his artificial right leg from the knee down.
>
> We have witnessed the horse cavalry bounding over watch from spur to spur to attack Taliban strong points—the last several kilometers under mortar, artillery and PK fire. There is little medical care if injured, only

a donkey ride to the aid station, which is a dirt hut. I think (the Uzbek Mujahadeen) are doing very well with what they have. They have killed over 125 Taliban while losing only eight.

We couldn't do what we are (doing) without the close air support. Everywhere I go the civilians and Mujahadeen soldiers are always telling me they are glad the USA has come. They all speak of their hopes for a better Afghanistan once the Taliban are gone. Better go. (The local commander, Dostum) is finishing his phone call with (someone back in the States).[8]

Wolfowitz obviously appreciated the irony of the fact that the first victory in "the first war of the twenty-first century" had been won by horse-mounted Special Forces riding alongside Central Asian "tribesmen" seemingly from the Middle Ages.

However, in the media frenzy that followed the subsequent "conquest" of the Texas-sized land of Afghanistan by no more than 350 US special operators (there was no Iraq-style mass US invasion of Afghanistan), the role of the indigenous Uzbeks was soon forgotten.[9] Downplaying the Northern Alliance Uzbeks' contribution, CENTCOM (US Central Command) Commander General Tommy Franks, was to proclaim:

Tiger 02, the Special Forces team supporting General Abdul Rashid Dostum—led by a young captain, a seasoned master sergeant, and a lanky sergeant first class, whose *noms de guerre* were Mark, Paul, and Mike—fought one of the most tactically skillful and courageous small-unit actions in American military history. Facing determined enemy resistance, terrible weather, and mounting casualties among their indigenous troops, these Green Berets used maneuver and air power to destroy an army the Soviets had failed to dislodge with more than half a million men.[10]

This sort of reporting tended to overlook the decisive military role of the indigenous Uzbek ground forces, whom Tommy Franks acknowledged took "mounting casualties."[11]

Off record, however, one US Defense official admitted that without the help of Dostum's Northern Alliance Uzbeks, "I'm not sure where we'd be."[12]

As this sort of low-key report suggests, the Uzbeks were more than just the exotic backdrop for American heroism; they had provided the United States with the surrogate fighting force desperately needed to mop up the Taliban on the ground.[13]

Recalling the Afghan campaign a year and a half after the event, it occurred to me that it had actually been more than just an inspiration for the subsequent "light" invasion of Iraq by fewer troops than many wanted. It had also been the ultimate Afghan-style juxtaposition: illiterate Uzbek horsemen mounted on sixty-dollar horses, coordinating their cavalry charges with state-of-the-art US bombers flying from distant aircraft carriers. The extraordinary turn of events defined this people's casual habitation of worlds both ancient and modern.

But the Afghans themselves did not blink an eye over the whole affair. No one in Afghanistan—not even the Uzbeks' legendary commander, General Dostum—found the confluence of Medieval-style cavalry tactics and satellite-guided ammunition to be at all odd. Dostum's riders had simply considered the American Special Forces to be vengeful *malaks* sent by Allah to rain his vengeance down on the Taliban.

What *had* struck General Dostum as strange was the fact that he and his men had not been properly thanked by their coalition partners when the campaign was over. Their crucial role in providing the ground force that helped deprive al-Qaeda of its sanctuary went largely unrecognized by their American allies.

Far from acknowledging Dostum's contribution to the "transformational" campaign, critics of George W. Bush had discovered in Dostum "the blood-thirsty warlord of Mazar," a whipping boy to be used for obliquely criticizing the American president. As the White House's opponents pounced on the neoconservatives in the Bush administration for diverting the war on terror from al-Qaeda in Afghanistan to Baathist Iraq, Dostum's Taliban-killing Uzbeks became a public relations liability. While Dostum was to proudly proclaim of Central Command's head, General Tommy Franks, "He is my friend. He is a great warrior," Franks and other US military and civilian leaders decided to wash their hands of their Uzbek ally.[14]

The bad press on General Dostum soon reached proportions worthy of the *Namas*, the Central Asian battle epics of the Middle Ages. General Dostum was now defined as a warlord, and, in the new scheme of things, warlords were defined not as friends but as a threat to Afghanistan's future. As the memory of 9/11 faded and the media turned to Iraq, America no longer had the stomach for allies who were accused of killing *too many* Taliban.

War correspondents out to make a name for themselves were soon competing with one another to write outlandish stories of a bear-like general and his bizarre behavior. Their accounts invariably described him as something between Attila the Hun and a Klingon villain from an episode of *Star Trek*. The American public believed the exaggerated reports simply because few really knew Afghanistan or its various ethnic groups.

But when one American journalist claimed to have heard the sounds of people being "skinned alive" during a visit to General Dostum's compound, my commonsense meter ticked toward skepticism.[15] No one who was trying to win the support of the powerful Americans would commit the unforgivable mistake of skinning humans alive, especially with inquisitive American journalists in his compound.

But the skinning story was just the tip of the iceberg. Another journalist described Dostum as a drug baron who had blatantly built a giant concrete statue of a heroin-producing poppy plant in the center of his compound.[16] This came at a time when Afghanistan's powerful American overlords were deciding whether to launch a nationwide crackdown on opium production.

If this report did not give cause for skepticism, an Irish filmmaker soon accused Dostum of blatantly slaughtering not hundreds but as many as five thousand Taliban prisoners of war. Of course, few Westerners could travel to Afghanistan to carry out systematic investigations of his claims, and to date no investigation has been carried out.[17]

But in what was to become the most famous of these "Dostum the Warlord" stories, he was accused of running over a looter with a tank.[18] Appearing in Ahmed Rashid's 2001 bestseller *Taliban: Militant Islam, Oil, and Fundamentalism in Central Asia*, this secondhand story was to be told over and over again by subsequent writers, each time with a bloody new twist. Scott Carrier described Dostum as "a powerful warlord who is reportedly so strong that he crushed a man's skull with his bare hands, so evil that his laugh has frightened men to death, and so cruel that he tied a man to the treads of a tank and then watched as he was crushed."[19]

My favorite Dostum story, however, has to be Andrew Bushell's account of his ogreish culinary behavior. If running "prisoners," "enemies, "ethnic opponents," and others over with tanks (plural) was not bad enough, Bushell described the Uzbek warlord as a "massive man who can eat twelve chickens and drink more than two quarts of vodka at one sitting."[20]

While naive foreigners could be forgiven for believing that Afghan warlords drove tanks over their own soldiers, crushed men's skulls in their hands, built statues of opium plants in their homes, laughed people to death, and ate twelve chickens in a setting, Afghans knew better.[21] For this reason, when members of the Afghan government began to spread these outlandish stories about Dostum, I sensed something deeper afoot. As a historian, I was familiar with Afghanistan's ethnic blood feuds and had traced some of them back centuries; I began to suspect they had as much to do with the bizarre accusations as anything else. It was clearly in someone's interest to encourage the character assassination of Dostum, an ethnic leader who was as loved by his own Uzbek people as he was hated by his Pashtun enemies. My hunch was that the Americans and their NATO allies were being manipulated by hidden ethnic forces that had ruled the multiethnic country for centuries.

At that stage I was not sure who was behind the shadow campaign, but if my instincts were correct, it had wide-ranging implications for what would soon be called the forgotten war of Afghanistan. At that very moment the down-but-not-out Taliban were regrouping in the south and preparing to launch a bloody insurgency while the Americans were distracted with a new campaign known as Iraqi Freedom. Soon the Taliban would begin burning girls' schools, sending suicide bombers into crowded markets, beheading teachers, and launching swarm attacks against coalition troops. Weakening

Dostum's hold over the nearby shrine of Mazar-e-Sharif and his northern realm would facilitate a Taliban reinfiltration of this strategic area.

In this unstable atmosphere, I felt it was extremely shortsighted to antagonize such anti-Taliban leaders as Dostum, even if he was a bona fide warlord. This was an especial concern when vital American resources, including Predator aerial drones, translators, look-down spy satellites, and Special Forces troops were already being diverted from Afghanistan to the new war in Iraq.

For all of these reasons, I felt that it was imperative that I meet with General Dostum in person that summer of 2003. I needed to see for myself whether he was a genocidal drug-dealing butcher, a respected leader of a persecuted sub-Afghan ethnic group, or something in between.

If my theory was correct and he was *not* a modern-day Genghis Khan, then my hope was that he would protect me while I investigated his role in the war on terror. Only by immersing myself in his world could I uncover the truth and see if he was a threat to Afghanistan or a potential ally for the upcoming war against the regrouping Taliban insurgents. But still, I had to ask myself, *What if I was wrong about him? What if all the things that had been written about him were true?*

Pondering the very real risks involved in my lone mission, I reminded myself how vulnerable I was in this place that the US State Department had declared a no-travel zone. Regardless of what the AK-47-toting Uzbek "GI Joes" guarding Dostum's compound thought about me as I emerged from our dusty truck and approached them, I was no Special Forces operative. Truth be told, I was a thirty-five-year-old history professor at a small university in New England. For me, meeting Dostum was more than just an opportunity to engage in fieldwork on the missing ethnic history of the Afghan war. My journey was the culmination of a lifelong fascination with the nomadic heirs of the greatest conqueror of all time, Genghis Khan. It was my chance to tell the story of how the Uzbeks, the direct descendants of the Mongol Golden Horde, had charged into battle to alter the course of modern history.

Thinking back on the long journey that had taken me from my safe home in Boston to this little-traveled corner of Central Asia, I once again asked myself if I was out of my league.

But as my Uzbek guard gently nudged me toward the entrance to Dostum's compound, I knew it was too late for second-guessing. By now the general would know that an inquisitive American had made the journey over the Hindu Kush to his front door in search of answers. My future was no longer mine to decide. It was time to resign myself to my kismet and see what Dostum "the Tank Crusher" had in store for me.

2

HOW TO MEET A WARLORD

"The Department of State warns US citizens against
travel to Afghanistan. The security threat to all
US citizens in Afghanistan remains critical."

—US State Department travel advisory

I N THE GLOOM of the entrance to Dostum's compound, several Uzbek soldiers frisked me and checked the film pockets on my journalist vest for weapons. One of them discovered my camcorder and fiddled with it for a few seconds before handing it back to me with an apology. With that, I was inside the headquarters of General Dostum, the warlord who was not only the most powerful man in northern Afghanistan but one of the most important players in the ongoing political battle to decide the future of the country.

"*Kel khoja*," my gunman said to me as he led me into the compound's inner garden. Blinking as I entered the crowded, sunlit courtyard, I noticed in the center a two-story concrete building with a balcony running its entire length. I was led inexorably toward it by my guards, who appeared to grow increasingly nervous as we approached their famous general. Suddenly, a voice greeted me in English, and I recognized Ehsan Zari, Dostum's prized translator and majordomo.

"Welcome to General Dostum's home, Ibrian," he said, stumbling over my awkward-sounding foreign name so that it sounded more like the Afghan equivalent of Ibrahim. I had earlier met Zari, a linguistic wunder-kind who spoke Turkish, Uzbek, Tajik Persian, Urdu, Pashto, and English, and he had helped me arrange this meeting.

"I've told the general you are here," Zari told me, "and he has promised to meet with you. Please feel free to ask him any questions you'd like. But I should warn you, the meeting will be short. Many important *aq saqals* [tribal elders] and *qomandans* [commanders] are gathering in the court-yard for a *shura* [council meeting]. He must tend to them."

A thrill coursed through me as we made our way onto the balcony and through the crowd of distinguished *aq saqals*. I was actually going to interview General Abdul Rashid Dostum, the commander who had over-thrown the Afghan Communist government in 1992 and fought nine years later alongside the horse-mounted Green Berets of Tiger 02 to destroy the Taliban regime. It would be a coup for me, a historian, to pull off an inter-view with a man whom I defined, for better or worse, as living history. How many people could say they'd met a Turko-Mongol warlord whose resume included bringing down two Afghan governments and fighting against bin Laden back when the Saudi terrorist and the United States were still on the same side?

I realized that my awareness of the consequence of what I was about to do would give me the sense of self-importance necessary to talk to Dostum as an equal. While I was a mere assistant professor of history back home at the University of Massachusetts–Dartmouth, here in Afghanistan I would be perceived as a representative of the greatest military power on earth. I sensed that being an American gave me a certain clout with the *aq saqal* chieftains gathered on Dostum's porch. They respectfully opened ranks before me with greetings of "*Salaam alaiukum*" (peace be upon you) as I passed by.

Moving through the assembled crowd, I noticed that the elders placed their hands on their hearts and bowed their heads slightly to me as a sign of respect. I found this simple gesture touching and responded in kind, saying "*Wa alaikum es salaam*" (and peace be upon you).

Notwithstanding the respect the *aq saqal* elders directed toward me, the real focus of their attention was clearly the man sitting in a throne-like armchair at the far end of the balcony. As the crowd opened and allowed me to see him, I instantly recognized the roguish face of General Dostum. With his graying, crew-cut hair, trademark mustache, large frame, and unmistakable aura of power, he appeared even more impressive in real life than in the footage I'd seen over the years.

But on this occasion he was not dressed for war. He was wearing a tailor-made black suit with a white collared shirt rather than the army fatigues or *chapan* Uzbek riding coat I had always seen him pictured in. Comparing his suit to the turbans, beards, and padded riding coats of the village elders around him, I was once again struck by the way old and new worlds effortlessly coexisted in Afghanistan. Unlike Dostum, who appeared to be at ease wearing a modern suit to a tribal *shura*, I felt strangely anachronistic in the presence of the village elders.

I suddenly realized that I was about to be propelled from outside observer to active participant in their lives. The historian in me found this switch from an observatory to a participatory role to be somewhat unsettling. But for all my newfound reluctance to insert myself into their world, it was too late to turn back. I was now caught in the flow of history and was about to become a part of it.

Approaching Dostum respectfully with his right hand on his heart, Zari informed him that the American "correspondent" had arrived, and the general directed his gaze toward me for the first time. As he did so, all conversation on the porch ceased, and the only sound I could hear was that of my heart beating.

For some of the longest seconds of my life, Dostum stared at me without saying a word, and I had the distinct feeling he was trying to read me. As I held his gaze, I found it hard to forget that the man before me had once possessed an army of fifty thousand men. His enemies accused him of being responsible for much of the stupendous destruction I had witnessed back in Kabul before my long journey here over the Hindu Kush.

Despite his fierce reputation, Dostum seemed to be strangely approachable as he signaled for me to come through the crowd and join him.

"Welcome to Mazar-e-Sharif, my friend. I hear you've made a long journey over the mountains from Kabul to find me here," he said to me in Turkish. "I'm sure you have many questions for me because you've come all the way from America."

Then his eyes narrowed slightly, and he spoke bluntly. "But I have a question for you, my friend. Why should I trust you?"

As his eyes bored into my own, I struggled to come up with a suitable response, for I knew he had no reason to do so. I was an American, and my government had seemingly turned its back on him and his people after using them to fight the Taliban. This, after hundreds of his men had died fighting against our common enemies in a war the American media was now trumpeting as a "seamless American conquest."[1]

Knowing that the Uzbeks had heard of American news reports that had described the campaign as a "transformational victory for light US forces," I crafted my response carefully.

"There is only one reason I can think of for you to trust me, Pasha [General], and that is for the simple fact I know you and your people. You see, back home in America I am a *khoja*, a scholar. I'm not a war correspondent traveling the world in search of the story of the day. I'm a historian who is devoted to patiently unraveling the past in order to understand the present, and perhaps the future.

"I know about the *baturs* [heroes] of Shaybani Khan and their struggle to defend the holy Mazar from the Iranian Red Turbans of Shah Ismail in the ancient times. I know about the evil time of the Afghan Pashtun tyrant Amir Abdur Rahman, who subjugated your once free people.

"I've also heard about your people's suffering under the Taliban fanatics and know of your role in defending the people of the north and the holy tomb of Mazar-e-Sharif from the Talib oppressors."

Then, almost in desperation, I threw out my final pitch. "I've also heard the bad things about you and want to hear your side of the story. If you trust me and share your story with me, I'll try to be objective."

I willed General Dostum to believe me even as I heard the crowd murmuring to convey my unexpected response to those in the rear. As the impact of my words rippled through the audience, I searched Dostum's face to try to gauge their effect. But I realized with a sinking heart that there was no sign of a reaction on his countenance. For what seemed to be an eternity he stared at me without expression. The seconds crept by in painful slow motion, and it dawned on me that my whole journey might have been in vain. In the awkward silence I even began to contemplate ways to extricate myself from this potentially dangerous situation.

Then, just as I began to accept that I had said something disastrously wrong, I noticed a twinkle in Dostum's eye. Gazing at me intently, he turned slightly and spoke to one of the two commanders sitting in a place of honor by his side.

"Who would have imagined it? Perhaps a man who knows of Shaybani can write my story?" he said. "Although I am no Shaybani Khan."

Then, with a hint of humor, he gestured to me again. "But he is an *American*. Our American friends live in a world without a sense of past. Can an American write the history of an Uzbek? What do you think, Lal?"

Turning to the turbaned warrior by Dostum's side, I realized that he must be none other than Commander Lal Muhammad, Dostum's second-in-command. Lal Muhammad was the gruff field commander who had led the flank cavalry assault on Mazar-e-Sharif in November 2001. Scores of Taliban had died in his thrust on Mazar-e-Sharif, and he was almost as feared as his general. Now it seemed Commander Lal Muhammad was to determine my fate as well.

Looking at me carefully, Commander Lal made a point of assessing me before breaking into a sly grin.

"I trust him, my pasha. Allah knows it's time *somebody* from the outside heard what we have to say."

Commander Lal's words appeared to have their desired effect on Dostum, for he motioned for me to come sit by his side. As I tentatively sat down next to him, he gruffly signaled for everyone else to leave. Everyone, that is, except for Commander Lal and one other turbaned commander, whom he introduced as Fakir. I realized that the general had decided to honor me with a private interview, and I quickly retrieved my camcorder to film the whole thing. I hoped to learn how this simple Uzbek villager had risen to become the last of the four powerful warlords who had battled for control of Afghanistan.

I was brimming with questions I was not sure Dostum would be willing to answer. What was it like to have waged war alongside both the Soviets *and* the Americans? How did it feel to have consistently fought against Osama bin Laden back when the Arab fanatic was on the same side as the United States? What was his childhood like? How did one rise to become a warlord? Was it true that he was driven by painful memories of a lost love? Did he have any regrets about the lives he had taken over the years?

As a historian I wanted to record the entire interview, for I knew Dostum had rarely shared such personal details with an outsider. I also realized that no one would believe I had actually met Dostum—the warlord known to frighten men to death with his laugh—if I did not bring the evidence home with me.

As Dostum said good-bye to the departing elders, I sensed that this would be no ten-minute interview like the ones he'd granted to journalists in the past. Every instinct told me I was going to be one of the first Westerners to hear the story of the last of the quadrumvirate of warlords who had fought to control Afghanistan. As the last turbaned *aq saqals* left bowing to Dostum, he finally directed his full attention to me. Saying nothing, he motioned for one of his servants to bring me tea and something to eat. In this land, which prided itself on the rituals of hospitality, such formalities were of utmost importance.

It was only after I had a cup of green tea in my hand and Turkish biscuits on my plate that Dostum finally addressed me, speaking in an unexpectedly disarming fashion.

"These are my right-hand commanders, Lal and Fakir. If you truly want to hear it, I'll tell you a story of myself and my people, and these men will help me. They have the right to speak because they have shed their blood fighting to free us from the Taliban. They are heroes in their own right, and they've been with me from the start."

As Dostum spoke I placed my video camera on the couch beside me to film the whole thing. To my relief, he seemed neither to notice nor to care.

"I'll go back to the beginning and tell you the story of how I rose from being a simple villager to defender of the great Mazar [Tomb] of Ali and the people in the north. I will also tell you many stories of the arrival of the Pashtuns, the Russians, the Taliban, al-Qaeda, and your own countrymen in our lands."

And as he called for one of his servants to bring me some more tea, he looked me in the eye and added with a broad smile, "Make yourself comfortable, *khoja*, and I'll tell you a story of Afghanistan."

3

THE APPROACHING STORM

"America will set Afghanistan on fire."

—MULLAH MUTTAWAKIL, TALIBAN SPOKESMAN

T HE ERA OF the warlords had begun back in the final days of the 1980s jihad to expel the *Urus* (Russian) invaders from Afghanistan. While the Soviets were still in Afghanistan, most of the country's competing ethnic groups put aside their own differences and fought against the foreign forces. In the northeast, the indomitable mountain Tajiks (Persians) fought under their legendary commander Massoud, the Lion of Panjshir. In the center of the country were the Shiite Mongol Hazaras, who lived in the heights of the Hindu Kush and sometimes fought with the Soviets when not fighting amongst themselves. In the south were the fierce Aryan Pashtun tribes, Afghanistan's ruling people. While not as dangerous as Massoud's Tajiks, they turned their southern tribal lands into a killing zone for Russian *kafirs* (infidels).

In the north, however, the Turkic-Mongol Uzbeks largely fought *for* the Soviet invaders. They did so to gain independence from their Pashtun rulers, and because they were enticed by the progress made in the lands of their kin living across the border in the Soviet Socialist republic of Uzbekistan.

When the Soviet invaders withdrew and the local Afghan Communist regime finally fell in 1992, warlords like Dostum the Uzbek and Massoud the Tajik fought to gain control of the country. While these two leaders ruled their own people fairly, in the Pashtun tribal lands in the south and east, chaos prevailed. Warlords preyed on the common people and forever soiled the name of the mujahideen (anti-Soviet guerilla fighters). In the early 1990s, the Pashtun warlords carved the southern lands up into personal fiefdoms and terrorized the very people who had once supported them in their struggle against the Soviets.

Into this chaos in 1994 came a new Pashtun cleansing force—the Taliban, the Students of Islam. Moving steadily through the Pashtun tribal lands of the south, the Taliban declared jihad on the mujahideen guerillas who had recently defeated the Soviets. While many in the West mistakenly conflated the two groups, the Taliban actually began to hang ex-mujahideen "freedom fighters" who had preyed on the simple villagers ever since the Soviet retreat.

In these early days, the Taliban offered hope to the people living in the war-torn southern province of Kandahar, along with a reprieve from the excesses of the mujahideen warlords. The Taliban's reclusive leader, Mullah Omar, captured the mood of his cleansing movement when he claimed he was "fighting Muslims who had gone wrong."[1] The Taliban were the only ones capable of ridding the troubled southern provinces of the anti-Soviet warlords who had turned their weapons on their own people. While the Americans saw the mujahideen through rose-colored lenses as anti-Soviet "freedom fighters," most Pashtun tribesmen had come to see them as thugs and gunmen. For this reason, when the Taliban hung Pashtun mujahideen warlords from the barrels of their tanks, the people of the south cheered and greeted them as liberators.

But the Pashtun Taliban soon betrayed the very people who had initially believed in their mission. It quickly became obvious that the price the people of Kandahar and other southern provinces would pay for the establishment of order would be total submission to the Taliban's warped interpretation of Islam. This version of Islam was even more extreme than that of the fundamentalist mujahideen. Far from bringing hope, the Taliban puritans began to envelop the people of Kandahar in a dark version of Islam that had been incubated in the Saudi-funded madrassas of Pakistan. Gradually the Taliban switched from being liberators to oppressors.

Despite all the horrors they inflicted on the people of the south, the Taliban's policies had not initially bothered the other moderate ethnic groups living in the center and north of the country, such as the Tajiks, Hazaras, and Uzbeks. The Taliban were ethnic Pashtuns who were subjugating fellow Pashtuns in the anarchy-ridden south.

But this began to change when the Taliban started to range beyond the Pashtun lands. By 1995 the Taliban were swarming over the other ethnic provinces like a cult of medieval holy warriors. Wherever the Taliban went, they enforced draconian laws that surpassed even those of the Saudis in their severity. In a series of fatwas (religious decrees), the Taliban supreme council announced that it intended to impose a form of Saudi Wahhabi-style fundamentalism on all of Afghanistan's traditionally moderate ethnic groups. Their stated goal was to "cleanse the land of its un-Islamic practices" and inaugurate "God's rule on earth."

For most average Afghans, the fundamentalism instituted by the Taliban and sponsored by their mysterious Saudi guest, Osama bin Laden, was hell on earth. With the arrival of the black-turbaned Taliban, women who dared to work outside of the home or to walk the streets without a male relative were arrested. Men who did not grow full beards and attend mosque five times a day were publicly beaten with iron cables. And those who watched "satanic" television sets or listened to music were fined and whipped.

But that was not all. Soon the town squares and stadiums of Afghanistan became the scenes of weekly executions; those accused of being prostitutes and adulteresses, apostates, elopers, murderers, and thieves were put to death. The Taliban's harsh laws quickly transformed southern Afghanistan into a grim religious prison camp.

Beneath the fanatical Islamic exterior, the Taliban movement was also a militant ethnic movement. While few outsiders understood it, on many levels the Taliban's religiosity was a smokescreen for the re-empowerment of the Pashtun ethnic group that had long ruled Afghanistan. In this sense the Taliban were more than just Islamic fanatics. They were Pashtun ethno-warriors who used fundamentalist Islam to justify their atrocities against other ethnic groups they labeled heretics. As events were to vividly demonstrate, there were plenty of "unbeliever" ethnic groups in the multiethnic cauldron of Afghanistan deserving of "divine punishment."

But for all the success the Taliban had in overcoming the various mujahideen warlords of the Pashtun south, the flames of resistance had not been completely extinguished in the north. The northern plains and central mountains were still claimed by an alliance of non-Pashtun warlords that included Dostum the Uzbek, Massoud the Tajik, and Mazari the Hazara. Dostum controlled the northern plains from his "capital" at Mazar-e-Sharif. Mazari controlled the central Hindu Kush mountain plateau from Bamiyan, and Massoud controlled the mountains of the northeast around the Panjshir Valley.

The continued existence of this so-called Northern Alliance opposition infuriated the Taliban leadership and was considered an affront to their claim to represent God's will on earth. Not surprisingly, the Taliban came to consider crushing the ethnic opposition to be their primary mission.

And no enemy was higher on their hit list than Dostum, the secular "unbeliever" whose Uzbeks had fought *against* the mujahideen in the 1980s. The Taliban could not forgive the Pasha for daring to oppose "Allah's will on earth" during the anti-Soviet jihad when he fought for the Russians. The Taliban's reclusive one-eyed leader, Mullah Omar, had placed a price on the *kafir* leader's head soon after his forces began their conquests.

But in the years following the emergence of the Taliban, Dostum had been unwilling to part with his head. On the contrary, he seemed to have a knack for collecting those of the Taliban. Dostum held off the Taliban conquest of the northern Afghan plains for three long years with his secularist army of fifty thousand tough Uzbeks. During that period thousands of Taliban corpses were sent back to grieving Pashtun families in the south. Time and again Dostum's tough Uzbek fighters had cut off and annihilated the Taliban's incursions north of the Hindu Kush. The Pasha seemed invincible in his northern realm; whether riding into battle on horseback or leading his tank divisions, Dostum had appeared to be a modern embodiment of the Mongol khans of old.

Western military analysts at the time had felt that Dostum's skilled leadership and sheer bullheaded determination would enable the secularized lands of the north to resist the Taliban fundamentalists indefinitely. It was as if the wrath of Dostum's former Soviet masters lived on in the pro-Communist warlord as he took great pleasure in sending Taliban holy warriors to meet their paradise.

But Dostum was betrayed in 1997 by Malik, one of his own subordinates, who let the advancing Taliban armies through his front lines in the midst of a bloody battle. When the Taliban broke through his defenses, Dostum's flourishing sub-state in the north finally fell. After one bloody attempt to regain his fiefdom failed, Dostum was forced to leave his people to the mercy of the fanatics in 1998.

With his departure to exile in Turkey, the strongest member of the anti-Taliban Northern Alliance had been removed. Soon after Dostum fled, the Hazaras were overwhelmed by the Taliban as well, leaving only Massoud's Tajiks in the northeastern regions around the Panjshir Valley to fight the fanatics.

Following Dostum's defeat, the Taliban triumphantly swept through the flat lands of the north, brutally subjugating his realm and enveloping its inhabitants in their fundamentalist time warp. By the summer of 1998 the white standards of the Taliban flew over the sacred blue-domed mosque of Mazar-e-Sharif, symbolizing their belief that they had a God-ordained right to rule the plains of the north and all Afghanistan. In the process, over one hundred years of Pashtun rule was reestablished over an area known as Afghan Turkistan, and the Uzbek upstarts were put back in their place. Dostum's departure from the scene left no one in the northern plains who could lead a united resistance to the Taliban.

Facing no real, viable military opposition, the Taliban demonstrated their power with impunity via public executions of "enemies of God." Borrowing a page from the Saudi Wahhabi fundamentalists, who had perfected the spectacle of public punishments, the Taliban even took to publicly stoning their victims—often women—to death with cinder blocks. On occasion the horrified people of the north were forced to watch their own daughters or wives be crushed to death for such "crimes" as leaving the house without a *mahrem*, a male family member. Women caught wearing fingernail polish had their fingers cut off, and those who revealed bright shoes beneath their burqas were mercilessly bludgeoned with iron rods.

In response to these calamities, the people of the north made pilgrimages to the Shrine of Ali in Mazar-e-Sharif to ask for succor. But it was to no avail, for the shrine had been closed by the Taliban. The Taliban puritans hated the blue mosque. They saw its ancient rituals as a Shiite-Sufi mystical abomination and suspected that they were pre-Islamic heresies. They also understood that the shrine provided a common bond that united the diverse people of the north. To stamp out any spirit of collective resistance, the Taliban banned the ancient ceremonies and fertility rituals associated with the shrine.

As the years of torment passed, a deep sense of gloom began to permeate the occupied villages and towns of the north. Despair was especially prevalent among the previously free women who could no longer leave their homes without fear of arrest. The Uzbek and Hazara men were also humiliated by the Taliban's harsh treatment of their womenfolk. The Taliban's public whipping of their wives, mothers, and daughters infringed upon their sense of *namuz*, or pride in their ability to protect female relatives.

Behind all of these calamities, the Afghans sensed the hidden hand of the mysterious bin Laden and his army of foreign fanatics, the 055 Brigade. The Saudi terrorist had been a guest of the local Taliban since 1996 and seemed to have undue influence in their councils.

But for all their resentment toward bin Laden and Mullah Omar, the subjugated people of the north realized resistance was futile. The Taliban had the full support of the neighboring Pakistanis, the Arabs, and Afghanistan's largest and most powerful ethnic group, the Pashtuns. The northerners also realized that the odds of Western military intervention on behalf of the obscure Uzbeks, Tajiks, and Hazaras were nil. The great powers that ruled the earth were indifferent to their suffering—only Allah heard their prayers.

But as the years passed by with no signs of deliverance, it seemed to them that He did not see fit to answer their prayers. It seemed as if bin Laden's dream of transforming their homeland into an al-Qaeda al-Jihad (Base for Holy War) would be realized. With no help from the uncaring Western powers, the evil that was manifesting itself in al-Qaeda's state-within-a-state would soon spread from the Taliban Amirate of Afghanistan across the globe. When Massoud, the last Northern Alliance resistance leader left standing, was overrun, the Taliban could claim to be the only government in Afghanistan. In the process, the grand vision of a cataclysmic war of the faith that had driven bin Laden ever since his baptism by fire as an Arab mujahideen volunteer against the Soviets in the 1980s would finally be fulfilled. With the impending defeat of Massoud's Tajik rebel enclave, the light of freedom in Afghanistan would be extinguished.

4

RAIDERS

"Long before the Americans came to Afghanistan,
we were fighting the Taliban in the mountains. It was a
lonely battle that few of us thought we could win."

—GENERAL ABDUL RASHID DOSTUM

DARYA SUF (RIVER OF THE CAVES) VALLEY. SPRING–SUMMER 2001.

Even as bin Laden and the Taliban hatched their plans for a final offensive against the outgunned Massoud in the spring of 2001, an unsettling rumor began to make its way through the villages of the north. It was whispered that a leader known only as the Pasha had returned from exile in Turkey to assist Massoud's Tajiks in their lonely battle. With a mixture of fear and excitement, the people of the northern plains furtively spread the news from village to village: Massoud had played his last card and brought the Pasha back from exile to join the battle.

The Pasha brought with him a simple message: anyone who wished to fight back against the Taliban and al-Qaeda 055 Ansars (supporter fighters) should make his way to the inaccessible Hindu Kush. He promised he would open a second front there and grant them their wish.

It did not take long for the Taliban's intelligence services to put a name to the mysterious Pasha. When they did, it fulfilled their worst fears. There was only one leader who went by that title: Abdul Rashid Dostum.

Emboldened by the news of Dostum's return, hundreds of Uzbek farmers, shepherds, and townsmen retrieved their hidden AK-47s and mounted family horses to join his band of rebels high in the peaks of the Hindu Kush. Those who made it to the highlands undetected gathered in predesignated spots under local commanders and proceeded to rendezvous points higher in the mountains. It was time to raise the banner of resistance among the Uzbeks.

In a timeless pattern that would have been recognizable to Uzbek khans of the Middle Ages, the various subcommanders then led their regional forces to a mountain base known as Balkhab to serve their master, General Dostum. Within a matter of weeks, the Uzbek militia had mustered, and Massoud's outgunned Tajik fighters had one of Afghanistan's greatest military strategists on their side.

But Dostum was hardly the only leader of repute among the Uzbeks. The various Uzbek subcommanders who brought their levies to serve under him in April 2001 were as colorful as any band of medieval dukes or barons. They included such legends as Ahmed Khan, a powerful Uzbek mujahideen leader who had fought with great distinction in the 1980s; Commander Lal, the greatest cavalry commander in all of Afghanistan; Commander Fakir, a burly half-Arab, half-Uzbek warrior known for his sense of humor and almost suicidal fury in battle; and Kamal, an Uzbek *qomandan* who was also said to be fearless in battle.

Under such tried and proven war leaders as these, the Uzbek militiamen gathered in their remote mountain base and prepared to wage war against their people's enemies. Their ultimate aim was to stir up a rebellion in the Taliban's rear and take some of the pressure off Massoud's defensive lines protecting the Panjshir Valley in the east.

Despite their determination to raise a diversionary rebellion, the lightly armed Uzbeks knew they could never confront their powerful foes on the open field of combat. Dostum's men lacked armor, heavy artillery, aerial support, foreign benefactors, and, most important, numbers. All those who joined the Pasha's war band of no more than two thousand isolated *cheriks* (raiders) knew that the odds were stacked against them that spring of 2001.

They realized that, in contrast to their own meager forces, the Taliban army numbered between fifty thousand and sixty thousand fighters. The Taliban war machine was financed by wealthy Arab fundamentalists in the Middle East and trained and equipped by neighboring Pakistan. Pakistani technicians maintained the Taliban's fleet of dilapidated MiG fighter jets, and Pakistani Inter-Services Intelligence (ISI) funneled millions of dollars and hundreds of noncommissioned officers into bolstering this movement, which served their own ambition of building a strong Islamic state next door. While the Pakistanis officially denied their involvement in supporting the Taliban cause, US intelligence services claimed, "Pakistan's ISI is heavily involved in Afghanistan (and their) Frontier Corps elements are utilized in command and control; training; and when necessary—combat."[1]

The Taliban were also armed with Uragan multiple rocket launchers, Soviet-built T-55 and T-62 main battle tanks, heavy artillery, communications equipment, and fighter-bombers.[2] While many Westerners had a misconception of the Taliban as a band of tribal warriors, in truth their artillery was second to none in Afghanistan, and their officers were trained by Pakistani professionals.[3]

And one could not forget the Taliban's allies, the al-Qaeda elite jihad foreign legion known as the 055 Brigade, or Ansars. These fanatics were known to storm enemy positions with grenades strapped to their bodies. Having a unit of kamikaze-style fighters who aspired only to be *shaheeds* (martyrs) gave the Taliban a military and psychological edge over their Northern Alliance adversaries.

The Uzbek mountain rebels knew that meeting such a well-equipped, trained, and numerically superior enemy in open combat would be tantamount to suicide. But this lack of battlefield parity did not dampen their enthusiasm. Far from waging a conventional war, the Uzbeks' plan called for a hit-and-run guerilla campaign. Their strategy would be to strike at their enemies in lightning raids from the mountains and then escape back into the sheltering heights to elude pursuit.

Once in the hills, Dostum's horsemen, who were intimately familiar with the terrain, could evade their foes by riding up dizzying mountain trails. These narrow mountain paths were all but inaccessible to the Taliban pickup trucks and armored personnel carriers that dominated the plains.

The key to the mobility of Dostum's rebels in the peaks of the Hindu Kush was their Qataghani steppe horses, which they referred to as Uzbek Humvees. Few riders in the world could match these scions of the ancient nomads of Eurasia for skill in horsemanship when they were mounted on their beloved steeds. Moving like ghosts in the mountains and striking at isolated Taliban garrisons and checkpoints, the Uzbek rebels began to wage a war of attrition that would sap their Taliban enemies' strength and confidence

Riding through the mountains on their sturdy horses, Dostum's sharpshooting horsemen appeared to be everywhere and nowhere. As their confidence rose, they began to launch small-scale offensives against such Taliban-controlled territories as the mountain district of Zari. Much to the Taliban's fury, Dostum's skirmishers even began to come down out of the mountains and overrun Taliban outposts before disappearing back into the Hindu Kush. During a particularly daring raid, Ahmed Khan's nephew, Commander Hikmet, wiped out a large Arab al-Qaeda 055 Ansar unit near the plains town of Aibek before escaping to the mountains.[4] The Arab fanatics did not stand a chance against the horse-mounted descendants of Genghis Khan who rode out of the hills to ambush them.

When the Taliban discovered the blackened bodies of their Arab allies and hoofprints disappearing into the mountainous wastes, they were driven blind with rage. Attacking the nearby villages and killing innocent women and children, they vowed revenge. But killing unarmed civilians was one thing; tracking down armed Uzbek *cheriks* in the barren mountains was another. All attempts to punish Dostum's horsemen were frustrated by the unimaginably rugged terrain of the Hindu Kush. The Taliban's fleet of fast-moving Toyota pickup trucks known as *ahus* (deers) simply could not penetrate the endless ridges and ravines.

But as Dostum's successes mounted so, too, did the attention he garnered from the Taliban leadership in the political capital of Kabul and spiritual capital of Kandahar. The Taliban realized all too clearly that if they did not respond to Dostum's bold challenge, their authority would be undermined throughout the north. In Afghanistan, tribal allies and supporters gravitated toward those who were perceived as strong. Dostum's defiance of the Taliban's authority had to be met decisively to prevent defections.

The Talibans' fears were not far-fetched. Even though music had been banned by the Talibans' ubiquitous moral police, their spies admitted that the *bakshis*, the bards of the mountains, had begun to sing the ballad of "Dostum the Taliban Slayer."

For all these reasons, in the fateful summer of 2001 the Taliban Supreme Command reluctantly diverted an army of four thousand desperately needed foot soldiers into the mountains to crush Dostum's rebels. But in so doing, the Taliban leader, Mullah Omar, inadvertently fell for the ploy laid for him by his warlord enemies. Dostum's goal had not been simply to harass the Taliban. His real objective was to force the Taliban to siphon off troops from their primary military front against the Tajik commander, Massoud, the Lion of Panjshir.

Later events were to show that this diversion of the Taliban's precious resources in men and matériel from the Panjshir front could not have come at a more crucial time. Dostum's diversionary feint gave Massoud's troops the reprieve they needed to survive the Taliban's much-heralded summer offensive of 2001. While the Taliban had loudly proclaimed that they would finally crush Massoud's forces that summer, their offensive was subsequently repulsed, with great loss of life. The last free portion of Afghanistan was saved from the Taliban, and a tantalizing 10 percent of Afghanistan remained beyond their control.

By easing up the pressure on Massoud's Tajiks, Dostum's band of Uzbek peasant-fighters made a major contribution to keeping their joint struggle alive on the eve of 9/11. While they could not have known it at the time, their actions were laying the groundwork for the destruction of the Taliban during the subsequent US invasion known as Operation Enduring Freedom.

But in the first week of September 2001, no one in the godforsaken land of Afghanistan—least of all Dostum's equestrian mountain guerillas—could have imagined that their diversionary tactics would have such important ramifications for what would later be billed as the war on terror. On the contrary, Dostum's *cheriks* knew all too well that if their small force was annihilated by the Taliban, few in the outside world would know or care about their deaths.

A lonely death appeared to be an increasingly probable fate for Dostum, for the Taliban were determined to crush him. By the first week of September 2001 the Taliban's retaliatory force of four thousand fighters was finally able to push Dostum's lightly armed fighters out of Zari, the mountain province they had recently gained. In the bloody battle the Taliban's reliance on aerial bombardments, light artillery, and sheer numbers proved decisive.

As Dostum's horsemen staged a fighting retreat back to higher mountains, the inhabitants of Zari paid a heavy price for having supported his fighters. Across the mountain district, houses and crops were burnt, innocent villagers gunned down, women raped, and scores of villagers dragged off as prisoners.[5] The Taliban were sending a clear message: efforts to support Dostum and his rebels led to swift collective punishment.

As the Taliban reasserted their authority in Zari through mass executions, they also sent their spies deeper into the Darya Suf Valley to track down the elusive Uzbek pasha. With the net closing in, it became obvious that the Taliban would sooner or later achieve some results.

Finally, on the evening of September 8, a spy reported that Dostum was said to be spending the night in a mountain village in the Darya Suf Valley. According to the spy, that night the Pasha would be coming down from the heights above the valley to a local village to get fodder for his fighters' horses.

It was too good a chance to pass up. With one MiG air strike the Taliban could take out the Uzbek leader and deliver a crippling blow to the Northern Alliance's efforts to establish a second front. Buoyed by their success in killing the legendary leader, the Taliban could then refocus their efforts on crushing Massoud's fragile sanctuary and bringing the last remnants of Afghanistan under their "God-ordained" rule.

The Taliban had cause to be optimistic as they prepared to destroy one of their most hated enemies and channel their forces to overrunning another. The dream of Mullah Omar and bin Laden appeared to be back on track as the Taliban MiG 21s passed over the Hindu Kush and descended down the Darya Suf Valley to take out the Pasha.

5

LAST LINE OF DEFENSE

———————

"He funds his war with emeralds from his valley homeland;
commands a part-guerrilla army of often vying tribal
chiefs; he has fought the Soviet Army, Afghan and Arab
fundamentalists as well as Pakistani regulars. After 22 years
of fighting, he is the world's most experienced tactician."

—*TIMES* (LONDON), DESCRIBING MASSOUD

**KHOJA BAHAUDDIN, NORTHERN ALLIANCE HQ, TAKHAR PROVINCE.
SEPTEMBER 9, 2001.**

It was not Dostum's kismet to die on September 8. Less than an hour before
the MiGs bombed the village that had given him sanctuary, he and his turbaned raiders had made their way back into the sheltering mountains. Dostum and his number two, Commander Lal, actually witnessed the bombing
of the village from a mountaintop perch and prayed for its inhabitants.

As the Taliban MiGs rained fiery destruction down on the unsuspecting
village in the Darya Suf Valley, far to the east, Massoud the Lion of Panjshir

41

met with his Tajik field commanders to discuss the Taliban's strange troop deployments against his own lines. Like his Uzbek allies operating in the bleak mountains, Massoud was worried about the dispersal of thousands of Arabs from bin Laden's camps at Farouq, Badr, Khadad, Al Jihad, Tarnak, Darunta, and other jihadi terrorist compounds. Massoud also fretted that al-Qaeda was planning another overseas terrorist operation like the ones bin Laden had already carried out in east Africa and Yemen. The last time bin Laden had scattered his men from his camps had been days before he attacked the US embassies in Kenya and Tanzania in August 1998.[1] Massoud wondered if Dostum and his men had any intelligence on the Arabs' strange deployments in early September.

Despite the fact that Massoud and Dostum were now allies in the joint war against the Taliban, it should be stated that they and their battles were very different. While Dostum and his Uzbek *cheriks* held their furtive war councils in mountain caves and lived on scraps of naan, Massoud's commanders sipped chai and dined on mutton in the relative comfort of their fallback headquarters at Khoja Bahauddin. While Dostum was operating furtively behind enemy lines, Massoud's commanders were ensconced in the last free portion of Afghanistan. For the time being at least, they were safe in their protected mountain enclave.

This safety was largely due to the fact that Massoud's realm was protected by defensive trenches that snaked hundreds of miles down from the border of Tajikistan in the north to the Shomali Plain north of Kabul. These defensive lines were bolstered by high mountain peaks, fields of landmines, artillery emplacements, and thousands of entrenched soldiers who constantly monitored the enemies' movements. In many ways the combat between the Taliban and Massoud's Tajiks along these static lines resembled that seen in the trench warfare of World War I. For years the Taliban had sent waves of warriors over Massoud's trenches in an effort to break into the Panjshir Valley and overrun the Tajik provinces behind it, but to no avail.

No matter how hard they tried, Mullah Omar's Taliban troops had been unable to conquer this last Northern Alliance foothold. A frustrating

10 percent of Afghanistan thus remained beyond Mullah Omar's control, depriving the Taliban of Afghanistan's seat at the United Nations. Afghanistan was a divided land, and the government was officially recognized as existing in the pocket of territory controlled by Massoud.

While unbridled fanaticism ruled on the southern side of his powerful defenses, in Massoud's protected government sanctuary, the Taliban's writ was not recognized. Sheltered in the Panjshir Valley and the stunning mountains of Badakhshan Province, the timeless rhythms of Afghan life continued as they had before the advent of the Talib darkness. In the safety of these peaks, activities that were unthinkable in the Taliban-controlled provinces were a daily occurrence. Local Tajik girls attended school; villagers danced to traditional music at weddings; and children continued to fly that "satanic device" banned by the Taliban, the kite. But Massoud's slice of free territory was limited. He desperately needed Dostum's operation in the central Hindu Kush to succeed in order to preserve his fragile Tajik sanctuary.

But while Massoud relied on Dostum for help, he personally had very little in common with his Uzbek ally-of-the-day other than a shared hatred for the Taliban. While Dostum was a barrel-chested peasant scrapper who had been a champion wrestler, skilled *buzkashi* (the rough Uzbek sport similar to polo) player, and oil-rig worker in his youth, Massoud was the lean son of a general who spoke passable French. While Dostum favored bold frontal assaults and the gruff company of his soldiers, Massoud preferred to read Persian Sufi poetry and practiced warfare the way he played chess, with subtlety and grace.

There were also ethnic differences as well. Massoud hailed from Afghanistan's second-largest ethnic group (25 percent of Afghanistan), a self-proclaimed "noble" race of east Persians known as the Tajiks. The Persian Dari–speaking Tajiks proclaimed that their lineage went all the way back to Spitamenes, Zoroaster, Jalaluddin Rumi, and the Persian "Kings of Kings," such as Cyrus, Xerxes, and Darius, who had fought against both the Spartans and Alexander.

Dostum's Uzbek forebears, by contrast, had been horse-mounted herds-men who roamed the vast plains of Inner Asia from Mongolia to Russia. The Uzbeks (10 percent of the Afghan population) proclaimed that they, not the Tajiks, were the descendants of the greatest conqueror of all time, Genghis Khan.

While both groups shared a common sense of "Afghanistani" iden-tity, they had their differences. The various races in Afghanistan's ethnic cauldron differed one from the other as much as the Germans, Italians, and French of Switzerland differed from each other. But Afghanistan's eth-nic groups had not united voluntarily to create their multiethnic state the way Switzerland's Germans, Italians, and French had—they had been con-quered by the dominant group, the Pashtuns, who made up 40 percent of the population.

For this reason the Uzbeks, Tajiks, and even the Hazaras—a mixed Mongol-Persian race of Shiite "heretics," who inhabited the highlands of the Hindu Kush and made up about 10 percent of Afghanistan's popula-tion—all agreed that the Pashtun Taliban were a threat to their ancient freedoms. All three northern ethnic groups found the Taliban's puritanical interpretation of the faith to be as offensive to their Islamic folk beliefs as the Taliban's policies of Pashtun dominance were to their ethnic pride.

This common understanding had allowed Massoud to finally overcome their lack of unity and forge the anti-Taliban coalition known as the North-ern Alliance. As Massoud patiently explained to the other ethnic leaders, time was not on their side, it belonged to the enemy. The moment had come for the warring tribes of the north to put aside their differences and make common cause against their shared Taliban foe before they were all overrun for good.

It had taken time for Massoud to implement his elaborate multilateral plan, but with the insertion of Dostum into the Hindu Kush in April 2001, his strategy finally began to bear fruit. To Massoud's utter delight, the Tali-ban's much-heralded summer offensive against his own embattled enclave had wavered and broken by early June. No one could doubt that Dostum's diversionary activities had helped lift the pressure on the Tajiks' lines. As predicted, the Taliban had been forced to put out brush fires started by Dostum's hard-riding Uzbek guerillas.

And it was not only Dostum who had begun to create diversions as part of the anti-Taliban Northern Alliance. Massoud had also invited another exiled anti-Taliban warlord, Ismail Khan, the legendary *amir* (commander) of the western city of Herat, back to Afghanistan from his exile in Iran to help fight the Taliban. Ismail Khan had started a similar uprising in the mountainous Ghor Province in the western Hindu Kush that had begun to spread toward Herat.

As Ismail Khan struck at Taliban targets in the west, a fellow Tajik commander named Ustad Atta Mohammad Noor and two Hazara leaders, Karim Khalili and Mohammad Mohaqeq, launched attacks in the mountains near Bamiyan in conjunction with Dostum. For Massoud these strategic assaults were poetry in motion. These small resistance pockets checked his enemies' advance against his own lines and gained a desperately needed reprieve for his hard-pressed troops.

But Massoud knew all too well that the Northern Alliance's future was still precarious. Something had to be done to garner Western support for their cause before the Taliban extinguished his brush fires. In a fit of desperation, Massoud decided to fly to Strasbourg, France, in the spring of 2001 to plead for Western assistance. While in France, he warned the European Union of the terrorist threat manifesting itself in the al-Qaeda training camps located in the Pashtun lands of southeastern Afghanistan. Massoud presciently stated, "If President Bush doesn't help us, then these terrorists will damage the United States and Europe very soon, and it will be too late."[2] He also hinted that al-Qaeda's "objectives are not limited to Afghanistan." In a secret memo to the CIA, Massoud warned that al-Qaeda was planning "to perform a terrorist act against the US on a scale larger than the 1998 bombing of the US embassies in Kenya and Tanzania."[3]

But Massoud's entreaties fell on deaf ears. No Western leader, not even the newly elected American president, George W. Bush, was inclined to offend the Taliban regime by openly training and equipping its Northern Alliance opponents. While several key US officials, including National Security Council (NSC) counterterrorism chief Richard Clarke and CIA Counterterrorism Center chief Cofer Black, favored sending covert aid to the Northern Alliance opposition, such discussions were never translated into action by the Clinton or Bush administrations. As al-Qaeda plotted to overwhelm Massoud's bastion of resistance and kill thousands of innocent Americans, the CIA "showed no sense of urgency in supporting the Northern Alliance." Washington's assistance to Massoud was expressly limited to "nonlethal" aid and shared intelligence.[4]

For all its platitudes and hand-wringing about the repression of women under the Taliban's misogynistic mullahs, Washington had tacitly written off the Northern Alliance as a "doomed, ragtag band of holdouts" by late summer of 2001. In the fateful days before 9/11, the Americans were seemingly resigned to a Taliban victory over Massoud, and the Bush administration showed no interest in openly attacking Mullah Omar's al-Qaeda "guests."

The Americans' lack of concern about the looming al-Qaeda threat troubled Massoud in the final days of August and early September 2001.[5] As usual, America's actions, or lack thereof in this case, mystified him. Like many Afghans, he wondered if the Americans' shortsightedness was perhaps part of a scheme to ally themselves with the Taliban. It was widely known that the American oil company Unocal had courted the Taliban in hopes of building pipelines across its lands to oil and gas fields in Central Asia and Russia.

Although he had been a mujahideen freedom fighter against the Soviets, Massoud himself personified the moderate form of Islam that Americans officially claimed to support in the Middle East. Wearing his trademark *pakol*—the round woolen hat that he had made famous as a symbol of the anti-Soviet resistance—Massoud symbolized the tolerant strain of Islam that had traditionally defined Afghanistan. He felt that the United States should have supported him not only out of principle, but out of self-interest.

But US Central Command had not seriously devoted itself to planning a military campaign in distant Afghanistan, nor had it made plans to support the anti-Taliban resistance. The daunting logistical problems related to the projection of US forces from the Indian Ocean to the heart of land-locked Central Asia had not been addressed by early September of 2001.

The end result of all this dithering in Washington and the European capitals was that the Northern Alliance was essentially hung out to dry on the eve of 9/11. Despite his gentle eloquence, Massoud returned home from his trip to Europe empty-handed.

As he toured his battered front lines following his diplomatic failure, his sense of unease increased. Those who were with Massoud in the early days of September 2001 recall that he worked feverishly to save his life's work.

But even as Massoud desperately sought to bolster his defensive lines, bin Laden prepared to carry out a plan of his own that was to change the history of Afghanistan and the United States forever.

The Death of the Lion

KHOJA BAHUDDIN, NORTHEASTERN AFGHANISTAN. SEPTEMBER 9, 2001.

Massoud began September 9 much as he did any other day. Following his usual routine, he woke early to pray toward Mecca and then spent several hours reading reports from the previous night's skirmishes. His troops had just lost control of the Shoki and Khan Aqa districts in Kunar Province the day before, and it looked as if the Taliban were on the offensive. One of his most trusted commanders, Bismillah Khan Mohammadi, had almost been overrun by Taliban forces that very night. Massoud had spent hours on his radio frantically directing assistance to the battle to prevent Kunar from falling.

One of Massoud's closest aides, Khalili, who was with him that night, recalled that Massoud later asked him to read a ghazel by the great Persian poet Hafiz when the battle finally finished at 4 AM. The poem Khalili chose to read was oddly prophetic and included these lines:

Like the candle, I died, suffocated by my own tears.

Like the candle, I have become silent.

When Khalili was done reading, Massoud did not comment for a while as he absorbed the words' beauty. "God, how beautiful," were his only words before he retired for the night.[6]

But if Massoud was exhausted from his sleepless night, the man whom the CIA described as "unassuming and soft-spoken" did not show it that morning.[7] He dismissed his commanders and made his way out onto the porch of his headquarters to collect his thoughts. As always his mind cleared when he breathed the warm air and surveyed the dun-brown hills surrounding his northern headquarters at Khoja Bahauddin.

Listening to the sounds of a stream gurgling below and taking in the familiar village noises, Massoud reminded himself that these fragile treasures were what he was fighting for. Every woman who found medical treatment or schoolchild who was exposed to something other than strict religious indoctrination was for him a minor victory. It was Massoud's dream of extending this moderate Islamic vision to the rest of Afghanistan that led him to fight on when the odds were against him.

With the West seemingly resigned to his defeat, the Pakistanis arming and financing his Taliban enemies, and the Arabs openly fighting in the 055 Brigade to destroy him, he knew he was in the battle of his life. If he was not strong, the last light of freedom in Afghanistan would be extinguished.

It was in the hope of ending Arab support for the Taliban that Massoud agreed to meet with two Tunisian reporters at his compound on September 9. For three weeks the journalists had been pestering his staff for an interview, insisting that they wanted to share his side of the story with the Arab world. While Massoud's intelligence chief, Engineer Arif, distrusted the reporters because they were Arabs, Massoud finally agreed to grant them an interview. He was intent on convincing them that—contrary to reports in the Arab media—the Taliban, not his own forces, were filled with foreign mercenaries.

The reporters were finally admitted to Massoud's headquarters to meet a leader who had a unique distinction of being the target of both the Soviets' and bin Laden's wrath. As the Arab correspondents made their way through the Lion's bodyguards to his inner sanctum, it was obvious that no leader in Afghanistan, not even Dostum, was more beloved by his followers than Massoud.

This adoration was not limited to the soldiers who had fought under his command. As the reporters had previously seen when Massoud had walked the streets of Khoja Bahauddin sharing melons with laughing children or advising village headmen on how to build new schools, he was adored by the common people. The villagers called him Amir Sahib (Lord Commander) and knew that without his leadership their fragile safe haven would fall to the Taliban fanatics.

Among Massoud's greatest traits was the pride he took in the treatment of his guests. Mindful of the Afghan obligation to offer hospitality, he made a point of putting his own concerns behind him when he greeted his Arab guests that fateful September afternoon.

Knowing their commander's sense of hospitality, none of Massoud's bodyguards thought it strange when their commander invited the two Arab reporters to come and join him in his personal quarters. When the Arabs entered Massoud's headquarters, one of his aides claimed they did so, "not as journalists, but as guests."[8]

As one of the reporters sat before Massoud that fateful morning, the Lion of Panjshir even honored him with the symbolic gesture of passing him chai with his own hands. He graciously asked the reporters if they had encountered any difficulties in traveling to his province from the lands of the Taliban. He appeared to be amused when one of them replied that they had. The reporters had been disappointed that Mullah Omar refused to give them an interview after declaring that television was *haram* (religiously forbidden) in his realm.

But the Arabs did not appear to appreciate the irony of the story. Instead they seemed offended that the Lion was enjoying himself at the expense of the Taliban. It was not surprising, therefore, that the lead reporter began the interview in an aggressive fashion. He bluntly asked Commander Massoud what he would do to bin Laden if he were able to capture him. The implication was that Massoud had no right to be hostile to bin Laden when the Saudi and his Arab fighters had fought to defend the Afghans as volunteer mujahideen in the 1980s.

Made uncomfortable by the reporter's rude question, Massoud paused to mull it over, and his thoughts must surely have been filled with anger. Massoud knew that Osama bin Laden and his band of militarily useless fanatics had brought little to the war against the Soviets other than their Saudi Wahhabi extremism. On the day the Soviet invaders had left Afghanistan, Massoud had proclaimed, "We don't need armed Arabs wandering around our country. They have no place here; they should leave."[9]

But his efforts had been in vain. The Arabs had seemed strangely bent on taking over "their" Afghan homeland and converting it into an al-Qaeda al-Jihad. Massoud could not, however, vocalize his deep disdain for the fanatical Saudi Wahhabi, who seemed to be better at waging terrorism than frontal combat. The reporters were Arabs, and such sentiments might offend them.

So Massoud bit his tongue and tried to craft a diplomatic response. As he did so, he suddenly noticed that the journalist with the camera was sweating profusely even though it was pleasantly cool inside. This set off alarms in the back of Massoud's mind. As his eyes met those of the cameraman, some sixth sense told Massoud something was amiss, and he prepared to abruptly end the interview.

But at that precise moment the journalist before him muttered a prayer and triggered a switch on the side of his camera. For a split second no one in the room moved as everyone grasped what was happening. In that frozen instant a powerful bomb hidden in the camera and power pack on the journalist's waist exploded. The resulting blast blew the cameraman and his equipment to bits of flying bone, tissue, and metal. The shrapnel sprayed Massoud before he could react. As the blast enveloped him and his friend Khalili, pieces of shrapnel pierced his heart and eye and he fell over backward in anguish.[10]

Hearing the explosion, the Lion's horrified bodyguards rushed into his chambers. Charging through the smoke, they saw that nothing remained of the first assassin except the bloody stumps of his legs and his upper torso. The guards gunned down the second journalist in cold blood as he frantically tried to escape through a window.

With tears of fury in their eyes, Massoud's soldiers ran to their leader, hoping against hope that the Lion had survived this attempt on his life as he had so many others before. But as they reached his side, they were confronted with the sight of their mortally wounded commander fighting for his last breaths.

Overwhelmed by pain, Massoud issued his final command. Turning to his badly burned friend, Khalili, he ordered his men to forget about him and tend to his friend. Then he fell silent.

As he was carried away from the bomb-blackened room to an awaiting helicopter, Massoud, the greatest of the mujahideen freedom fighters and the last hope for unifying the anti-Taliban resistance, fell unconscious and died. With his death, an era in Afghan history came to a close. What the Afghan Communist Army, Soviet Fortieth Limited Contingent, neighboring warlords, and hordes of Taliban fighters had been unable to accomplish in two and a half decades of frontal combat, the Arab assassins had finally achieved through base treachery.

In killing Commander Massoud, the man who had humiliated the USSR and repulsed the Soviet "infidels" from the Dar al-Islam (Realm of Islam), the Arab assassins had slain one of the greatest defenders of the Muslim world since Saladin. In so doing, they brought shame upon their cause, for Massoud was the true embodiment of the gentlemanly Muslim warrior ethic forged by Saladin's medieval warriors; bin Laden, who slaughtered unarmed men, women, and children and called it holy war, was not.

But such obvious truths offered little consolation to Massoud's grieving followers. Many in the Lion's inner circle were overwhelmed by fear and panic. Everyone knew that Massoud had been the heart and the soul of the resistance to the Taliban. With his death, their lonely battle for Afghanistan's future was one step closer to defeat by the Taliban and al-Qaeda.

As for Massoud, no one knows what he thought or felt in his final seconds of life. But it is likely that he felt a deep sense of sadness and failure. With his death, the Afghanistan he had fought so hard to protect was now sure to be overrun by the forces of ignorance and fanaticism. In his last moments of life Massoud must have surely known that, with his departure from the scene, his troops' resolve would crumble. When it did, the peaceful sanctuary he had fought so hard to preserve would finally fall to the Taliban–al-Qaeda alliance. On that day his beloved Panjshir, like the rest of Afghanistan, would be transformed into a base for al-Qaeda's never-ending terrorist war. After so many years, Osama bin Laden and Mullah Omar had finally won.

His fears would not have been far off from the truth, for at the very moment of his death, the Taliban and al-Qaeda 055 Brigade commenced an assault on his front lines with a fury that caught the Tajik defenders by complete surprise. From Takhar Province in the north to the Shomali Plain in the south, the Taliban artillery opened up on the Northern Alliance and thousands of troops surged forward. Covered by artillery fire and bolstered by waves of Arab fanatics and Pakistani jihad volunteers, the Taliban threw themselves against Massoud's lines.

In the face of this unexpected onslaught, the Northern Alliance's lines began to waver. On the far northern front the Taliban swarmed toward the strategic town of Farkhar, the key to Takhar Province and gateway to Badakhshan. As the Taliban surged over their defensive lines, Farkhar's Tajik defenders fought back ferociously. The defenders prepared to die defending their positions, for they knew that if Takhar fell the Northern Alliance would follow.

But against all odds the Taliban offensive was repulsed by a Northern Alliance tank and machine gun crew, which valiantly held a strategic ridge against wave after wave of Taliban fighters. It is no exaggeration to say that the band of Tajik fighters saved the Northern Alliance that day. Had

Farkhar fallen, the Taliban would have poured into Badakhshan, the largest and most important free province left to the Northern Alliance. From there they would have been able to enter the Panjshir from the rear and overwhelm its defenders. As one shaken Northern Alliance fighter put it afterward, "We were literally one tank away from being overrun that day!"[11]

As the Taliban regrouped and prepared to launch more assaults, Massoud's intelligence services frantically commenced an investigation into the murder of their commander. They quickly determined that the Arab "journalists" sent to interview Massoud had actually been Tunisian al-Qaeda agents dispatched from Kabul by Osama bin Laden. One of bin Laden's bodyguards openly admitted as much when he recalled his master asking his followers, "Who will take it upon himself to deal with Ahmad [Shah] Massoud for me, because he has harmed Allah and his sons?"[12] This cryptic appeal had sealed the Northern Alliance leader's fate, and with it the hopes of millions of Afghans living in misery under the Taliban mullahs.

With Massoud out of the picture, the Northern Alliance was destined to fall. It was now time for bin Laden to celebrate his victory over his moderate Tajik rival and assume the title of Lion (*Osama* means "lion" in Arabic). It was also a signal for the Saudi billionaire terrorist to launch the second and most audacious part of his elaborate scheme: a surprise attack on the distant United States known in al-Qaeda circles as the September Operation. This attack would change the dynamic of the war in Afghanistan overnight and transform the final battlefield in the Cold War into the first battlefield of a new global conflict known as the war on terror.

Laying the Trap

AFGHANISTAN. SEPTEMBER 9–11, 2001.

While most Americans remained largely unaware of Massoud's death, feverish activity was taking place in bin Laden's terrorist camps on September 10, activity that would soon grab their attention. On the eve of the worst terrorist attack of all time, bin Laden was doing more than just supporting the Taliban's attacks on Massoud's lines. He was quietly dispersing his 055 Ansar (Arabic for "helper") fighters to towns in the north of Afghanistan in anticipation of a probable US counterattack.

As the foreign jihadis who were not involved on the front lines with Massoud were dispatched to Mazar-e-Sharif and Kunduz in the north, it became obvious to the Northern Alliance that something big was in the works. But it was only two days later, when news of the terrorist attack on the World Trade Center and the Pentagon came from New York and Washington, DC, on September 11, that they understood the full significance of Massoud's assassination. The killing of the Northern Alliance overlord was probably a final signal to launch the 9/11 attacks on America's military, political, and economic heart.

Bin Laden, it seems, had correctly foreseen that the unprecedented slaughter of Americans in their greatest cities would lure the US military to Afghanistan in search of vengeance. He dreamed of leading a glorious 1980s-style Afghan guerilla jihad against the American "paper tiger" that would bleed the United States to death in the Afghan mountains, just as it had the USSR.

In the upcoming battle, bin Laden foresaw that the arriving Americans would have found an indigenous ally in the Northern Alliance's most charismatic leader. With Massoud's intimate knowledge of the local terrain, ability to field thousands of seasoned fighters, and control of vital staging grounds, he would offer the Americans the perfect partner. For this reason, bin Laden understood all too clearly that Massoud, even more than Dostum, had to be eliminated before al-Qaeda operatives attacked the "far enemy," the United States. Bin Laden was confident that, without the charismatic Massoud, the Northern Alliance would lose its morale and crumble as a potential pro-US proxy force before the Americans arrived.

With the Taliban's front lines freed up from fighting the weakened Northern Alliance, bin Laden predicted his battle-hardened Arab jihadis could transform Afghanistan into a quagmire for the Americans. It would be death by a thousand cuts as his al-Qaeda and allied Taliban fighters turned the mountains of Afghanistan into a graveyard for the last remaining infidel superpower. Bin Laden told his followers, "We must carry out painful attacks on the United States until it becomes like an agitated bull, and when the bull comes to our region, he won't be familiar with the land, but we will."[13]

But for all of its self-obvious brilliance, Bin Laden's grandiose plan for a civilizational struggle in the mountains of Afghanistan was predicated on two false premises. The first was that the Tajik component of the Northern Alliance would disintegrate within hours of Massoud's death. The second was that his own al-Qaeda paramilitaries and Taliban tribal allies would subsequently be fighting a mujahideen-style guerilla war against a full-scale US ground invasion.

While bin Laden would not be made aware of his second flawed assumption until November 2001, his first misread quickly became obvious when the Northern Alliance failed to collapse—far from it. The Northern Alliance's front lines held their ground despite the pummeling fighters took on September 9 and 10.

Massoud's brother, Ahmed Wali, deliberately misled bin Laden and the Taliban in order to buy the Northern Alliance more time. Denying that Massoud had been killed, he announced that his condition remained grave, "but the doctors are optimistic about him."

Only later did bin Laden discover that the Northern Alliance leadership had deliberately kept the news of Massoud's death from their troops. Knowing the fighter's deep devotion to their leader, Northern Alliance spokesman Dr. Abdullah Abdullah had simply announced that Massoud had been wounded in a cowardly attack. Thus, even after Massoud's death, his Tajik troops fought on with renewed fury to avenge the attempt on their beloved leader's life.

But the word of Massoud's death could not be kept secret forever. Clearly the Northern Alliance needed American help to survive.

As the Northern Alliance reeled under the Taliban onslaught, the news of Massoud's assassination was secretly conveyed to the Americans in hopes of receiving some assistance. The CIA's Counterterrorism Center received a phone call from a Massoud intelligence officer named Amrullah Saleh on the evening of September 9.[14] Saleh could hardly speak through his sobs as he informed his American allies that the Lion of Panjshir was dead.

Before hanging up, Saleh asked the CIA to keep the news secret so the Northern Alliance would have a chance to regroup its forces and plan a post-Massoud strategy. But word was leaked to the press the following day and quickly made its way to the place where it would do the most damage: Afghanistan.

In no time the Taliban were informed by the US media of the glorious news of their greatest enemy's death. They quickly began to circulate the news to their jubilant troops and to demand that the Northern Alliance "surrender or die."[15] Afghanistan was now at their feet, and the Taliban's power reached its apex. As one Northern Alliance official recalled it, the Taliban radios began to gleefully announce, "Your father is dead, you can't resist us now!" When Dr. Abdullah heard the news, he "was one hundred percent sure that the resistance would be over in a matter of days."[16]

In the West, the news of Massoud's death was greeted with dismay by those few individuals who knew or cared about the long-suffering people of Afghanistan. Most of them understood that it signified the triumph of bin Laden and the end of the anti-Taliban resistance. The BBC's James Robbins reported on the evening of September 10, "The future of armed resistance to the Taliban now hangs in the balance. Without Massoud as commander, it will probably collapse, and the strictest of all Islamic regimes will remain unchallenged."[17]

From there it did not take long for the sad tidings to reach Northern Alliance fighters desperately manning their lines in the Shomali Plain. By the morning of September 11, local Tajik commanders were worriedly radioing Massoud's headquarters at Khoja Bahauddin asking if the rumors of the Lion's death were true.

As the word of Massoud's murder continued to spread, the Northern Alliance high command knew it was only a matter of time before the news filtered down to the rank and file. And no one could predict how the men on the front lines would react when they heard of their leader's assassination.

But it was not only the Tajiks who would be impacted by the news of the Lion's death. Massoud had comrades-in-arms from other ethnic groups who were waging diversionary campaigns behind enemy lines. These dangerously exposed allies would be devastated by the news that Massoud, the overall commander of the Northern Alliance, had been slain. Chief among these allies was General Dostum, who had himself narrowly survived the Taliban MiG bombing raid on the Darya Suf Valley.

When word of Massoud's death reached Dostum's liaison officer in the Panjshir on September 11, he was shocked. With a sick feeling, he realized that the Pasha had just been elevated to the unenviable position of Afghanistan's "most wanted man." When the news of the Lion's assassination reached Dostum, he would surely realize that the pressure on him would increase. Common sense dictated that Massoud's death would seriously weaken his Tajik army and free up thousands of Taliban troops to overwhelm Dostum in the mountains.

As the sun rose over the Hindu Kush on the morning of September 11, it appeared as if the Northern Alliance had lost the desperate battle for Afghanistan. With the death of Massoud and the inevitable destruction of Dostum's smaller forces, the evil that had been growing in Afghanistan would soon spread to surrounding regions.

While the people of Afghanistan could not have known it at the time, they would not be mourning alone for long. Millions of Americans would soon join them in grieving as the long-ignored evil that had been festering in Afghanistan struck across the globe and arrived on their shores, just as Massoud had predicted it would.

But history would show that despite the sorrow that swept Afghanistan following the assassination of Massoud, his death had not removed the last hope against the Taliban. High in the mountain peaks overlooking the Darya Suf Valley, the Pasha and his two thousand Uzbek *cheriks* held a *kurultay* (council meeting), grimly gathering to reaffirm their commitment to the struggle. While the odds against them had just increased, none of Dostum's commanders were inclined to end their blood feud with the Taliban. After saying prayers for Massoud's soul, Dostum's horsemen voted in the ancient Uzbek *kurultay* tradition and decided to continue the battle.

The decision by this small band of Uzbek raiders to fight on regardless of the odds was crucial in deciding the fate of Afghanistan. It would soon become apparent that in failing to kill the other great Northern Alliance commander, al-Qaeda had left the Americans with the perfect proxy for destroying bin Laden's Taliban hosts and depriving him of his Afghan sanctuary.

6

THE EVIL COMES TO AMERICA

"Something really spectacular is going to happen here,
and it's going to happen soon."

—RICHARD CLARKE, NSC COUNTERTERRORISM CHIEF, JULY 2001

MANHATTAN, THE UNITED STATES OF AMERICA.
SEPTEMBER 11, 2001.

As the morning sun rose over Afghanistan on September 11 (the twenty-third of Jumada al-Thani, 1422, in the Muslim calendar) and shone down on the opposing Afghan forces, events were taking place across the globe that were to drastically change the dynamics of the war in this land that had been forgotten by Washington since the Soviets left. Unbeknownst to the slumbering Americans, bin Laden's elaborate plan to strike at "soft targets" on the American mainland had been set in motion. Once bin Laden's sleeper cells had been activated, there was no turning them back.

At that very moment, nineteen Arabs spent their last morning on earth praying and going over their plans. These nineteen hijackers were to propel

Afghanistan from the status of forgotten Cold War battlefield to ground zero in the war on al-Qaeda.

But on the morning of September 11, 2001, few of the inhabitants of distant Afghanistan could have foreseen that their country was about to become the focus of the largest US military buildup since the 1991 Gulf War. Only bin Laden and a few in his trusted inner circle knew that the al-Qaeda sleepers had awoken in North America and were about to strike later that day.

As dawn crept over the eastern seaboard of the United States, thousands of unsuspecting Americans went to work in the World Trade Center towers, the Pentagon, and the US Capitol building, or boarded flights for California, unaware that their fate had been sealed. But bin Laden knew what was to come, and he awaited news from the land of the "arrogant infidels" with great anticipation. Two days earlier he had ordered his driver, a Yemeni named Salim Hamdan, to take him and his family from their easily identifiable compound near Kandahar up to Kabul, where he could hide himself in the capital's masses.[1] There he stayed with a small group of friends in the Wazir Akbar Khan district before going on to Khost Province to await news from the distant shores of America.

When the first garbled news reports of an airliner crashing into a building came from New York, bin Laden knew it had begun. The attack known in fanatical jihadi circles as Holy Tuesday had commenced. When it was over, the world would never be the same.

By the afternoon of September 11, there were few Americans who did not have a theory about who had attacked them. In the stunned aftermath, some tried, with varying degrees of success, to pin the blame on the Palestinians or the secular dictator of Iraq, Saddam Hussein.

But more knowledgeable voices quickly prevailed. The CIA, National Security Agency (NSA), Defense Intelligence Agency (DIA), and State Department came forward with evidence irrefutably linking the terrorist network of one Osama bin Laden to the attack.

As the evidence mounted, President Bush's job description changed drastically. The Texas Republican who had been elected on his domestic agenda prepared to deal with a foreign-based terrorist crisis of unparalleled proportions. By the evening of September 11, President Bush appeared on television to promise his stunned nation that those who had brought down the buildings would be punished.

In the sorrow-filled days following the attack, President Bush made it resoundingly clear that the United States was at war with the terrorists. He also let it be known that he held one man accountable: Osama bin Laden. Calling upon the Taliban to hand over their Arab "guest," Bush swore to bring him to justice. If that failed, he promised, he would bring justice to bin Laden, whom he wanted "dead or alive."

The Taliban initially reacted to the stunning news from America by panicking and denying their Arab guest's guilt. Far from turning bin Laden over, Mullah Omar proclaimed, "Osama bin Laden will be the last person to leave Afghanistan," and warned his people not to be "cowards."[2] The Taliban, it seemed, were determined to share al-Qaeda's fate.

When confronted with news of the Taliban's intransigence, the Bush administration had no recourse but to move against the clear and present danger emanating from Afghanistan. As the Taliban drew a line in the sand, Richard Armitage, the deputy secretary of defense, summed up America's position as follows: "We told the Taliban in no uncertain terms that if this happened, it's their ass. No difference between the Taliban and al-Qaeda now. They both go down."[3]

Infuriated by Mullah Omar's decision to stand by al-Qaeda, President Bush ordered his top general to "rain holy hell" on them.[4] As for Bin Laden, Cofer Black, the head of the CIA's Counterterrorism Center, was more blunt. Black ordered his Special Activities operatives to "capture Bin Laden, kill him, and bring me his head back in a box on dry ice."[5]

By late September the die was cast, and the Taliban's fate was sealed; the United States of America and its powerful NATO allies were at war with Afghanistan's fundamentalist Pashtun rulers as well as their al-Qaeda "guests."

The White House responded by marshalling its intelligence, military, and political resources to understand the nature of the enemy. In so doing, the American diplomatic, military, and intelligence communities not only avoided the elaborate trap being laid by bin Laden and his followers but began putting the pieces into place for one of the greatest victories in modern military history. History would know the subsequent US mission in Afghanistan in the fall of 2001 as Operation Enduring Freedom.

7

SEARCH FOR A PLAN

"These men [Dostum and other Northern Alliance warlords] were not saints, but then saints are in short supply in the world."[1]

—US Secretary of Defense Donald Rumsfeld

LANGLEY, VIRGINIA (CIA HEADQUARTERS), PENTAGON, WHITE HOUSE, AND FORT CAMPBELL, KENTUCKY (HQ FOR THE FIFTH SPECIAL OPERATIONS GROUP). SEPTEMBER 15–20, 2001.

By resisting the urge to act rashly, the United States ultimately formulated a sound strategy for "eviscerating" the Taliban regime—one that was more thought out and nuanced than bin Laden could have foreseen. The multifaceted response crafted by America's military, diplomatic, and intelligence services would ultimately see the Taliban regime overthrown and al-Qaeda deprived of its sanctuary before Christmas—at the cost of roughly a dozen American lives. Success came on a scale, and with a rapidity, that bin Laden, who was eagerly expecting a full-scale military invasion, could not have foreseen.

The dynamics behind this 2001 stealth victory are still not fully understood to this day, and this has led some to underestimate ex post facto the
very real problems that the US military faced at the time. But the speed with
which America's response to 9/11 achieved its immediate goals should not
lead to a retroactive discounting of the real obstacles it encountered. British admiral Sir Michael Boyce described the impending Afghan conflict as
"the most difficult operation ever undertaken by this country post-Korea."[2]

The task given to Central Command—destroy an entrenched and determined tribal foe dispersed across a Texas-sized, mountainous land located
in the heart of Central Asia—was considered impossible by many skeptics,
who predicted a Vietnam-style quagmire of mass casualty. Even the opti-
mists expected a long winter campaign that could not be won without the
deployment of at least fifty thousand troops from the US Marines, the 101st
Airborne, the Tenth Mountain Division, and others.

As CENTCOM began to assess the difficulties involved in projecting
US forces deep into the wintry mountains of landlocked Afghanistan, US
generals desperately sought the means to crack the Taliban while avoiding
the pitfalls of a full-scale invasion.

It was at this stage that the CIA came to the forefront of the war planning. Although CIA Director George Tenet was later criticized for his role
in the groupthink effort on Iraq's nonexistent weapons of mass destruction, his advice on Afghanistan proved to be dead on target. He and Cofer
Black understood all too clearly that "this war would be driven by intelligence, not the pure projection of power."[3]

They had a plan that would follow this principle. As it happened, one
farsighted US official had already drawn up an outline for an intelligence-
driven war against the Taliban. Eight months prior to 9/11, NSC Counterterrorism Chief Richard Clarke had provided the CIA with a plan known
as the Blue Sky Memo, which called for arming the Northern Alliance and
using it to attack al-Qaeda.[4] This memo, which was shelved until 9/11, called
for "massive support to anti-Taliban groups such as the Northern Alliance
led by Ahmad Shah Massoud," as well as winning Pakistani support and
the targeted killings of al-Qaeda leaders using Predator aerial drones.[5] As

this once-secret memo makes clear, it was the CIA that suggested linking the Northern Alliance opposition with US Special Forces, not the military, which had no contingency plans for invading Afghanistan.[6]

Considering the urgency of the task at hand and the glacial speed at which US ground forces typically deployed, US Secretary of Defense Donald Rumsfeld overcame his distrust of the CIA and signed on to Clarke's plan. The final green light was given by Chairman of the Joint Chiefs of Staff Richard Myers, who was well suited to lead the war. Myers had made it clear that he was not about to launch an ill-conceived mass invasion of one the world's most heavily land-mined and armed tribal nations just to appease the bloodlust of a few American ultrapatriots. Wasting American lives to simply occupy the mountains of Afghanistan would not bring back those who had died on 9/11, nor would it punish those who had killed them.

With his Air Force background, Myers felt that the best way to implement Clarke's covert plan was to channel the awesome might of the US air forces against the enemy using Special Forces spotter teams on the ground.[7] This "surgical" approach would enable small US Special Forces teams to act as "force multipliers" and avoid the risks of a full-scale invasion of a hostile tribal land.

The disastrous Afghan wars of the British and the Soviets provided the most obvious cautionary tales indicating what might happen if the United States launched a frontal invasion. In 1842, in one of their single greatest defeats ever, the invading British had lost sixteen thousand men to Afghan hill warriors. The seemingly invincible Soviet Red Army had lost more than fourteen thousand servicemen in its 1979–89 invasion. One British author wrote of Afghanistan and its indomitable fighting men, "The Afghans are extraordinary fighters, tough and resourceful and cruel, and they know their business inside out. On their own territory they are unbeatable. They love fighting and dealing with invaders. It is almost a game to them. The country is Death Valley 10 times over."[8]

Notwithstanding the risks of a full-scale invasion of Afghanistan as highlighted by the British and Russian debacles, there were valuable lessons to be learned from their mistakes—especially those of the Soviets, who had acted unilaterally. As President George H. W. Bush had previously demonstrated during his UN-authorized attack on Iraq in the 1991 Gulf War, winning the support of the world paid dividends.

President George W. Bush took seriously his father's advice on the need to build a coalition, and this became his first priority once it had been decided that America would launch a "light footprint" invasion instead of a full-frontal invasion. In implementing this approach, the United States would not follow in the clumsy footsteps of the Soviets or British. Much to bin Laden's chagrin, America would act cautiously in conjunction with its allies and with the full support of the global community.

By mid-September 2001 Bush had dispatched Colin Powell, the widely respected secretary of state, and Donald Rumsfeld, the sharp-spoken secretary of defense, across Eurasia on a diplomatic blitz designed to rally support for the impending campaign by the CIA, Special Forces, and Air Force.

American diplomats found it easy to gain the support of their NATO allies in Europe, all of whom (including the Turks, Germans, French, and Belgians, who would later vote against the American invasion of Iraq) were extremely sympathetic in the aftermath of 9/11. For the first time in its history, NATO even invoked Article 5 of its founding charter, which states that an attack on a member is an attack on the alliance.

American diplomats, however, placed even greater emphasis on winning the support of Afghanistan's immediate neighbors, the strategically located countries of Uzbekistan and Pakistan. US Central Command had impressed upon the State Department the importance of acquiring basing rights in these countries for covert operations.

Donald Rumsfeld led the effort to gain the support of Uzbekistan's leader, President Islam Karimov. By late September, America had received basing rights in an ex-Soviet airbase located in southern Uzbekistan at Karshi-Khanabad (code named K2). K2 subsequently became a major staging ground for covert Special Forces "infil-exfil" (infiltration and exfiltration) into Afghanistan.

As the Pentagon mulled over its limited options and prepared to send approximately 350 CIA and Special Forces operatives into harm's way, US generals furiously sought to draft a "subtle" strategy to destroy al-Qaeda and its Taliban hosts. Taking into consideration all the risks and limitations involved, this was no small task. It was made all the more vexing by the realization that there really was no high-tech standoff solution to rooting the Taliban and al-Qaeda out of the Afghan cities and countryside. For all America's vaunted killing technology, the Pentagon planners realized that they could not defeat an army dispersed over Afghanistan's mountains, deserts, and towns by means of an aerial campaign alone. While America's air power could be used to destroy troop concentrations and communication facilities, Afghanistan was clearly not, in Air Force jargon, a target-rich environment. As Donald Rumsfeld put it, "B-52s are powerful and can do certain things within reasonable degrees of accuracy, but they can't crawl around on the ground and find people."[9] As in Vietnam, sooner or later somebody would have to deploy boots on the ground to flush out the dispersed enemy. At some point, the United States would have to supplement the small groups of Special Forces with light infantry to carry out larger search-and-destroy missions.

As September rolled toward October, all those involved in planning America's strategy knew that the clock was ticking. Snow was already dusting the highest peaks of the Hindu Kush, heralding the arrival of Afghanistan's notoriously harsh winter. The American president and people were also growing impatient; they were demanding results.

And these were not the planners' only concerns. As it became obvious that America was going to war against Mullah Omar's Taliban regime, the CIA reported that thousands of Pakistani Pashtun jihadi volunteers were flooding across the border into Afghanistan to support the Taliban. Most of these tribal fanatics were being deployed in convoys to the north, a strategic area where most analysts felt the battle for Afghanistan would be decided.

For this jihadi rabble, the brutal suppression of "bad Muslim" Uzbeks, Tajiks, and Hazaras in the north and the killing of American invaders was more than just a religious obligation, it was an opportunity to fight alongside fellow Pashtuns on the Afghan side of the border. As the number of

Pakistani Pashtun volunteers in Afghanistan swelled, the CIA feared that the clash of civilizations that bin Laden had dreamed of was fast becoming a reality. The CIA fretted that its window of opportunity for swiftly toppling the Taliban regime using special operatives was closing.

But all that was about to change. In the midst of the frantic search for a subtle plan, the CIA received a most unexpected phone call from an American expat living in Uzbekistan. The caller was a former employee of the US oil firm Unocal. He claimed to have kept in contact with various tribal leaders in northern Afghanistan since his company's departure in the late 1990s.

Much to the CIA's amazement, he also claimed to have a message from an isolated Northern Alliance commander operating deep in the Hindu Kush. According to the expat, the rebel commander had heard of al-Qaeda's attack on America and had promised to say prayers for the "martyred" Americans.

But that was not the most interesting part of the message. The Northern Alliance commander also offered to make his small force of two thousand riders available to the Americans in punishing the Taliban and al-Qaeda. In his own words, he offered to be "the means for the Americans to achieve their vengeance on the al-Qaeda slaughterers of both our people's women and children."[10]

The Northern Alliance commander did not speak in vague, hypothetical terms, for that was not his style. He was a man of action and had a bold plan. Introducing himself as a "son of Afghanistan, named Abdul Rashid Dostum," he offered to wage a lightning war against the Taliban. Specifically, he would strike from his remote base in the Darya Suf Valley of the Hindu Kush toward the city of Mazar-e-Sharif, the holiest city in northern Afghanistan. If his fighters could capture the Shrine of Ali in Mazar-e-Sharif, he claimed, they would fulfill a prophecy going back to the time of medieval ruler Shaybani Khan. According to Dostum, this symbolic act would prove to the Afghans that the wheels of fate had turned against the Taliban; their army would quickly break up and defect to the Northern Alliance. With one symbolic strike, the United States and its Afghan ally could decapitate the Taliban regime in a matter of weeks.

The electrifying message ended with Dostum's promise to attack the Taliban regardless of what the Americans did. He seemed determined to move against the Taliban with or without US support. His forces had already reinvaded the Taliban-occupied mountain province of Zari and were pushing Taliban forces out.[11] Thus the first commander to conquer territory from the enemy in the war on terror was the Uzbek leader Dostum.

As the stunned CIA analysts mulled over the message, it took them little time to grasp both its military and political implications. Here was an indigenous leader—a Muslim—with intimate knowledge of the local terrain offering to provide the United States with an aggressive fighting force to help it fight *on the ground* in Afghanistan.

While few in number, Dostum's small force could provide the American special operatives with the force protection they needed to move about and target the Taliban with satellite- and laser-guided bombs. And when the Taliban melted into the countryside or hunkered down in their shelters or trenches to avoid aerial bombardments, Dostum's men could flush them out. In essence, Dostum and his small force could provide the surrogate army called for in Richard Clarke's Blue Sky Memo.

For the US planners, this was the obvious solution to the problem that had bedeviled them since it became apparent that the Taliban regime could not be removed by a full-scale, frontal invasion. Namely, how do you deploy boots on the ground in Afghanistan without leaving a heavy footprint?

Dostum's knowledge of the lay of the land and local superstitions related to the shrine of Mazar-e-Sharif made his offer all the more enticing—especially since the Tajik component of the Northern Alliance opposition was in disarray following Massoud's recent death. Only Massoud had been able to keep the fractious Tajiks together, and now he was gone. His lackluster replacement, General Fahim Khan, was having difficulties keeping the Badakhshani and Panjshiri components of the Tajik opposition united.

In light of the United States' previous abandonment of Afghanistan after the Soviets left in 1989, Fahim Khan did not trust America's long-term intentions. For obvious reasons he was reluctant to throw his divided Tajik force against the Taliban in a war of vengeance on behalf of a fickle Christian superpower from across the globe.

To make matters worse, the Tajiks' political head, President Burhanuddin Rabbani, was a fundamentalist known to make anti-American pronouncements. American intelligence also suspected him of having close ties with the Iranians, who were ethnic kin of the Persian-speaking Tajiks.

Dostum, by contrast, had close ties with Turkey, America's secular NATO partner. Unlike the Iranian-linked and militarily stalled Tajiks, Dostum was a secularist who seemed eager to go on the offensive. Dostum also claimed to have been fighting *against* the fundamentalists all along—even when the United States was supporting them against the Soviets back in the 1980s.

In the stunned aftermath of Dostum's message, the CIA, NSA, and DIA mobilized their considerable "humint" (human intelligence) and "techint" (technical intelligence) resources for the task of finding out everything there was to know about the mysterious Northern Alliance commander. It quickly became apparent to the CIA that America's greatest weapon in the war on terror might not be the 917th Bomber Wing, the 82nd Airborne Division, or the USS *Enterprise* battle group, but two thousand Uzbek horsemen operating somewhere in the high peaks of the remote Hindu Kush, armed with little more than AK-47s and their belief in the sanctity of the shrine of Mazar-e-Sharif.

Fully aware of the importance of Dostum as a covert indigenous ally, the CIA took the lead in developing a way to use his forces to destroy the Taliban. As the CIA and Special Forces began to synchronize their plans, CIA head George Tenet sent a secret memo to President Bush that said:

> We need to go in fast, hard, and light. Everyone, including al-Qaida and the Taliban, are expecting us to invade Afghanistan the same way the Soviets did in the 1980s. Bin Laden and his followers expect a massive invasion. They believe we will withdraw in the face of casualties and never engage them in hand-to-hand combat. They are going to get the surprise of their lives.[12]

The Pentagon's response to the new orders for a covert invasion of Afghanistan in conjunction with the Northern Alliance was almost instantaneous. Within a matter of hours it had begun to put together a special operations force known as Joint Special Operations Task Force–North (aka Task Force Dagger) to be sent into the mountains of northern Afghanistan. Its task was to provide Dostum and other Northern Alliance leaders such as Ustad Atta Mohammad Noor, Fahim Khan, Ismail Khan, Mohammad Mohaqeq, and Abdul Karim Khalili with close air support.

In the skies far above the Darya Suf Valley, Lacrosse terrestrial radar-imaging spy satellites and MQ-1 Predator spy drones began to record every feature of the unknown land below in preparation for the US deployment.

Meanwhile, at CIA headquarters, Counterterrorism Center chief Cofer Black chose a CIA operative named Henry "Hank" Crumpton to oversee the light operations in Afghanistan. Crumpton, a CIA veteran with field work experience in Africa and an interest in history, looked to the campaigns of the legendary Lawrence of Arabia for inspiration. The Welsh-born Lawrence had infiltrated the deserts of Arabia during World War I and galvanized the Arab tribes to fight as proxy warriors against Britain's Ottoman Turk enemies. Lawrence had famously advised his British superiors, "Do not try to do too much with your own hands. Better the Arabs do it tolerably than that you do it perfectly," and this would be the approach the joint CIA-Special Forces teams would follow.[13] That, and the tactics of sixth-century Chinese military strategist Sun Tzu, who had advised, "The expert in using the military subdues the enemy's forces without actually having to commit his own forces to the battle."

Crumpton summed up his vision for the CIA-spearheaded operation as follows:

I focused on our Afghan allies. I knew they would be the key to our victory. Only they understood the terrain, only they would be able to recruit other Afghans to join us, only they could penetrate the Taliban at all levels, and only they could move immediately. The US military knew little about Afghanistan, because there was no conventional threat. And our military was overwhelmingly conventional. They would take many months to mobilize a sizeable force.[14]

Far from being Soviet-style invaders, the CIA and Special Forces would be acting in the role of insurgents against the dominant Taliban. In Crumpton's words, "We would be the accelerant helping to fuel an uprising."[15]

As the CIA prepared to be inserted into Afghanistan to liaise with the mysterious Dostum and lay the framework for the subsequent arrival of Special Forces A-Teams, the machinery of America's all-powerful military-intelligence community kicked into overdrive to find the answers to several key questions. The information would be crucial in keeping America's Special Forces alive in the terra incognita of the Hindu Kush and leveraging Dostum's riders to act as a surrogate army. The Americans desperately needed to know: What was the significance of the mysterious tomb of Mazar-e-Sharif? Why had Dostum and his men fought *against* the CIA-funded mujahideen in the 1980s? And, most intriguing of all, what were Dostum's people doing riding *horses* into combat?

Everyone involved realized that America's human resources on the ground in Afghanistan were limited and that there were no high-tech answers to these questions. As one US military officer put it, "Our intelligence is zero. We don't know who is the good guy and who is the bad guy."[16] In order to find out who the "good guys" and "bad guys" were, the United States would have to engage in old-fashioned historical research. While such background research went against the American grain (especially in the high-tech climate of the US intelligence community), the CIA analysts realized they would have to explore dusty history books, interview anthropologists, master the differences among Afghanistan's various ethnic groups, and unravel local legends to gain mastery of the Afghan battle space.

This investigative journey would provide the American analysts with the key ingredient they would need to win the upcoming battle in Afghanistan: namely, a mysterious Afghan warlord known as Abdul Rashid Dostum.

8

KHOJA DOKO VILLAGE, 1954

"Once we had the power. It was our turn then, and from
the time of Timur [Tamerlane, the fourteenth-century
Turkic-Mongol warlord] no one could stop us. No one else
had so many horses. No one could ride them so well. We
had it all. It was our turn then, but now the turn has passed.
It's the turn of the Pashtuns, now they have the power."

—Uzbek Buzkashi rider interviewed in 1978[1]

**JOWZJAN PROVINCE, DESERT PLAINS OF NORTHWESTERN
AFGHANISTAN. 1950.**

Abdul Rashid, the man who would later become known as Dostum, came into
the world in a three-room domed house made of dried clay bricks in conditions
that defined the word "primitive." Lacking electricity, furniture, and running
water, it had few of the amenities a Westerner would expect in a house; with
only a rudimentary dirt floor, his home could easily have been mistaken for a
stable or storage shed by someone from another part of the world.

73

A peek outside revealed a world that had changed little since the time of Shaybani Khan and his conquering Uzbek horde. Situated on a dirt path used by farmers on their way to their fields, Abdul Rashid's home and the village surrounding it would not have been out of place in the Middle Ages. The rhythms of life continued unchanged despite the changes in the wider world. Khoja Doko's men still worked in the fields using basic implements and lived according to the course of farming seasons and ancient Muslim and pre-Islamic festivals. Donkeys were still used to carry *devedikeni* (camel thistle) from the desert to feed the animals. Hay was trampled into grain by horses, and life-giving water was transported to the dry fields in earthen jars. Local khans dominated village life, and in the evenings the village men occasionally came together to play the *dambura* (lute) and hear *bakshis* (bards) recount stories of ancient heroes, such as Amir Nogai, Yedige, Alp Amish, Ubaidallah, and Shaybani.

But there had also been changes since the time of Shaybani Khan's conquest of Central Asia, largely related to the Uzbeks' gradual adaptation to sedentary life from the eighteenth to the twentieth century. As the nomadic Uzbeks settled down on the plains around Mazar-e-Sharif, they came under the influence of the neighboring Persian Tajiks. While the Uzbeks kept their yurt-tents as summer dwellings, they began to build clay-walled settlements called *kishlaks* (winter camps), which became more permanent villages over time.

As they settled down along the riverbanks that cut through the dry northern plains and began to cultivate local grains, the Uzbeks also adopted Tajik agricultural techniques. As these processes unfolded, the Uzbeks began to merge with their Tajik neighbors and plant both real and symbolic roots in the plains of what was then known as Turkistan.

But in the mid-1700s, the ruler of the Uzbek sub-khanate of Faryab made a fateful alliance with a group of foreign warriors from south of the Hindu Kush. These warriors with long faces and light-colored eyes were known as the Afghans or Pashtuns.

While the Afghan fighters eventually departed, they never forgot the rich lands of the Uzbeks, Tajiks, and Turkmen of the north. They would one day use this temporary alliance with the Uzbek khan of Faryab as a pretext for claiming that he had surrendered all the lands of the north to them.

But it would take one hundred years for the Afghan Pashtuns to make good on their claim to Faryab and the other Uzbek-dominated lands of Turkistan. Their moment came when the Uzbek Ming and Qataghan tribes clashed in the mid-1800s. As the infighting took its toll on both sides, the Pashtuns considered the moment ripe to destroy the Uzbeks' independent khanates once and for all. Swarming over the Hindu Kush, the fierce Afghan warriors staked their claim to rule Turkistan by conquering the holy shrine of Mazar-e-Sharif.

In response to this sacrilege, the indomitable Uzbek horsemen from the small khanates of Kunduz, Mazar-e-Sharif, Shiberghan, Maimana, Andkhoy, Sar-e-Pol, Tashkurgan, Balkh, and Akche set aside their differences and rode out of their clay-walled citadels to defend their land.

For their part, the invading Afghans knew they were up against a semi-nomadic enemy that was in many ways their superior. One nineteenth-century Afghan Pashtun observer wrote, "An Afghan rolls in his saddle, an Oozbeg is part of his horse, and he takes an Afghan out of the saddle with his spear as you would take meat with a spoon. I have seen the battle of both of them and I know that my countrymen cannot stand before an Oozbeg horse."[2]

But the Pashtuns had a surprise for their horse-mounted Uzbek foes. As the Uzbek *sowars* (cavalrymen) rode into battle wielding their compound bows, spears, and sabers, the Afghans unveiled a host of secret weapons: thousands of modern breech and muzzle-loading rifles and lethal field cannons. These had been provided by the invading Christians who controlled India—the British. Not knowing what was in store for them, the Uzbek horsemen rode to their destruction. As they attacked the Pashtun invaders, rank upon rank of Uzbek rider fell to the withering fire of the Afghans' guns and cannons. The battle was a massacre.

When the smoke finally cleared, the Afghans' ruler identified himself as Abdur Rahman, the Iron Amir. He was quick to demonstrate why he had earned such a fearful moniker. Slaughtering the Uzbeks and allied Turkmen and Tajiks in the tens of thousands and deliberately spreading famine to break the spirit of the northerners, Abdur Rahman crushed all resistance. Southern Turkistan, the Uzbek lands south of the Amu Darya River, were his by 1881. From that year forth he proclaimed himself to be the ruler of the "God-Granted Kingdom of Afghanistan, Turkistan and Their Dependencies." (In 1920, "Turkistan" was removed from the country's title, and in 1967 the name officially disappeared from the map as well.)

Following their conquests, thousands of Uzbeks, Turkmen and Tajiks, and Hazaras were subsequently led in chains from their burning villages to the Afghan Pashtun capital, Kabul. Many were cut to pieces, strangled, poisoned, hanged, dismembered, boiled, crucified, disemboweled, sawn in half, or left to bleed to death after having their mouths slit open.[3]

When the butchery was over, the Afghan ruler built an imposing fort known as Qala-e-Jangi (the Fortress of War) to the west of Mazar-e-Sharif as a symbol of his power. To man Qala-e-Jangi and other fortresses built with British help, Abdur Rahman brought in tens of thousands of Pashtun settlers.[4] These "internal colonists" would help him and his heirs subjugate Uzbek rebellions right up until the 1930s.

For generations after their conquest, the Uzbeks sought to understand why the Christian British had worked to destroy their ancient independence. Only much later did they realize that the slaughter, enslavement, and conquer of their people had been a chess move in the Great Game, a cynical struggle for power and influence in Central Asia. To preempt any possible Russian moves toward India, their crown colony, the British pushed Abdur Rahman to conquer the surrounding peoples and create a buffer state south of the Amu Darya River. The Afghans were then encouraged to centralize or "Pashtunize" this tribal conglomeration so it could serve as a cohesive shock absorber between the Russian and British empires. And thus was born the multiethnic Kingdom of Afghanistan.

Having done as his British allies requested, Abdur Rahman had the Uzbeks' *aq saqal* graybeards arrested and humiliated. But this was not enough for the conqueror, whose brutal policies have been compared to those of Vlad the Impaler and Ivan the Terrible. Having publicly humiliated the Uzbeks' elders, he then had them chained across the barrels of field cannons and blown to bloody bits over the heads of their terrified families and communities.

Thus the nineteenth-century Afghan Pashtun ruler Abdur Rahman was able to solidify his people's rule over the north and begin the process of Afghanizing them. As the Uzbeks adopted the ways of the dominant Pashtuns and local Tajiks, the men increasingly came to wear distinctive turbans wrapped around *tubeteikas* (skull caps), and the women to don veils. While the Uzbeks did not subscribe to the laws of *namuz* (the pride in protecting the women in one's clan) and *purdah* (the confinement of women to protect their clan's honor) to the same degree as their Tajik and Pashtun neighbors, Uzbek women nonetheless lost much of their former nomadic independence. In the process, they gradually took to wearing the blue or white burqas of the Pashtuns and Tajiks, except when they were working in the fields.

While the vast majority of the Uzbeks had been forced to end their seasonal migrations into the Hindu Kush, their love of horses and the culture that surrounded them lived on. This passion for horses, more than anything else, allowed the Uzbeks of the twentieth century to maintain links to their former steppe homeland to the north. Like their nomadic forebears who roamed the open plains of Central Asia, Afghanistan's Uzbek shepherds continued to live on horseback. They also continued to play the horse-mounted game of *buzkashi* (literally "goat grabbing"), which had been used by their Mongol ancestors as a war game to develop raiding skills.

In addition to *buzkashi*, Uzbeks also gathered to watch their ancient form of wrestling known as *kurash*, which, like their horse-mounted games, taught them how to fight. It is no coincidence that some of the best *chapandaz* (*buzkashi* players) were also famous *pahlawans* (wrestlers), a claim that could be made by few polo players.

While women watched these events from the rear of the crowd, they usually did not play a prominent role in the public life of Uzbek rough-and-tumble *buzkashi* politics. The village women tended to stay at home, where they sewed clothes, took care of domestic chores, sought out brides or husbands for their children, kept track of the village gossip, and made traditional food: naan, *manti* (similar to raviolis), *somsa* (pies with meat and onions inside), *lagman* (noodle soup with meat and vegetables), and rice pilaf.

The Uzbek women also bore the important responsibility of raising the children in an unforgiving land that was most unpropitious for child rearing. Trying to keep their children alive in a country where infant deaths were all too common was a heartbreaking task.

Those Uzbek children who survived infancy went on to play barefoot in the melon patches and fields surrounding their *kishlak* until they were five or six. Then they were put to work. It was not uncommon to find young children, who in the West would be attending elementary school, working in the fields and engaging in full-time manual labor.

In all these aspects Khoja Doko, which lay to the west of Mazar-e-Sharif, was typical of the Uzbek villages of Afghan Turkistan. Its men played *buzkashi*; its women rolled the dough for *manti*; and its children died young of a variety of diseases. But there was one thing that separated Khoja Doko from the other mud-walled villages on the plains and hills of Turkistan. Despite the fact that the backwater village of Khoja Doko appeared to be consigned to inconsequence, in the late twentieth century it was to be home to a leader who would go on to bring down two Afghan governments and awaken his people to reclaim the heritage of Shaybani and his warriors.

9

THE FIRST BATTLES

"He was always a fighter. He never had the sense
to back down, even as a child."

—Mohammad Omar, Abdul Rashid Dostum's older brother

KHOJA DOKO, JOWZJAN PROVINCE, THE KINGDOM OF AFGHANISTAN. 1955–70.

From the day Abdul Rashid came into a world dominated by ancient traditions and poverty, his life was a struggle. His initial battle, as for all children born in Afghanistan, was merely to survive. Afghanistan of the mid-1950s had an infant mortality rate that was among the highest in the world. Like Abdul Rashid's sister, Anar, who died at the age of two, many children did not survive their first years of life. For this reason, Afghans give each child a false name for the first three days after birth, when he or she is still weak, to trick the devil into stealing the soul of the wrong child.

In Afghanistan newborn babies died from such evils as diarrhea, malnutrition, disease, lack of proper medical facilities, ignorance, and superstition.

Infants who had diarrhea were far more likely to be treated by a mullah than a doctor. Rather than provide an IV to replenish lost fluids, mullahs prescribed *taweez* (protective amulet) or drinking chicken saliva to protect their patients from the evil eye or *almastis* (female spirits).

Those infants who beat the odds and survived drinking water filled with microbes and living on leftover scraps of fly-covered food grew up to be tougher than their pampered Western counterparts. Condemned by the lottery of birth to a world devoid of children's safety seats, toys, preschools, baby food, physicians, pediatricians, clean water, and hospitals, Afghanistan's children either became strong or perished.

Those who not only survived in this world but came to dominate it were the fighters. The fighters have always shaped Afghanistan's history, especially when the weak central power of the day has collapsed.

By all accounts, the future warlord Abdul Rashid was born a fighter. In a household filled with nine siblings, including stepbrothers and stepsisters, it was almost a given that he would have to fight just to get his share of the food.

Abdul Rashid's early struggle to survive is best illustrated by a story from his youth. When he was only six, he was filling a jar with water from an irrigation canal. Suddenly a flash flood caused by melting snow in the Hindu Kush filled the ditch and swept him away. As the brown waters overwhelmed him, he took deep breaths and struggled to push himself to the surface. As he repeatedly rose up to catch his breath in the torrent, his lungs finally filled with dirty water, and he began to drown.

He was saved only by a villager. The villager saw a child's limp body being carried away by the current and snagged it in the branches of a dead tree limb. Before returning the child's body to his parents, the villager decided, almost as an afterthought, to try pumping the water from the boy's lungs. As the man pressed up and down on the boy's tiny chest, Abdul Rashid suddenly vomited water and came back to life. When the color came back to his face, the boy opened his eyes and grabbed the grinning villager's hand in terror.

When the villager brought Abdul Rashid home, his father Rahim's only reaction to the news of his son's brush with death was to beat him harder than usual.

Abdul Rashid managed to stay out of trouble for almost a year. As a reward for his good behavior, his father let him attend Koran lessons with some of the other children in the village. Three times a week Abdul Rashid, Mohammad Omar, and his other brothers (Abdul Kadir, Rustem, Amir), and his sisters (Kizlar Shah, Aysultan, Zuleyha, and Sherafet) would go to the village mosque to learn the principles of their people's faith.

Abdul Rashid and his siblings were extremely fortunate. While many village mullahs were illiterate, close-minded, and fanatical, Khoja Doko's village priest, Mullah Chakbashi, had traveled far and wide learning about Islam. Whereas the average mullah simply aimed to force his wards to memorize Arabic scriptures (without actually teaching them the foreign language), their mullah genuinely wanted them to appreciate the beauty of their religion.

The moderate message that was imparted to Abdul Rashid was one that, sadly, the younger mullah who replaced Mullah Chakbashi after his death—a zealot named Ahmed—derided as being "too open to accommodation with unbelievers and infected with dangerously lax ideas." Mullah Chakbashi was one of the last generation of teachers who were to pass on the ancient Sufi-mystic traditions of Central Asia to their pupils.

But in small villages like Khoja Doko across the north there were still a few Uzbek Sufi sheikhs or *ishans* who taught the ancient ways. These holy men worshipped God through poetry, meditation, singing, and *zikirs* (whirling dancing and chants), all of which were designed to achieve a deep sense of oneness with the Creator. Where the Uzbek Sufi sheikhs still held sway, women were not treated as chattel created just to tempt men. When Mullah Chakbashi was still alive, the village girls were included in the Koran classes—at least until they reached puberty and were sent into the confines of the burqa by their families.

Only one person seemed to mind this arrangement: Abdul Rashid. But it should be stated that his dissatisfaction stemmed not from his dislike of girls in general, but one particular girl in his classes, Khadija.

Khadija lived several dirt streets over from Abdul Rashid and had played with him and his brothers and sisters when they were younger. But as Abdul Rashid grew older he no longer found girls to be worthy playmates.

Khadija was not the only annoyance in Abdul Rashid's life in Khoja Doko, however. As a child he seemed incapable of accepting the bullying of older boys in the village. When he was attacked, he fought back every time, regardless of the outcome. By the time he was ten, older boys who had the strength to thrash him soon learned that it was not worth it. No matter how badly they beat him, Abdul Rashid always managed to get some blows of his own in.

But not all of Abdul Rashid's time was spent getting into trouble. As a youngster he was permitted to attend school until he was twelve. This kept him from engaging in further mischief. With the other students attending the simple village school on the hill above Khoja Doko, he learned the Arabic script and soon began to read and write words. All of the words he learned to write in the Arabic alphabet were of course common words in Persian Tajik, the language of interethnic communication in Afghanistan. And it was in this respected lingua franca, known as Dari (Dari and Pashto were Afghanistan's only recognized languages), that he learned rudimentary math, geography, science, and, most important, Afghan national history.

But the history he was taught was not the sort of enlightened multiculturalism a Swiss student would have been exposed to. From his first days in school, Abdul Rashid's teachers taught him and the rest of the students that Uzbek history was unimportant and their peasant language was fit only for farm work. They were also taught that the Uzbeks and neighboring Turkmen were uncouth Turkic invaders of the Kingdom of Afghanistan. Their glorious Afghan homeland, they were told, was founded by Ahmed Shah Durrani, an eighteenth-century Pashtun who began the "unification" of the various "Afghan" peoples. By 1884 the "lost" province of Afghan Turkistan was "reintegrated" into Afghanistan.

Regardless of the accuracy and content of the lessons he received, Abdul Rashid's education was, like that of all students in Khoja Doko, extremely basic. He was forced to share just a handful of books with the other children in a school that was devoid of heating and lacking in desks, pencils, paper, and other supplies.

As the students grew older, even this simple education ended for many. The poorer ones were gradually forced to quit school to work in the fields, and this number soon came to include Abdul Rashid. When he turned thirteen his father sat him down and told him that his prolonged education was over. "There are mouths to feed in this family. Reading and writing will get you nowhere in life. You need to work to help feed the family and find your own way in the world."

While Abdul Rashid desperately wanted to continue his studies, a son did not argue with his father in Uzbek culture. Lowering his head in respect, Abdul Rashid resigned himself to his fate. The next day he walked up the hill to his classroom, returned his pen and writing pad, hugged his favorite history teacher, Sharif Khan, one last time, and said good-bye to his classmates. By the following morning he was hard at work in the fields, enviously watching his more fortunate classmates march up the hill to continue their educations.

But Abdul Rashid's submission to his father's will did not mean that he had lost his fighting spirit. As he grew into his teens he continued to refuse to back down to people outside his immediate family. On one occasion, when he was fifteen, three older boys decided to gang up on him and beat him with sticks after an argument in the village square. Warned in advance by his best friend, Yar Muhammad, Abdul Rashid armed himself with a stick of his own and went in search of his ambushers. When he found them, he fought all three with the same fury he had always fought with as a child. By the time the fight was over, Abdul Rashid was covered in blood: his own—and that of his opponents.

While Abdul Rashid's wounds were limited to a damaged hand, a cracked tooth, and a few bruises, two of his opponents suffered broken bones. When their parents saw their condition, they furiously reported Abdul Rashid to the authorities and had him dragged down to the local police station. When the teen was brought in, the police commander found himself in the presence of a proud but respectful village lad who seemed to be incapable of lying in his own defense. When asked if he had beaten the other two boys whose parents had filed the complaint, Abdul Rashid replied in the negative. He explained that he had actually beaten three individuals, not two. He confessed to having beaten them thoroughly, but only in self-defense.

Exasperated by the thickheaded lad even as he admired his self-defeating honesty, the police chief declined to press charges no matter how hard the other boys' parents demanded it. Instead, he had Abdul Rashid sent home and ordered his father to keep him out of trouble.

This proved to be easier said than done, though, for Abdul Rashid was by this time developing skills as a leader among the poorer lads in the village.[1] With his friend Yar Muhammad by his side, he and his gang were even prone to fight back against the sons of the khans, the landowning class.

Abdul Rashid, whose family came from a long line of poor sharecroppers who worked on a local khan's lands, found himself unable to endure the taunts of "*Kara diqon!*," which meant "black peasant." When the local khans from the nearby town of Shiberghan came in their American- or Russian-built cars down the dusty dirt road to check on their village's lands, it hurt Abdul Rashid's pride to see his father and other respected villagers bow their heads in submission to them. And he was infuriated to see his own people's khans ingratiating themselves with the more powerful Pashtun khans and government employees from Kabul.

As the fights with the khans' sons grew worse, Abdul Rashid's father decided the time had come to send his son away from his village to earn money. In truth, Rahim was also worried that the family's khan might evict them if he knew Abdul Rashid was fighting with the landowners' sons. As

Rahim and the other hardworking peasants saw it, Allah had placed some men in charge of others. To question the timeless order of things was to question God himself. That was not only blasphemy, it was dangerous.

So at an age when most Western teenagers are focused on the minor traumas of growing up in affluent societies—competitive school sports, acne, braces, difficulties in dating, and disconnect from their parents—Abdul Rashid did as he was told. Setting out to find work under a dark cloud, he began a journey that was to eventually free him from the khans and mullahs of his youth. In the process Abdul Rashid, a simple peasant with no claims to high birth or advanced education, would become more powerful than any of the leaders who dominated his childhood.

10

THE SOLDIER

"For me the army was the only way to gain respect
and serve my country."

—ABDUL RASHID DOSTUM

KABUL, JALALABAD, THE REPUBLIC OF AFGHANISTAN. 1970–78.

As Abdul Rashid grew older working in the oil and gas fields, the peasant lads of the village seemed to be drawn to the jovial brawler with the proven reputation as a hard-to-beat *buzkashi* rider and *kurash* wrestler. By this time he was already establishing his *nam* (Persian for "name" or "reputation"). While he was not the son of a khan, he seemed to have a remarkable ability to exert influence over those around him. He clearly did not need the benefits of a powerful or wealthy father or clan to earn his own followers.

Despite leaving his village behind, one of Abdul Rashid's favorite pastimes remained fighting with the sons of khans. It seemed more than probable that the local police would sooner or later throw him in jail for his unruly behavior.

Matters came to a head one day when Abdul Rashid found himself arrested and jailed for a crime of some sort. This is a period of some mystery in Abdul Rashid's life, and one that he simply passed over on many occasions in our conversations by saying that "unjust accusations were made against me."

Soon after his release from jail, Abdul Rashid made his way to the great capital of the northern plains of Turkistan, Mazar-e-Sharif. There, for the first time, he beheld the blue-domed shrine that the locals believed held the body of Ali, the son-in-law of the Prophet Muhammad. While the original building from before the time of Shaybani Khan had been repaired over the centuries, the shrine appeared much as it would have during the time of the Uzbek conquests. The marble courtyard surrounding the mosque was still filled with white doves, Sufi dervish mystics still begged for alms in the entrance to the inner tomb, and pilgrims and supplicants from far and wide still came to pray at the shrine and crawl around a sacred relic known as the Dik-Ali cauldron in hope of receiving a miracle. Fully aware of the importance of the shrine to the local population, the Afghan state had wisely decided to protect Ali's tomb and now served as its custodians.

Abdul Rashid's arrival in Mazar-e-Sharif was just before the great festival of Nowruz. For the people of the north this New Year's festival had all the connotations that Westerners associate with both Easter and New Year's. Every year on that festive day, tens of thousands of pilgrims came to Mazar-e-Sharif to celebrate the return of life to the earth after the long winter. As the ancient Aryans and Bactrians had done for centuries, the people of the north watched horse games, prayed for rains and a fruitful year, gave gifts to loved ones, and listened to musicians.

The highlight of the ceremony was the raising of the *janda* (pole), a tradition whose origin was lost in the mists of time. For the farmers, this ceremony was a vital part of the planting season. Everyone believed it blessed the soil with another year of rain. They believed that, if the pole was not raised and the prayers were not said, the land would be cursed.

For this reason when the pole was finally raised, thousands of people raised their voices in joyous celebration and roamed the streets listening to music, meeting friends from other provinces, thanking God and Ali for their good fortune, and eating *sumaliak*, a special soup. Shiite mixed with Sunni and Uzbek, Turkmen, Aimaq, Pashtun, and Hazara all mingled together in a joyous celebration where ethnicity and religion did not matter.

While he was in Mazar-e-Sharif, Abdul Rashid, who had turned eighteen, was forced to do his national service in the army. He, like all the local recruits, was subsequently transported over the mountains from the only homeland they had known, Turkistan, for military training. There was little that Abdul Rashid, or anyone else, could see from the enclosed military vehicle on the long journey over the Hindu Kush and down to the capital.

Things did not get better when they finally got to Kabul. To his dismay, Abdul Rashid and the recruits were confined to the base as they learned how to follow orders, shoot various weapons, speak Dari and Pashto, and work with heavier military equipment. While the training was difficult and on occasion led to beatings, Abdul Rashid seemed to excel. After several months his skills were duly noted, and he was promoted to squad leader. This, however, did little to break up the monotony of a life spent in constant training.

But one day their drill sergeant came to announce that they had the day off to celebrate Pashtunistan Day. Unable to contain their excitement, the recruits were driven through the city to enjoy the afternoon at the Bagh-e Babur. The Bagh-e Babur, or Babur Gardens, was a series of terraced gardens in western Kabul built in the shadow of the tomb of one of Central Asia's greatest military legends, Babur Zahiruddin, the famous Timurid Tiger.

On the way to the garden, the recruits took in the sights of modern concrete buildings, government architecture, airliners coasting into Kabul International Airport, the occasional foreign tourist, and hundreds of women out and about wearing makeup and stylish Western clothes. Of course the city was also filled with the more mundane sights and sounds they all knew as well. There were the usual donkeys, beggars, women in burqas, blacksmiths, bazaars, mullahs, and goats eating refuse on the side of the road. But for a simple Uzbek from the provinces, entering the Afghan capital was like stepping into another world. Abdul Rashid instantly loved Kabul and everything it stood for. In the provinces ignorance prevailed, but here the government was working to bring the people of Afghanistan into the twentieth century. It seemed, however, as if Abdul Rashid's fate belonged to the provinces, where ignorant mullahs and tyrannical khans ruled.

Abdul Rashid returned to his barracks that evening with little expectation that things would change for the better in his life. But the next morning the drill sergeant came in with an announcement: "Three soldiers from among you have been chosen to serve out the remainder of their training in the elite 444 Commando Unit based in Jalalabad. You'll be trained to fight the enemies of Afghanistan by some of the greatest military experts in our country."

Everyone held their breath as the names were called out, but no one seemed surprised when Abdul Rashid's name was read first. His aptitude for weapons, hand-to-hand fighting, obeying orders, and leading others had not gone unnoticed by his superiors or his peers.

As the twenty-one-year-old from Khoja Doko was led away with the other two specially chosen recruits, his head spun with excitement. For the first time in Abdul Rashid's life his hard work and talents had been officially recognized by a superior. That moment began the transformation of the young man from a peasant into a general.

When the convoy pulled into their base in the eastern city of Jalalabad, Abdul Rashid was filled with enthusiasm and eager to begin his training. But as he and other commando recruits began their courses, it became obvious that they still had much to learn. Before they learned their fighting craft they needed the proper political education. For Abdul Rashid, whose schooling had ended at the seventh-grade level, this next phase was to be a fascinating exposure to the political developments that would one day tear his homeland apart.

On the first day, his commander—a tough commando who had been trained in the Soviet Union—gave them a history lecture the likes of which

Abdul Rashid had never heard. The historical journey the commander took him on was strongly shaped by a watered-down version of Communism that many Afghan officers subscribed to. In Afghanistan the army was the liberal voice of reform and progress, and Communism was seen as the antidote to the religious fanaticism and ignorance the military felt held their country back. The speech was an outline of various reformist governments' failed efforts to improve the lot of the peasants and modernize the country. The villains in this telling were always the conservative village mullahs, who considered everything novel to be *bid'ah* (heresy), and the khans, who kept the landless peasants in a state of poverty. It was the mullahs who called for the public stoning of women and the khans who had peasants thrown off their land if they did not work as sharecroppers. Together these forces worked to keep Afghanistan in the Middle Ages.

For Abdul Rashid, the bold words spoken that day were electrifying. He had never heard anyone speak out against the powers of the conservative countryside with such fiery determination and confidence. What his commander was proposing was both heresy and a call for revolution.

Abdul Rashid's political indoctrination in the army did not go much deeper than that; but as perfunctory as his introduction to Communism was, it inspired him. He gradually came to identify with the modernist agenda of a moderate Communist faction known as the Parchamis (the "banner" group), even if he was unable to understand the complexities of Marxism-Leninism.

For most Parchamis, Communism did not mean enforcing Soviet-style atheism or extending the Soviet workers' revolution across the planet. It meant forcefully ending poverty, social inequality, ignorance, fanaticism, and misogyny in their own homeland. While some of the Parchamis were more versed in the complexities of Marxist rhetoric, most were practicing Muslims who, in another context, would be called liberals, modernizers, or reformers.

But this was the Afghanistan of the early 1970s. In this time and place, anyone who wanted to increase women's literacy, end peasants' debt to their oppressive landlords, or whittle away the power of the mullahs and Sharia law was a "Communist."

Naturally the mullahs and khans considered the Communists to be their mortal enemies. While the Communists secretly moved to exert their power and enforce their will on the country, the khans and mullahs mobilized the provincial masses to resist them. In Kabul University the new breed of Muslim conservative fanatics threw acid in the faces of unveiled, liberated women and clashed with Communist militants who dreamed of forcefully unveiling women. It was a culture war in the extreme.

By the mid-1970s the battle lines had been drawn. In the impending struggle for Afghanistan, the traditionalists would eventually gain control of the mosques and the countryside while their progressive Communist foes would control the government, cities, and military. One side claimed Allah, centuries of tradition, and the support of the Arab Muslim Brotherhood. The other maintained a grip on the urban centers, universities, schools, the army, and the support of the Soviet Union.

But before the cataclysmic war for Afghanistan commenced, an Afghan Uzbek conscript named Abdul Rashid completed his national service and returned home with his head held high. When his elite commando unit delivered him to his home village after a two-year absence, the people of Khoja Doko saw a changed man. Gone was the angry teenager who had clashed with the khans' sons and fought to earn his reputation by wrestling and playing *buzkashi*. In his place the villagers found a thoughtful, confident young man who brought with him new ideas.

As his best friend Yar Muhammad and his other village friends gathered around him to hear of his adventures, Abdul Rashid sought to share with them all that he had learned. While the village elders called his new ideas dangerous, the younger men eagerly imbibed them. They were thrilled by Abdul Rashid's stories of "naked" women without veils in Kabul, strange lands lying beyond the Hindu Kush, and men who boldly challenged priests and khans.

But mostly they envied Abdul Rashid the fighting knowledge and experience he had acquired as a member of the elite commando unit. This was as exciting as his tales of miniskirt-wearing Kabuli women, soldiers who were not afraid of mullahs, and dreamers who planned to overthrow the old order.

Word of Abdul Rashid's return quickly made its way to Khadija, who had grown to be a strong-willed woman in the years since he had last seen her. This was best demonstrated in her relationship with her father. When he had decided to marry her off to a khan twice her age in order to acquire new lands, she had threatened to kill herself. Seeing that his daughter meant it, her father relented—but only after rendering a brutal beating. For months afterward he had refused to speak to her, until one day he came home with a new focus for his anger. Abdul Rashid, the local troublemaker, had returned to the village.

The fact that Abdul Rashid could drive her father to fits of anger without even knowing it appealed to Khadija. In his own gruff, oblivious way, Abdul Rashid was creating ripples in Khoja Doko, and Khadija liked what he had to say.

But Abdul Rashid did not spend long discussing politics among the village youth. He was first and foremost a "hands-on" man, not a politician. Soon after his arrival his experience as a noncommissioned officer leading a unit of one hundred elite commandos landed him a well-paying job. He was hired to work for the state-run gas and oil company in the nearby town of Shiberghan. Soon the money he brought in from this work and the respect he earned from his employers gave him a newfound stature among the poorer villagers. He was one of them, and he had made it.

Abdul Rashid was of course thrilled by the responsibility that had been placed on him and soon began to earn the praise of his employers. For the next few years he threw himself into his work with the same single-minded energy he had brought to the army, and he seemed to have a bright future ahead of him.

Content with his challenging, well-paying job as a driller, Abdul Rashid might well have spent the rest of his life working in the gas fields of Shiberghan. But on April 27, 1978, events larger than him would change not only Abdul Rashid's life but those of millions of his countrymen. On that day the tired young man came home from work and was summoned by his uncle to his family's main room.

"You've traveled beyond the borders of Turkistan to Kabul and other faraway Afghan lands—tell us what this terrible news means!" his uncle ordered, pointing to the family radio with a distraught look on his face.

His curiosity aroused, Abdul Rashid sat down on the floor cushions between two of his brothers, Mohammad Omar and Abdul Kadir, and listened to the radio. Sitting in rapt silence, he heard someone on the radio claiming to be from the "Revolutionary Council of the Armed Forces" and repeating the same shocking words over and over again in Tajik Dari: "People of Afghanistan, today is the dawning of a new era. Today President Daoud has been overthrown!

"For the first time, power has come to the people. The last remnants of the imperialist tyranny, despotism, and the royal dynasty have been ended. A glorious future awaits you in the People's Republic of Afghanistan! Long live the People's Republic of Afghanistan!"

As he heard the stunning news, Abdul Rashid had no way of knowing that the message portended a time of horror that would take the lives of over one million of his countrymen. Nor could he have foreseen that the rash act of Afghanistan's small Communist Party would lead to the intervention of both the United States and the USSR in an internal Afghan civil war between the conservatives and the modernizers. But somewhere deep inside, Abdul Rashid knew that this momentous event would shape his own destiny—for better or worse.

Looking at his uncle, Abdul Rashid suddenly remembered his commando trainer's words about dragging the country into the modern era one beard at a time. "My God," he whispered under his breath, "those Communist dreamers actually did it. They overthrew the president!"[1]

Seeing the frown on his uncle's face, he added, "Forgive me, Toga [Uncle]. I am not sure what it means—but I think it means the old ways are coming to an end. I believe it means that a new wind is blowing across the land."

Nodding in silence, his uncle stroked his beard and said nothing. Everyone sat listening to the disturbing message over and over again. Finally his uncle got up to leave, and the three brothers rose in respect.

But as he left the room, their uncle looked back and spoke directly to Abdul Rashid: "Mark my words and pay heed. You may think you know the world, but you do not. I am older and have earned my wisdom over the years and decades. The old ways exist for a reason: they are ordained by God to keep order here on earth during our short lives. I have seen enough to know that no good will come of this overthrow of the old order. Ordinary men have no right to remove kings and presidents. It is arrogance, it is immoral, and it is against the will of God. These impetuous men are consumed by *gharur* [the sin of pride], and they will bring calamity down on us all. May God protect us from their folly."

Then, as an afterthought, he said the words Abdul Rashid would remember years later when the country of his youth had been reduced to burnt fields, refugee camps, mass graves, and burning cities: "If new winds are really coming this way, Abdul Rashid, let us pray to God that they do not blow us all away with them."

The Uprising

JOWZJAN AND SAR-E-POL PROVINCES, THE PEOPLE'S DEMOCRATIC REPUBLIC OF AFGHANISTAN. 1978.

At first the new Communist regime was cautiously welcomed by the simple people of Khoja Doko and other villages of Jowzjan Province. Well aware of the country folks' deep-seated conservatism, the moderate Parchami faction of the People's Democratic Party of Afghanistan tried to move gradually in implementing its revolutionary social policies. When government teams arrived in northern villages, they were respectful to the mullahs as they opened up health clinics and began literacy programs.

Inspired by their Soviet comrades, who had offered privileges to the oppressed non-Russian ethnic groups of the former Russian Empire in their ethnic Soviet republics, the Parchami Afghan Communists tried to reach out to the non-Pashtun minorities. These outreach programs were soon felt even in out-of-the-way places like Khoja Doko. One day Abdul Rashid was summoned to the living room by his father, who had tears in his eyes. "They are speaking our language on the radio!" he exclaimed in shock. "Come quickly before it ends—the news is being given in Uzbek!"

Although skeptical, Abdul Rashid followed his father into the room and for the first time in his life heard his tongue being spoken over the airwaves. When a woman came on the radio afterward and began to sing about the Afghan homeland in Uzbek, he was overwhelmed with emotion. Having heard nothing but Pashto or Dari on the radio since his childhood, the moment had a tremendous impact on him.

That was not all. The new Communist government soon began to publish the first Uzbek language newspaper, *Yulduz* (the star). In the evenings Abdul Rashid would sit with his extended family and listen as his younger brother, Rustem, who was much better at reading, went through the paper. Among the most interesting bits of news was that the new Communist government would allow non-Pashtuns to enter the high ranks of the army for the first time.

For Abdul Rashid, whose superiors in the army and at work had all been Pashtuns, this news was hard to grasp. But it told him one thing: the new Parchami Communist government appeared to be reaching out to the Uzbeks and other oppressed minorities in an effort to end Pashtun dominance. Like the wondrous USSR, which had given the Uzbeks north of the Amu Darya River their own socialist Soviet republic, the new Afghan Communist state appeared to be recognizing its downtrodden minority groups.

Many members of the growing Uzbek nationalist intelligentsia in Mazar-e-Sharif quickly came to the same conclusion. These intellectuals entertained novel ideas that the Uzbeks were not a race of peasants but a *millat* (nation) with a proud past. For this reason, they were drawn to the new Communist government. Many of them called to mind the loss of

Turkistan's independence a hundred years earlier and dreamed of reviving their oppressed nation.

Across the north, progressives who had liberal ideas about giving women and peasants more rights also came to support the new government. Of course the conservative mullahs muttered that God had not created women to be equal to men, and the khans ridiculed the notion that *kara diqon* had rights, but this discontent did not initially translate into action. Nor did the Pashtuns initially rise up against the new Communist regime, because its top leaders were all Pashtun like they were.

But for those who were not living in the cosmopolitan bubble of Kabul, it was apparent that the provinces were like dry kindling waiting for a spark to set them on fire. That spark came in the summer of 1978 when the moderate Parchami faction of the Communist Party was purged from power by a more extreme branch, the Khalqi (translation: "people") faction. Led by devout Marxists, the Khalqi faction was eager to pick up the pace of the reforms. Like Stalin, who had brutally secularized the conservative lands of Soviet Uzbekistan during the 1930s, the Khalqi Communist leadership dreamed of modernizing the country—at the barrel of a gun.

By the summer of 1978 the Khalqis had begun a series of reforms that would inadvertently ignite the flames of resistance in the countryside and drive the khans and mullahs to declare jihad. Considered to be among the most ungodly of the Khalqi Communists' decrees was their law forgiving landless peasants—who made up more than 70 percent of the country's population—their debts to their wealthy landlords. With the stroke of a pen, the new revolutionary regime claimed to have ended "the backbreaking burden of usury and mortgage" and announced that "millions of peasants were freed from the clutches of moneylenders." They also began to arrest khans and mullahs, even those who were not resisting the unpopular reforms.

But the real spark that set the blaze came when women activists from Kabul went into the villages to "liberate" other women. When the uncovered Communist women performed educational plays and spoke in public about women's rights to schooling, work, their choice of husband, birth control, and life without the veil, the conservative mullahs were driven over the edge.

Consistent with these views, the Khalqis issued the infamous Decree Number 7, setting off what had been bubbling just beneath the surface. The decree outlawed the forced marriage of young girls and lavish expenditures on *haq mehr* (bride price). To conservative onlookers, among the decree's most blasphemous pronouncements was its stipulation that a woman could not be bartered or married off against her will. For centuries, Afghans had paid large dowries for wives chosen for them when they were young. Girls as young as twelve were forced into marriages that ensured political or economic alliances. It had always been done that way, and by outlawing a custom that was deeply ingrained in the people's conservative culture, the Khalqis boldly declared war on the very traditions that defined the countryside.

It quickly became apparent that the village Afghans drew a line when it came to interference in their domestic affairs. As the decree became known, rumors began to spread that the Communists were empowering women in order to transport them to Moscow to serve as prostitutes. It was time for God-fearing Muslims everywhere to put an end to what they considered to be un-Islamic interference in their customs by the liberalizing Communists.

The reaction against the law began in the mountains of the eastern province of Nuristan but quickly spread to other tribal areas. By the late summer of 1978, bands of *ashrars* (rebels) led by their village khans or mullahs had begun to kill teachers and burn schools, health clinics, and other symbols of the detested Communist regime.

The Parchami Communist faction, which had been driven from power, pleaded with the Khalqis to moderate their policies. But the Khalqis made the fateful decision to fight fire with fire, determined not to allow the forces of ignorance and bigotry to defeat their glorious revolution. Taking a page from Stalin's book, the Khalqis sent their dreaded secret police across the land to arrest "counterrevolutionaries." Villages that resisted were surrounded by the army and bombed or assaulted. Tens of thousands of innocent people were arrested and taken to the notorious Pul-e-Charkhi Prison east of Kabul, never to be seen again.

By the winter of 1978, the government was engaged in a full-scale war with the provincial counterrevolutionaries who threatened their ambitious plans to modernize Afghan society. But unlike Soviet leader Josef Stalin, who had the might of the all-powerful KGB secret police and the Red Army to back up his *hujum* (assault on Islam), the Khalqi Communists' resources were limited.

In order to strengthen their military forces, the Khalqis came up with a drastic solution: increasing forced conscription into the army. The new draftees would be used to defend the revolution and prevent the mullahs and khans from stopping the march of Communism.

As these unsettling events unfolded, a deep sense of uncertainty descended on the village of Khoja Doko. While many of the poorer peasants were attracted to the Communists' egalitarian ideas, their powerful khans and mullahs declared their policies *bid'ah*. With mounting confidence, the provincial elites prepared their old bolt-action Enfield rifles to fight against the godless Communist government, and the simple folk joined them. If their mullahs said the new government was un-Islamic, who they were they to question them?

This struggle between two inflexible forces would shatter Abdul Rashid's family. Among those called up to serve in the Afghan Army was Abdul Rashid's bookish younger brother, Rustem. When Abdul Rashid returned home from work to discover the terrible news, he was horrified.

In the days following Rustem's call up to the army, Abdul Rashid grew sick with worry as he imagined his weak younger brother going through the brutal training he himself had experienced. While he had not minded the demanding physical instruction, hand-to-hand fighting, hazing, poor food, and officer brutality, he knew it would break Rustem.

"God forbid Rustem be sent into battle against the mullahs and *ashrars* in the provinces," Abdul Rashid confided to his older brother Mohammad

Omar. "The rebels are fanatics. They're publicly executing captured Afghan Army soldiers as infidels."

As the day of Rustem's conscription drew near, Abdul Rashid grew more concerned, and a deep gloom settled over the entire household. They all realized that national service now meant going to war.

On the day the army arrived in their village, Abdul Rashid's mother could not control her sobbing. While the young man put on a brave face and tried to act as if he were proud to be following in Abdul Rashid's footsteps, he could not hide the real fear in his eyes.

As the Afghan Army trucks that had rolled into Khoja Doko that afternoon dispersed soldiers out into the village to collect the recruits, Rustem began to physically shake. As his mother fell to the floor weeping, a squad of soldiers arrived at their door and demanded that he report to duty.

Watching his younger brother bravely walk out to join the soldiers, Abdul Rashid understood that there was a good chance he was sending his younger brother to his death. Thousands of village youth just like Rustem were being thrown into combat without proper training, and many would not be coming back.

Abdul Rashid had always been the black sheep in the family, whereas Rustem had been his parents' favorite. As he imagined his family coping with the loss of their precious younger son, he understood what he had to do. It was time to act to save his brother.

When one of the soldiers pulled his mother's hands off Rustem and began to take him to the awaiting transport truck, Abdul Rashid ordered him to unhand her. Though Abdul Rashid was unarmed, his voice carried a certain authority to it, and the soldiers' commander sensed that he was no ordinary peasant. Looking the tough Uzbek villager in the eyes, the troops' commander understood that this man would put up a fight if the men did not release his mother.

Placing his hand on his pistol to show who was in charge, the commander glared at Abdul Rashid for a few seconds and then ordered his men to unhand his mother. If nothing else, he was curious to see what made this peasant so confident.

Nodding his head in gratitude, Abdul Rashid stepped forward and gave the commander the salute he had been taught in the army. "I am Abdul Rashid, and I spent two years serving with the 444 commandos in Jalalabad as a noncommissioned officer. I have had extensive combat training and am volunteering to fight to defend our *watan* (homeland). The government has mandated that one person from our household report to service—I offer myself in the place of my brother. I request that you mark out his name on your roster and replace it with mine. You will find him to be of no use in combat, whereas I am a trained soldier."

After pausing to mull over the proposition and demonstrate who was in charge, the commander magnanimously consented. "*Bale* [OK]. You have permission to take your brother's place. You are now a member of the Army of the People's Democratic Republic of Afghanistan and will serve your country for two years."

Before his family could react, Abdul Rashid walked away from them and allowed himself to be hefted up into the back of the departing transport truck. Despite his outward calm, his ears were ringing from the shock of what he had just done. Looking back on his family, he realized he was leaving them, his job, his home, and everything he had dreamed of returning to back when he had previously been in the army. Now it would begin all over again.

Abdul Rashid realized that he had just made one of the most important decisions of his life, but then he understood that it was not he who had made the choice. As always, the rules of the land were controlling his destiny. While the wealthy could easily bribe their way out of the army, the price of getting out of military duty—300 Afghanis—was far beyond his family's means.

Abdul Rashid controlled himself as he saw Rustem running behind the truck, crying. Finally, Abdul Rashid lost sight of his brother, his family, and his home as the truck drove out of Khoja Doko and onto the dirt road to Shiberghan where he would begin his career as a fighting soldier.

First Command

DARYA SUF (RIVER OF THE CAVES) VALLEY, NORTHERN AFGHANISTAN. FALL 1979.

In the following weeks the Afghan Army trainers provided the recruits from Khoja Doko and other villages with a rushed training in how to use their Mosin rifles. It quickly became obvious, however, that Abdul Rashid was already an expert, and he was tasked with helping to train his fellow recruits. But before their training was complete, their commander decided to use them in battle against *ashrars* (rebels) who had just taken the city of Sar-e-Pol in the western plains of Turkistan. Long before the men were ready, they were thrown into combat.

In the subsequent battle Abdul Rashid fought well, and on two separate occasions rallied retreating Afghan Army troops to return to battle after they had been pushed back by the rebels. After several days of intense fighting he had become something of a leader for several platoons of new recruits. Abdul Rashid seemed to have the ability to think coolly in battle and was a natural commander. Considering the generally poor performance of the other recruits, this made him stand out, and he came to the attention of his superiors.

Soon after Sar-e-Pol had been retaken, Abdul Rashid's commanding officer took him to meet the general in charge of the *kandak* (battalion). The general belonged to the moderate Parchami Communist faction that had decided to create several all-Uzbek militias to fight against the *ashrars*. He felt that the Uzbek peasants would fight better if they were organized in ethnically homogenous units and led by commanders from among their own people. The general asked Abdul Rashid if he would be interested in leading one of these new Uzbek "homeland defense" *kandaks*, and he responded with alacrity that it would be his honor to serve his homeland as a commander. With that, Abdul Rashid received his first command, leading a six-hundred-man *kandak*.

Abdul Rashid was thrilled by his promotion and honored to be able to lead fellow Uzbeks in combat. By this time he had already acquired his nickname, Dostum (translation: "my friend"), for his tendency to address everyone in his unit with the term. It was to be under this nom de guerre that Abdul Rashid would subsequently gain fame as a skilled counterinsurgent.

While the other Pashtun generals were leery about giving command of a fighting force to an Uzbek, Dostum's Parchami commander made it clear that the Uzbeks would be organized as a fighting unit only on a temporary basis. This would eliminate the risk of them seizing power as the Turkic *ghulams* (slave warriors of the Arabic and Persian rulers) had in ancient times. The general made it clear that Dostum and his six-hundred-man "tribal unit" would only have one chance to prove themselves. If they succeeded, the Jowzjani Uzbek militia would be retained and expanded. If not, the battalion would be disbanded and scattered among several other multiethnic *kandaks*.

All too aware of the pressure on him, Dostum made his first command decision. He boldly approached his general and told him he wanted to choose his own men. When the general readily agreed, Dostum began a tour of Jowzjan Province to find the men he wanted. He traveled from the Soviet border in the north to the southern mountains in search of the perfect recruits. For incentive, the recruits would be offered something the earlier draftees had not been given: regular salaries and better weapons, including the fully automatic AK-47 assault rifle. Most important, Dostum, the *kara diqon* peasant, offered them the opportunity to fight under one of their own for honor, good pay, and prestige.

But Dostum did not choose the men his commanders expected. In every village he looked for the local scrappers, poor farmers' sons, tough *buzkashi* players, the roughest oil and gas men, and simple peasants who had nothing to lose. Many of these rough young men had grown to trust Dostum while working with him in the gas and oil fields; others came from his home district and knew of his reputation as a wrestler. Many simply saw Dostum and his militia as their only chance to make something of themselves in a society that offered them few opportunities for advancement. Yar Muhammad, Dostum's childhood second-in-command in his fights with the khans' sons, was delighted to join his unit.

This new brotherhood was bound not by any deep affection or loyalty to a government that had always suppressed its people, but to one another and to their commander. They all understood that their leader was one of them. He spoke their Uzbek language and knew of their struggles to survive as impoverished workers and farmers. He knew that few of them could read or write, fewer still owned land, and none of them was from the elite. Like Dostum, they knew this was their one chance to achieve something. War could kill them, but it could also provide them with unexpected opportunity if they had the skills and audacity to seize it. In a conservative Muslim society that believed in predestination, Dostum's newly formed unit gave simple peasants the uncommon opportunity to choose their own destiny.

Dostum made it clear that his men had to have one talent in particular to seize their destinies: the ability to ride. The reasons for this soon became obvious when Dostum gathered his men at their base in Mazar-e-Sharif to train. While the Afghan military manuals emphasized Soviet-style infantry tactics, Dostum envisioned something entirely different. He intended to tap into his people's greatest national asset and deploy horses in battle. While several of his commanding Pashtun officers dismissed the idea offhand, Dostum fought tenaciously for the right to use his people's horses.

Although several of the commanders mocked Dostum's plan, his commanding general finally conceded. Having seen the Uzbeks' rough-and-tumble version of polo, he liked the idea of harnessing their warlike spirit for the counterinsurgency against the rebels.

This seemingly minor victory further enhanced Dostum's confidence. But as he left his general's office, he overheard the commander's second-in-command quietly mock him. This contempt infuriated Dostum and drove him even harder as he trained his men for their first battle. As the tough

Uzbek *buzkashi* players honed their skills at shooting targets from the back of a moving horse, some of their skeptics began to see that they might have a chance against the rebels. Especially now that they had been armed with AK-47s and a few RPG-7 rocket-propelled grenade launchers.

Some time later Dostum rousted his men before dawn and led them out of Mazar-e-Sharif toward the Hindu Kush on their first mission. Watching them ride out of the base, some of the Pashtuns ridiculed them. Sensing the contempt in which the rest of the army held them, Dostum and his men rode with backs ramrod straight and proud. Their fellow soldiers' disdain only stiffened their resolve to succeed.

And succeeding clearly meant avoiding detection. Riding southward toward the snow-covered mountains, they avoided roads and settlements to keep their progress secret. It was only when they entered the foothills of the Hindu Kush a day later that Dostum met with his men and told them their destination.

"A group of *ashrars* belonging to the jihad party of a Pashtun named Hekmatyar has taken the town of Darya Suf in the heart of the Darya Suf Valley," Dostum explained. "You may have heard of this fanatic. These days he lives in Pakistan and works for their intelligence services. This man is not a warrior; he's a terrorist, and he is trying to spread his jihadi poison to our lands.

"His followers have infiltrated the Darya Suf Valley and are using it as a base to mount guerilla strikes down into the plains. We must destroy these *ashrars* who call themselves mujahideen [holy warriors] now and save Turkistan from the fanatics.

"As for my plan, it's nothing too complex. We'll simply ride until dusk, camp in an abandoned village for the night, then attack at the break of dawn. Our intelligence says the mujahideen rebels have set up their base on a hill outside the village of Darya Suf. We'll ride up the Balkh Valley, which leads to the Darya Suf Valley; once there, we'll attack the rebels. All we have to do is roll over their positions and destroy them before they destroy us. Simple as that."[2]

While no one thought it would actually be that simple, none of them was inclined to question his decision. Doing so would have been seen as unmanly and cowardly. Hearing no objections, Dostum silently led his men into the mountains, following sheep trails that took them up the Balkh Valley and into the hills. If any mujahideen spies were observing them, they would have seen his unit simply disappear into the mist-covered mountains of the Hindu Kush. There was no telling what their ultimate destination was. To keep their mission secret, the men tried to avoid all contact along the way, lest word of their destination leak out to the Islamist rebels.

For their part, the *ashrars* were on the lookout for Dostum and his men, but they were unable to discover where they were headed. They assumed the Uzbeks had ridden back home toward the capital of Jowzjan province, Shiberghan. The fact that Dostum and his men were on horses had misled the rebels, who concluded that the unit was simply on a routine patrol.

Thus when Dostum and his men finally arrived outside the village of Darya Suf in the valley of the same name, they found the rebel sentries sound asleep at their posts. Furtively moving through the morning mist, Dostum and his men tried to get as close as possible to the rebels' hilltop base before they were discovered.

But their stealth approach did not last long. One alert sentry noticed the shapes of horsemen moving through the morning mist and raised the alarm. As he yelled to alert his comrades, he was instantly gunned down. The gunfire quickly awoke the other rebels, and the game was up. The time had come for Dostum and his men to ride across the plain surrounding the rebels' hill and overwhelm them before they could react.

"Charge!" Dostum yelled as the sentries woke and began to fire on his men. In a second the Uzbeks were frantically whipping their horses forward, lying low in their saddles to avoid incoming rounds. Stunned rebel pickets at the bottom of the hill rushed out of their huts to see hundreds of enemy horsemen emerging out of the mist and charging toward them. Those mujahideen who did not rush back inside instantly were gunned down by the fast-riding Uzbeks.

Despite their initial disadvantage, the rebel defenders lost no time fighting back. As the *ashrars* fired on the incoming Uzbeks, Dostum watched several of his men tumble out of their saddles, riddled with bullets. Still, the Uzbeks rode over the trenches of the stunned enemy at full speed. At one point their fast-moving column was halted by return fire from a rooftop, and the men dismounted to rush it. The Uzbeks pushed forward, offering covering fire for three of their members, who charged straight into the enemy's fire and took them out. As the battle raged, a wounded rebel charged at Dostum and was gunned down. The air was filled with the sounds of men screaming in fury and fear as the Uzbeks rolled with their momentum.

Everything around Dostum appeared to be happening in a strange frozen world. He seemed to have lost his hearing, recognizing only the pounding of his heart, and he soon realized that they were running out of enemy to kill. Suddenly, as if sensing that they were on the losing side of the battle, the rebels began to emerge from their positions with their hands in the air. Seeing their surrender, Dostum quickly called for an end to the slaughter. In the blink of an eye, it was over. The mujahideen rebels surrendered to the mysterious horsemen who had emerged out of the mist to wreak havoc on their lines.

As his hearing came back with a roar, Dostum heard his men chanting his name. Dostum's childhood friend Yar rode up and tapped one of his prisoners on the head with his rifle. "What do we do with this riffraff?" he asked his commander.

Staring into the frightened captives' eyes, Dostum sought to decide their fate. As his hand stopped shaking, he walked before the cowering rebels and made what was perhaps the most important decision of his career. While the mujahideen were known to gun down "Communist infidel" captives from the Afghan Army, Dostum decided to embrace his prisoners and try winning them over to his side. As the enemy soldiers were disarmed and tied up for transport back to Mazar-e-Sharif, he made a point of publicly leading his men in a prayer of thanks so that their prisoners could see they were not atheists. With his men lined up behind him in prayer, Dostum loudly spoke the prayers taught to him as a child by Mullah Chakbashi.

But Dostum did not end his efforts to reach the rebels there. On the long journey back to headquarters, he carefully explained to the captured fighters that he and his men were not Communists. They were simply poor men fighting to enforce the rule of law as God himself ordained. He explained that none of his men cared about Communism nor even understood it, but they respected their ordained rulers as all good Muslims should.

Remembering the warning his uncle had given when he first heard on the radio that the Communists had overthrown the president, Dostum scolded the prisoners for not taking salaries to fight for their rightful ruler, the government. He also pointed out that the rebels' commanders were all local khans and mullahs who had abused them for generations before ordering them to wage jihad on their behalf.

While many of the bearded *ashrars* were too fanatical to be reached by his message, Dostum noticed that several of the poorer Uzbek captives were listening attentively. Many of them were superstitious and believed that victory went to him whom God had chosen. That Dostum was clearly a Muslim and an Uzbek peasant like them made his message all the more appealing.

"I have no idea what will happen to you lads when we turn you over to my commander in Mazar-e-Sharif," Dostum continued, "but if any of you are willing to mount up and join me and my men, I'll put in a good word for you. Perhaps the government will forgive you and pay you to fight for it. If your families vouch for you and offer themselves as hostages for your good behavior, I'm sure you'll be released to fight with me."

In light of the Uzbeks' well-known flexibility in making alliances, it came as no surprise that the vast majority of the Uzbek prisoners quickly saw the wisdom of joining with Dostum. Dostum clearly had clout and a *nam* (name); but most important, he had momentum on his side.

When Dostum and his column returned, the whole district came out to see the sight. Even the Pashtun generals who had earlier mocked him and his men came out to applaud them for their stunning success.

Dostum's commander publicly embraced the "peasant commander" and made a point of praising him. For Dostum the praise and tribute were vindication of his belief in himself and his battle instincts. He could not suppress a grin when he saluted his general and replied, "My general, I promised you I'd give you a victory or die trying. I'm happy to report that I am still alive. The town of Darya Suf is back in government hands, and I and my men await your orders!"

11

THE TRAITOR

"My men did not fight for Communism.
They fought for me and for one another."

—Abdul Rashid Dostum

KHOJA DOKO. WINTER 1979.

Dismissed from military duties for a temporary leave, Dostum once more returned to his village a hero. But he quickly realized that things had changed for the worse in Khoja Doko during his eleven-month absence. Everyone, it seemed, had a grievance. No sooner had he and dozens of his men arrived home to their village than the local elders invited him to a meeting to air their complaints. Dostum told the *aq saqal* graybeards that he had little or no clout with the provincial governor in the town of Shiberghan; nonetheless, the men saw him as a powerful government fighter who could intervene on their behalf with the Khalqi Communist authorities.

The village elders' complaints had to do with the new government's Communist policies. One elder whom Dostum had known since childhood complained, "The government has mandated a new policy limiting dowries to less than 300 Afghanis. What man who has pride would give away his daughter for a mere 300 Afghanis? This is against Islam and tradition!"

Another pointed out, "They're redistributing the land and taking it from those who have it and giving it to those who don't. This is against the holy Koran. Some men are born with land, others are not; this is Allah's will. Who are these men to change the fate that has been written on our brows at birth?"

Finally the village mullah complained, "The government has banned giving a tithe as is prescribed in Islam. This is blasphemy. They are preventing us from practicing our faith."

As Dostum heard the complaints, he sympathized with the villagers. The Khalqi Communists from Kabul tended to be a brutal lot who were unsympathetic to peasants' concerns. He promised the village headmen he would intercede on their behalf with the government delegation coming to Khoja Doko the next day. There had to be some middle ground between the extreme Communism of President Amin's Khalqi faction and the entrenched conservatism of the peasants. As someone who had led government soldiers into combat in defense of the revolution, perhaps he would be able to make the villagers' case.

As Dostum left the meeting he realized that he had become a leader among the three thousand inhabitants of Khoja Doko. Word of his success in Darya Suf had already spread to the village, and people were now calling him Commander Dostum instead of Abdul Rashid. The village's hopes seemed to be riding on him, and the new respect with which he was treated was empowering. But would he be able to sway the powerful men coming from the provincial capital of Shiberghan?

The next evening the government delegation arrived in Khoja Doko to hear the villagers' complaints, and hundreds of village men dressed in turbans and *chapans* came out to greet them. The crowd then moved to an open-air gathering hall at the base of Khoja Doko's hill for a meeting. All eyes were on the large young man in the green military uniform who was pressed forward by the crowd to represent them.

But as the government men came forward from their cars, Dostum's heart sank when he saw that one of them was Abdurezzak Khan, the older brother of his childhood playmate Khadija. Abdurezzak was not only Khadija's brother, he was also the son of a khan. In his youth Dostum had gotten into more than one scrap with Abdurezzak, and the man would doubtless still hold a grudge against his childhood enemy even though he had, like Dostum, gone over to the Communists.

Dostum was not far off the mark in his assumption. As the village men lined up to shake hands with Abdurezzak and the official next to him, known as Hara Juya, Dostum prepared to greet them. But when the two men came to him, they assiduously avoided shaking Dostum's hand. The public rebuff was meant to humiliate the village upstart who had dared to speak on behalf of the people. While Dostum inwardly seethed with rage, he outwardly held his composure as the two men walked to the center of a makeshift stage and began to speak to the people.

But nothing could have prepared him for what came next.

"Comrades and workers, we have come to hear your complaints," Hara Juya began. "But we have heard that you have asked the thief and brigand known as Dostum to represent you. Know that this man is unworthy of such an honor. He is an *ashrar* and a criminal who has no status in Khoja Doko. You believe you have chosen a hero to represent you when in fact you have chosen a traitor to the revolution as your representative."[1]

As Hara Juya continued in this vein, it became obvious to Dostum and the elders around him what the government's representative was trying to do. By discrediting Dostum, he was discrediting the villagers' complaints.

"If you don't shut this fool up, I will," Yar Muhammad snarled from behind Dostum as Hara Juya continued to berate him. And Yar was not the only one who was upset; more than two dozen of Dostum's fellow soldiers stood in the crowd, and they looked as if they had murder in their eyes. It was clearly time for Dostum to do something drastic.

Dostum made the second critical decision that would help him reach out to the mujahideen resistance in the area and begin to forge a middle road between the mujahideen rebels and the Communist government. As Hara Juya switched from berating Dostum to belittling the village elders' complaints, Dostum reached into the sheath on his belt and withdrew the government-issued knife hanging there. Then, before Hara Juya's guards could react, Dostum leapt onto the stage and rushed him. As the knife blade raced toward his throat, Hara Juya screeched in horror.

But Dostum merely held the knife to the official's throat as his own men disarmed Hara Juya's bodyguards. A ripple of surprise swept the crowd as everyone watched to see what Dostum would do next. With all eyes on the two of them, Dostum hissed into Hara Juya's ear, "Comrade, if you don't want me to slit your windpipe, you'll do exactly as I tell you. Tell the people that you rescind the laws on tithes, dowries, and land confiscations. Apologize for insulting their customs, and I'll let you live. Then return to your cars and drive back to Shiberghan before I change my mind."

With a face that was red from fury, humiliation, and fear, Hara Juya did as he was told. When he was finished, Dostum shoved him from the stage and watched as he and Abdurezzak Khan fled through the crowd back to their waiting cars.

As they drove off, Yar saluted Dostum. "Well, Abdur Rashid, I believe you've won the hearts of the people of the village; no one will ever call you a Communist again. But I suspect you'll have hell to pay when the governor finds out how you manhandled these two."

That night Dostum slept fitfully in his family house. The next morning his older brother Mohammad Omar gently woke him. "Good morning, 'traitor.' Once again trouble finds you, I see. You're the talk of the village after that little stunt last night. Now a messenger has arrived from the governor himself. It seems you are wanted in Shiberghan to answer for your actions. What will you do? Turn *ashrar* or go to your doom? Governor Besheryar is a murderer; you resisted his commands and threatened his representatives. I suspect you'll end up in a shallow grave like all the other so-called counter-revolutionaries he's killed if you go to Shiberghan."

Dostum mulled over his options. While the *ashrar*/mujahideen rebels would be delighted to have him come to their side, his *nam* had been built defending the secular revolution, not siding with those who killed schoolteachers in the name of Islam. And besides, he was not one to run away from a confrontation.

"I think you know the answer, Mohammad Omar. I have to go to Shiberghan to explain my actions to the governor. Perhaps I can show him how the government's actions are driving the people into the hands of the rebels. I was simply trying to placate the villagers before they went over to the mujahideen."

That afternoon Dostum arrived at the governor's headquarters in Shiberghan and was ushered into Besheryar's office. There he saw a furious Hara Juya, whom he noticed with satisfaction had a small bandage on the nick Dostum had put on his neck the night before.

"Here is the traitor Dostum who I told you about. He's the one who roused the villagers against the revolution and spoke out against President Amin!"

Dostum felt the blood boil in his veins. After saluting the governor, he tried to speak in his defense, but as he moved forward to explain his actions, the governor signaled for one of his guards. A second later Dostum felt a gun butt crash up against his face, and he fell to the floor, spitting blood. As he tried to rise, another guard hit him in the back of the head, and he blacked out.

He awoke later in the day in a jail with a gash on the back of his head and still spitting blood from the initial blow. It did not take him long to realize where he was. He was below the governor's office in the holding cell used for condemned men awaiting execution. His gamble had not paid off, and now he was going to pay the ultimate price for interfering in the government's policies toward the peasants.

A wave of despair overwhelmed him as he looked back upon his life and the few things he had accomplished in it. While he was, like many Afghans, fatalistic and resigned to his death, a part of him burned with rage. It burned with fury at the system that had allowed him to rise up and be someone, and then had taken it all away from him in an instant.

As the hours passed, Dostum tried to remember the death prayers Mullah Chakbashi had taught him. He was overwhelmed by the sense of having come so close to success. In the ultimate of ironies, Dostum and his men were to have been rewarded for their campaign in the mountains by their commanding general on that very day on the parade grounds in Shiberghan. It might well have been the beginning of a promising career. But now all that awaited him was an executioner's bullet and an unmarked grave. He would soon join the thousands of alleged counterrevolutionaries being killed across the land by the Afghan Communist government. Soon the very name Dostum would be forgotten and his unit would be broken up and disbanded.

Lost in his misery, Dostum did not initially notice the gunshots that rang out from the courtyard in front of the governor's office, nor the sound of horse hooves. Only when several agitated guards came downstairs to grab him did he realize that something was amiss.

"Get up, Dostum, you *ashrar* scum, and move! The governor has decided to release you. It seems that hundreds of your men have arrived out in front of the governor's office and are threatening to storm it if you're not released. The governor has signed a pardon for you, and you are to be spared. Now go and get that mutinous rabble out of here before the governor's own troops open fire on them and we have a civil war on our hands!"

With that, Dostum was unceremoniously led out of the dark cell and into the sunlit court, where it appeared that his entire *kandak* had gathered. When he staggered out into the sunlight, a roar swept across the mounted men, and Dostum saw a smiling Yar Muhammad at their head.

As Dostum grabbed the reins of the horse Yar handed him, he looked back into the governor's office. There he saw Khadija's brother Abdurezzak Khan staring out the window, wearing a strange expression that Dostum could not read. With a grin, Dostum saluted him and rode off in a cloud of dust.

The General

JOWZJAN PROVINCE, THE PEOPLE'S DEMOCRATIC REPUBLIC OF
AFGHANISTAN. 1979–84.

As all of these events were unfolding in Shiberghan, larger events were
taking place that would propel the newly minted Uzbek leader to the forefront of the war between the Communists and the mujahideen rebels.
What would ultimately become known as the Afghan war began when
the embattled Afghan Khalqi Communist ruler, President Amin, moved
too fast to try implementing Soviet-style five-year modernization plans
in his country. Soon a spontaneous rebellion spread from the mountains
of Nuristan in the east to the entire country. By the summer of 1979, the
mujahideen rebels controlled much of the countryside and began moving
on the cities. As the Communist regime in Afghanistan appeared close to
falling, the Soviets desperately sent in advisers, arms, and funds to stave off
a counterrevolution.

But things began to fall apart during a rebellion in the great western
city of Herat. Government troops led by a Tajik named Toran (Colonel)
Ismail Khan were sent to quell the rebellion. Instead they turned their guns
on their Soviet advisers and massacred them. Ismail Khan's men, proudly
bearing the heads of the Soviet advisers on sticks, then took to the western
Hindu Kush and created a mujahideen fighting unit.

In the east, a Tajik leader known as Massoud led a similar uprising in
the scenic Panjshir Valley and began to swoop down out of his mountains,
attacking vital supply columns connecting the USSR to Kabul. Massoud's
mujahideen soon gained control of much of the northeast and proved to be
a direct threat to Kabul.

From Pakistan, the fundamentalist leader Hekmatyar, who gained
great notoriety for throwing acid at unveiled women, responded with a
different tactic. He sent his terrorists into Kabul to gun down government
officials. Hekmatyar's fanatics also killed teachers in the countryside, burnt
schools, and assassinated government leaders. As Hekmatyar spread his

terror throughout the east, the Pakistanis and the Americans decided to sponsor him, and he became the number-one recipient of CIA covert funds.

In the south, a rebel by the name of Haji Latif attacked government troops in Kandahar. In the central highlands, a Hazara commander named Abdul Mazari began to attack government positions. And in the northern plains of Turkistan, Tajik mujahideen commanders named Zabiullah Khan and Ustad Atta began to launch attacks from the Hindu Kush.

As the countryside went up in flames, President Amin dawdled and talked of killing even more so-called counterrevolutionaries. By December 1979 it appeared to the Soviet leaders in the Kremlin that Amin had doomed the revolution by pushing it too far too fast. He had to be stopped and the rebellion suppressed, or else the fundamentalist rebels would seize the country and threaten the USSR's secularized Central Asian republics.

On December 25, 1979, in a move that was to haunt it until its dying days, the Soviet Union ordered the Soviet Fortieth Limited Contingent to invade Afghanistan, kill Amin, replace him with a more competent president, and help suppress the rebellion. The whole intervention was expected to take just one year, and then Soviet troops could be withdrawn home. Thus began the Soviet invasion that was to devolve into a nine-year proxy war between the Soviets and the US-sponsored mujahideen rebels.

Dostum's first indicator that the Soviets were invading the country came when he and his men began to see the white contrails of Soviet jets crossing the blue Afghan sky on December 26, 1979. Watching the high-flying planes from their base in Shiberghan, they all sensed that something big was taking place.

Three days later Dostum and his six-hundred-man fighting unit were deployed to Mazar-e-Sharif, where they reunited with their general, who had heard about Dostum's run-in with the governor of Jowzjan Province.

"Well, Dostum, no one can accuse you of not speaking your mind, but you would do best to keep your opinions to yourself in the future," said the general. "Now, to the task at hand. It appears as if we have a new leader. President Amin the Khalqi has been killed, and a member of the Parchami

Communist faction named Babrak Karmal has been put in power. As you know I am a Parchami banner man, and many of our faction have been given promotions."

Dostum congratulated his commander and eagerly awaited his orders. Everyone knew that the Parchami faction was the moderate faction of the Afghan Communist Party. It was also the faction that was most interested in working with minority ethnic groups like the Uzbeks.

"As it happens," the general told Dostum, "my commanders in Kabul have given me permission to upgrade your unit from three hundred to one thousand men and to designate it the 734th People's Self-Defense Regiment. Your job will be to defend the highways and gas and oil installations, the very ones that some of you helped build with Russian help. You are also to facilitate the movement of Soviet troops from Termez on the border of Uzbekistan to the Hindu Kush. There you will transfer protection of Soviet supply columns to a Hazara commander named Sayid Mansur Naderi in Baghlan Province. His Ismaili Hazaras have formed another pro-government tribal militia to help protect the revolution. You will probably come into contact with our Soviet comrades, who are here to help us suppress the counterrevolutionaries and end the *ashrar* rebellion. When you do, treat them as brothers; they are doing their internationalist duty to make sure that the rebels do not overthrow the glorious revolution."

As he left the meeting, Dostum was ecstatic. His hard work in training his men and establishing a pro-government tribal militia had paid off. Now he had orders to recruit more men in order to increase the size of his *kandak* to one thousand fighters. His *nam* was increasing, and it seemed as if he had risen from the pit of the governor of Shiberghan's jail. After his release he had been promoted to the rank of a full colonel.

For the next year Dostum did as he was ordered, traveling across Jowzjan Province and recruiting from the hardscrabble Uzbek villages of the north. While some reactionary mullahs spoke out against him, the fact that Dostum had fought to defend the Islamic traditions of Khoja Doko convinced many that he was a good Muslim. In the widening struggle for the future of Afghanistan there were moderates on both sides, and everyone knew that Dostum was not a hardened Communist like many of the Khalqi officials sent from Kabul.

This ability to play both sides allowed Dostum to regularly meet with local mujahideen commanders to negotiate cease-fires, encourage defections, and attempt to downgrade the violence in his home province. In the following months, Dostum proved to be the ultimate Afghan counterinsurgent. He knew the lay of the land and the local customs, had spies in the ranks of the rebels, knew how to use Islamic traditions against the mujahideen, and fought ferociously—but only as a last resort. On nearly every occasion that Dostum and his riders confronted the mujahideen, they came away victorious, but Dostum constantly tried to beat the rebels through nonmilitary means.

As whole districts in the Pashtun south fell to the mujahideen rebels from 1980 to 1982, Dostum's home province of Jowzjan remained comparatively secure. While there were sporadic attacks by mujahideen on the provincial capital of Shiberghan, they did not have the same impact on security as they did in other provinces. As Dostum and his Jowzjani militia co-opted mujahideen or crushed them throughout the province, Shiberghan became known throughout the country as Little Moscow.

Soon, the new governor of Jowzjan, a Parchami moderate, made the stunning decision to upgrade Dostum's unit even further and increase enrollment from one thousand to ten thousand. The new unit would be known as the Fifty-Third Division and would be the largest tribal militia in the country. This represented a drastic increase in the tribalization of the counterinsurgency in the north and made Dostum the second most powerful man in the province after the governor. Other pro-government militias that had been formed at the time, including those of the Uzbek commanders of neighboring Maimana Province, led by Rasul Pahlawan and Gaffur Pahlawan (aka the Wrestlers), came under Dostum's nominal jurisdiction as well.[2]

In 1983, as word of Dostum's success spread, Dr. Mohammad Najibullah, the head of the Afghan Intelligence Service (KHAD), invited him to come to Kabul for a meeting. It seemed that the Soviets had taken a direct interest in his success and wanted to know how they could export it to other regions.

By this stage Dostum had been fighting for three years and had grown in stature from being the "peasant commander" to one of the most successful anti-mujahideen leaders in the country. When Dostum arrived in Kabul he found a large cosmopolitan city where women worked as doctors and teachers and freely walked the streets without fear of mujahideen attacks. The university was filled with men and women learning secular subjects that had been banned by the mujahideen. To protect the city from the rebels who sought to disrupt this haven of safety, Soviet troops wearing their distinctive fur hats and tan military fatigues guarded the intersections and checkpoints leading into town.

The sky above Kabul was filled with Soviet transport planes bringing supplies in to keep their war effort going. The occasional flight of MiGs or Hind attack helicopters flew east to confront the Tajik and Pashtun rebels. Clearly the Soviets were expending considerable effort to keep Kabul safe from the rebels.

All seemed secure in the Afghan capital, but Dostum heard troubling reports from the provinces. Despite their efforts to crush Massoud and his Tajik rebels, the Soviets could not prevent him from ambushing their convoys once they left the Uzbek and Ismaili Hazara protected zones of the north. And in the southeast, the Pashtun mujahideen had made tremendous inroads into the provinces stretching along the Pakistani border. With rear-area supply bases across the border in Pakistan, the US- and Saudi-sponsored Pashtun mujahideen proved to be all but impossible to beat. Clearly Dostum's success in the north was the exception, not the rule, and the government had a keen interest in promoting his Jowzjani model elsewhere.

"Dostum, on behalf of the Revolutionary Committee, I want to thank you for your efforts on behalf of the workers and peasants of Afghanistan," Dr. Najibullah, a large Pashtun with a mustache, said as they began their meeting. He was curious about the reasons for Dostum's success, and Dostum was eager to share his secrets with Najibullah and a Soviet delegation.

"I was helped by the fact that the Tajik and Pashtun mujahideen factions operating from their sanctuaries in Pakistan didn't allow the Uzbeks and Turkmen to create their own mujahideen party," said Dostum. "There is no Uzbek mujahideen group. The Pashtuns and Tajiks had racist views toward our Turko-Mongol peoples, so our local mujahideen had to join Massoud's Tajik party or Hekmatyar's Pashtun party to fight. Many chose not to do so; instead they came over to me to fight for the government for salaries. We Uzbeks and Turkmen tend to be a pragmatic lot when it comes to such things.

"Then there is the terrain. Unlike the Tajik and Pashtun rebels who have mountains to fight from in the east, most of Afghan Turkistan is a flat plain. Although there are a few Uzbek rebels, such as Ahmed Khan of Samangan Province who operates from the mountains of the south, they cannot strike as far north as Mazar-e-Sharif. We catch them out in the open and easily destroy them. While half of my men still fight on horseback, recently we have been given artillery and Soviet-built tanks to fight the rebels, and we can beat them in both light and heavy attacks.

"To make matters worse for the mujahideen in the north," Dostum explained, "they cannot retreat across the border to rest, re-arm, and train the way the Pashtuns and Tajiks go to Pakistan. There are no cross-border sanctuaries for the rebels operating in Afghan Turkistan. By contrast my own pro-government forces can always be resupplied by our fraternal allies from across the border in the Soviet Union. For all these reasons, we've been successful in suppressing the rebellion from the town of Maimana in the west to Kunduz in the east.

"But once you enter the mountains to the east of Kunduz, you enter the realm of Massoud. His men fight well, and we respect them. Massoud's mujahideen are a match for my Jowzjani Division. But when Massoud tried closing the Salang Pass over the Hindu Kush, my men pushed them out in a bloody fight."

Najibullah appeared pleased by Dostum's response. Then he dropped a bombshell. "Well, whatever the secret of your success is, we have decided to increase the number of your troops to forty thousand, Dostum. It seems that the Afghan president himself has decided to entrust you with taking your force beyond the borders of Afghan Turkistan to crush the feudal insurgents elsewhere."

Dostum was stunned. Forty thousand men under the control of an *Uzbek*. Not since the time of his people's conquest by Abdur Rahman, the Iron Amir, had the Uzbeks fielded such a sizable fighting force. It was a tremendous honor, and he wondered if he was up to the task.

But there was more. That afternoon Dostum was invited to a cabinet session of the Afghan Communist Party. There, to his amazement, he was given a Hero of Afghanistan award, the highest honor granted by the People's Democratic Republic of Afghanistan. He was also promoted to the rank of four-star general. Clearly the upper echelons of the country had placed their faith in him. One general claimed that after the Russian Spetsnaz special forces and Hind attack helicopters, Dostum and his men were the most effective weapon in the Communists' arsenal.

And it became clear that the Parchami Communist government meant to use their new tribal weapon far from its northern base at Shiberghan. Najibullah announced, "Next month you and your men will be deployed to the south to Kandahar, the heart of the Pashtun insurgency. If you prove to be effective there, we'll try you in other zones as well."

Burning with a desire to prove himself worthy of the tremendous trust placed in him and his men, Dostum subsequently drove his Jowzjanis hard, fighting against Haji Latif's mujahideen forces in Kandahar. From there Dostum's Jowzjani Division was deployed to the forested mountains of Paktiya in the east, where they clashed with the Pashtun rebels of Jalaludin Haqqani.

After that they pushed out the Wahhabi forces of a Pashtun commander named Abdul Rasul Sayyaf, which were threatening Kabul from the nearby province of Paghman. For months Sayyaf's forces had been firing rockets down into Kabul, killing civilians. Afghan television featured images of Dostum's troops storming Sayyaf's positions and pushing his rebels out of firing range of Kabul. Once again Dostum was hailed as a hero. He had saved the people of the Afghan capital from the merciless bombardment of a fanatic.[3]

Time and again the Afghan Communist government found that Dostum's tough Uzbeks succeeded where even their Soviet allies could not.[4] And they noticed that Dostum and his men fought with much greater ferocity against the Pashtun mujahideen and their Arab volunteer allies than against fellow Uzbeks and Turkmen mujahideen in the north. As Dostum's Jowzjanis cleared the insurgents out of such provinces as Paktiya, Logar, Paghman, and Kandahar, his fame as a counterinsurgent spread throughout the land.

But not all of his press was favorable. In the Pashtun lands, Dostum and his rebel hunters became known as *gilimjans* (carpet thieves) for plundering the homes of their enemies. And powerful Pashtun Communists, such as the Khalqi faction minister of defense, Shanawaz Tanai, were alarmed by the prospect of Uzbeks killing Pashtuns, even though those particular Pashtuns were the mujahideen enemy.

But Dr. Najibullah, the head of KHAD, always defended Dostum from his Pashtun Communist detractors. Najibullah succeeded in convincing his fellow Pashtun Communists that the powerful Uzbek militias would be put back in their place once the war was over.

Oblivious to the fact that he and his men were being used by a Pashtun-dominated Communist Party, Dostum decided to return to his home village of Khoja Doko in 1984 to check up on his family. There his path would again cross with that of Khadija, the girl who had once shadowed him as a child.

12

KHADIJA

"Khadija was the only one who could
tame Dostum in those days."

—ABDUL KADIR, DOSTUM'S YOUNGER BROTHER

**KHOJA DOKO, JOWZJAN PROVINCE, THE PEOPLE'S DEMOCRATIC
REPUBLIC OF AFGHANISTAN. 1984.**

When Dostum returned to his village, he was greeted as a hero by most.
But one powerful family in Khoja Doko held a grudge against him. The
father, uncle, and brothers of Khadija resented Dostum's usurpation of their
authority following the now legendary knife-pulling incident during the
Communist delegation's visit years ago. Since that time Dostum's brothers and uncles had feuded with the family of Abdurezzak Khan, Khadija's
brother. Dostum's younger brother, Abdul Kadir, a spitting image of his
famous general brother, had been warned several times by the village elders
to cease the feud.

Upon hearing of Dostum's return and as the feud threatened to grow more violent, the village elders met to adjudicate. Dostum's father attended the *shura* (council) to see what the powerful *aq saqals* would decide. Meanwhile Dostum and his brothers waited at home for the council's decision.

Several hours later Dostum's father and the elders arrived, with Khadija's father and brother among them. The village mullah read his verdict to the assembled crowd.

"For years now your two families have fought and have spread dissension in the village. This feud of yours is against our customs and against Islam, which calls for peace. To keep the peace the council has chosen to bring your two families together."

"Abdul Rashid Dostum, your father and Abdurezzak's father have agreed to join your families in marriage. In four months time you, Abdul Rashid, will marry the second-eldest daughter of Abdurezzak's family, a fine young woman known as Khadija. Thus declares the council of Khoja Doko."

As the mullah's words echoed across the room, all eyes were on Dostum to see how he would react to the verdict. But no one expected the look of undisguised joy mixed with shock that appeared on his face. In the ultimate of ironies, his bold assault on the Communist delegation had brought him to Khadija, whom he knew had grown to be a beautiful, intelligent, educated woman.

While Khadija's father did not look thrilled by the prospect, he had to follow the will of the council or be ostracized. Besides, General Dostum was not the rabble-rouser of his youth; he had become the most powerful Uzbek in the land. Joining with Dostum would link him to a powerful family. Notwithstanding his faults, Khadija's father could not be called a bigoted village conservative. He had allowed his daughter to stay in school right to the end of high school and had even allowed her to take some classes at Balkh University in Mazar-e-Sharif. At least he and Dostum were on the same side in the war that was tearing Afghan society apart.

For his part, Dostum was ecstatic, but he tried to keep the joy off his face as he rose and bowed his head to acknowledge the elders' decision. "If it is the will of the *aq saqals*, I agree. It is good that there will finally be peace between our feuding families. I will be honored to marry Khadija in the interest of bringing our great families together."

Dostum and Khadija set a date for the wedding, and a jubilant Dostum was then called back to the army to fight a mujahideen offensive to the east. While Dostum's Jowzjani militia was off fighting in Mazar-e-Sharif, however, a local Uzbek mujahideen commander made the bold move of attacking Khoja Doko village. In a sign of things to come, he and his men closed the school on the hill in the center of the village and threatened to execute anyone suspected of being a Communist. The mujahideen also threatened Khadija's family for their links to Dostum.

As the pressure on him to call the wedding off mounted, even the *aq saqals* who had made the original decision appeared to be rethinking the wisdom of their ruling. With the mujahideen rebels strutting around the village, Dostum's improbable dream of marrying Khadija appeared to be fading. Dostum burned to return to his village and liberate it from the *ashrars*.

But the fighting in Mazar-e-Sharif had proven more difficult than anyone had expected. Ustad Atta, a member of Massoud's Jamiat Party, personified this boldness. Dostum took it as a personal insult that Atta's rebels should strike at the holy city of Mazar-e-Sharif, and he fought ferociously to push his men out of its suburbs.

As the battle for Mazar-e-Sharif unfolded in painful slow motion, the day of his marriage with Khadija fast approached, and Dostum fretted. What if he could not get there in time? Would he be able to clear out the rebels from Mazar-e-Sharif and free himself to return? What if her father or the village elders changed their minds during his absence? What if the mujahideen who had seized Khoja Doko had heard of his impending wedding and harmed Khadija?

Infuriated by the delay caused by the fighting, Dostum led Yar and the rest of his men into combat over and over again, only to have Atta's wily mujahideen evade them whenever the fighting got too tough.

As Dostum frantically sought a way to end the fighting and return to Khoja Doko, a messenger arrived from the village with a letter for him. When Dostum read it, his heart soared even as he was filled with fear. In it Khadija told him that she was planning to escape from the village on the following Wednesday and travel to Shiberghan to meet him at the governor's headquarters.

Dostum read and reread the letter. It was the first indication he had received from Khadija that she loved him, and it more than demonstrated her courage. Truly the sharp-tongued girl of his youth had grown to be a strong-willed woman. She was risking her life to escape her father and brothers—not to mention the enemy-controlled village—to marry him. He longed to return to the village with his men and crush the rebels, but his orders were to push Ustad Atta's men out of Mazar-e-Sharif first.

But could he escape his duties and make it to Shiberghan on the chosen day to meet her? Dostum finally forced the issue by leading a bloody charge into the Hindu Kush to wipe out the supply lines that were providing Ustad Atta and his men with their weapons. While scores of his men died in the process of storming the hornet's nest of a rebel bastion called Elburz, he finally felt confident enough to leave his troops on the morning of the anointed day. With their supply lines cut, Atta and his rebels retreated back to the mountains to lick their wounds, and Dostum prepared himself to see Khadija for the first time in years.

Dostum was now free to speed to Shiberghan in his Neva jeep to meet Khadija. But as he checked his watch he realized he was already running late. Would Khadija be able to escape the mujahideen in her village and her parents and make it all the way to Shiberghan undetected? With his heart pounding, Dostum and Yar and a small group of soldiers raced to get to Shiberghan in time.

Suddenly the governor's compound appeared before them, and Dostum leapt from the jeep, calling out Khadija's name to the various women in blue burqas selling items on the street. He ran along the rows of faceless women, frantically shouting her name.

But no one responded. Dostum grew sick with fear as ran up the stairs of the governor's compound and stared out at the crowd. But he could see no one that resembled Khadija in the sea of turbans and burqas. He was too late; he had missed her. Or worse yet, she had been caught trying to escape her father's household—or apprehended by the rebels in charge of the village.

Then he saw a face in the crowd staring at him, and his heart sank in horror. It was Khadija's older brother, Abdurezzak Khan. His presence could only mean one thing: he and his brothers had caught Khadija and taken her back to the village. Dostum was overwhelmed with despair and instinctively opened his hands in supplication to let Abdurezzak know that he, not Dostum, had all the power.

With his eyes locked on Dostum's, Abdurezzak moved through the crowd toward him. "Greetings, Abdul Rashid. I see you have come here today looking for something?"

Dostum's eyes bore into Abdurezzak's as he answered, "You know I have. I've come to Shiberghan from Mazar-e-Sharif for my betrothed. I have come here for your sister Khadija as promised me by the elders."

Then Abdurezzak spoke again. "I see that you love my sister, and she too would seem to love you. I caught her trying to sneak out of the house in the early morning hours to marry you. Of course she threatened to kill herself if she was not allowed to come here to meet you. It was a woman's foolishness. A woman cannot travel on her own, especially with the war waging around us—it's madness."

Abdurezzak continued to stare Dostum in the eyes. "But she is a strong-headed woman, of that there is no doubt. And Khadija is no fool. I have always been close to her and dreamed of having her meet a man that cherished her."

Dostum could not control himself as he absorbed the unexpected words. Spontaneously he grabbed the smaller man in a bear hug. Nothing else needed to be said. With that Abdurezzak and Dostum drove to a nondescript house in Shiberghan's back streets. As they entered, Dostum heard shuffling in the women's quarters.

They signaled to one of their host's sons to summon Khadija. Dostum waited anxiously for her to arrive. What would he say to her after all this time? How should he greet the woman that was to become his wife when he barely knew her?

Then she entered the room, with only a headscarf on her head, along with three or four younger girls who were similarly unveiled in the modern fashion. She said nothing, but her lively eyes conveyed a mixture of relief, shyness, and perhaps a hint of humor.

For his part Dostum simply grinned from ear to ear and felt like an idiot. Then Abdurezzak spoke.

"Khadija, are you sure you want to go through with this?"

Khadija paused, and then replied with a surprisingly strong voice, "I am sure, brother. This is the man I want to marry."

Abdurezzak then turned to Dostum. "Abdul Rashid, are you sure that you want to marry my sister?" he asked.

Dostum responded, "God knows, there's nothing in the world I want more than to marry Khadija."

His response seemed to satisfy both Abdurezzak and Khadija.

"Then let's go to the mosque and do this before anyone tries to stop us. If the mujahideen find out that we're holding a marriage for the notorious Dostum here in Shiberghan, there's no doubt they'll try to disrupt it."

With that the small party drove to the mosque and held a ceremony that was devoid of the usual festivities that characterized an Uzbek wedding, such as the kelin salon and other rituals. Once the ceremony began, the mullah read them their acceptance agreement, and Dostum and Khadija both nervously agreed. When it was over Dostum, Abdurezzak, Yar, and the other men gathered and sang Khadija a simple song that was traditionally sung for Uzbek women at their wedding. The lyrics asked her not to cry and encouraged her to be happy even though she was leaving the only home she'd known.

With that, the mullah blessed them with some verses from the Koran; a scribe from the governor's office recorded their marriage, and they were declared man and wife.

Not sure what to do now that the wedding was over, Dostum beamed and stared at Khadija. Khadija seemed to be equally at a loss for words. Dostum even noticed tears in her eyes; whether they were from excitement, joy, or fear he was not sure. Determined to keep his own tears from his men, Dostum gruffly ordered them to bring the car up.

But their quiet reverie was broken by the sound of distant gunshots. As Dostum cursed his men for celebrating by firing off their rifles, Yar came running into the room with a worried look on his face. "General, I have some bad news for you. Five blocks from here the mujahideen are launching an assault on the Shiberghan Prison; they're trying to release their friends inside. Every soldier is needed to push them back!"

Dostum's grin faded, and he instantly became serious. "You see what you've married," he said to his bride, "a man who has no rest from fighting."

Children and Death

SHIBERGHAN. 1984–87.

Dostum survived the battle for the Shiberghan Prison despite being wounded in the stomach and face from shrapnel. He later pushed the rebels out of Khoja Doko, where he was welcomed as a hero. In so doing he earned even further praise from Dr. Najibullah, the head of KHAD intelligence. As the Soviet's yearly casualty rate surpassed two thousand, both the Russians and the Afghan Communists came to rely upon the moderate Uzbeks to fight their war against the mujahideen.

But although Dostum spent months at a time fighting in the mountains, he always found time to be with Khadija. While their relationship was shy and tentative at first, they quickly became closer than most Afghan couples. Afghan men and women typically live in separate worlds, with married couples often barely interacting. But Dostum needed to be with Khadija, and at every opportunity he rushed to their home in Shiberghan to be by her side.

Khadija, who had more education than Dostum, taught him much of what she knew. And, most important, under Khadija's tutelage Dostum grew to respect the rights of women, a belief that he would maintain throughout his life. While he had been a secular modernist for many years, he became a staunch supporter of the Communists' battle to empower women at this time. Among the many projects that he ran while serving as a commander in the Afghan Communist Army was a school for girls in Shiberghan where Khadija taught.

In return, Dostum shared with Khadija his stories of the places he had seen, such as Kandahar, Kabul, Jalalabad, and even the Soviet republic of Uzbekistan, a modern land he had visited for a brief training exercise. As Dostum's salary increased, he showered Khadija with gifts: novelties from the USSR such as a Western-style table and chairs, jewelry, modern women's clothing, a television, and even a refrigerator.

But life was filled with more serious concerns as well. After several months together, Khadija became pregnant and gave birth to a girl, whom they named Rahila. Dostum doted on his firstborn, and enjoyed spoiling her. In his heart of hearts, though, Dostum had wished for a boy. But their second child, Ayjemal, was also a girl. When Khadija became pregnant a third time, Dostum visited the shrine of the Kizil Ayak Sheikh to ask for the blessing of a boy.

This time around, when Dostum took his pregnant wife to the hospital, he was confident their child would be a boy. To Dostum's delight, he was, and they named him Batur (brave warrior).

While Dostum spent as much time as he could with his wife and children, his duty demanded that he spend most of his days fighting in the field. By this time the mujahideen rebels had grown bolder. As the Soviet losses mounted, a new liberal Soviet leader named Mikhail Gorbachev sought a way out of the quagmire that he defined as a "bleeding wound."

One of the approaches he took was removing the Soviet leader Barbrak Karmal and replacing him with Dostum's KHAD sponsor, the notoriously brutal intelligence chief Mohammad Najibullah. In 1986, Najibullah was promoted to president of Afghanistan, and he began to rely more upon Dostum as his great praetorian guardsman. Dostum and his fierce Jowzjanis reported directly to the new president and went wherever the fighting was toughest.

At this time Dostum's Uzbeks also began to clash with Arab fanatics coming over the border from Pakistan. While the well-trained Uzbeks usually came away victorious from their clashes with the Arab mujahideen adventurers, they failed to destroy the Arab's mountain base in Jaji, an obscure village on the Pakistan border. This failure would give rise to the legend of one fighter named Osama bin Laden.

But bin Laden's subsequent terror war against Americans seemed unimaginable at a time when the CIA was funding the anti-Soviet mujahideen and arming them with the heat-seeking antiaircraft missiles known as Stingers. After 1986, as the Soviets' once invincible Mil Mi-24 Hind attack helicopters and their Mil Mi-8 Hip transport helicopters were shot down by the rebels, the Communist government increasingly relied upon Dostum's men to guard convoys that were forced to move on the ground to avoid antiaircraft missiles. In this, Dostum's men proved to be the most effective fighters in Afghanistan after the Soviet and Afghan special forces. While there are numerous accounts of the mujahideen from this time period, a UN representative provides a rare 1980s eyewitness account of Dostum's men that helps bring his tough Jowzjani militia to life:

Ethnically they are Uzbeks, reputedly the fiercest most primitive fighting force in Afghanistan. Some are teenage boys. Some are, of course, older and are veterans of a decade of warfare in this beautiful, ravaged country. It can be assumed that every one of them, no matter what his age, has suffered some losses within his family.

They are clad in various costumes. Some wear traditional shalwar-kameez, a two-piece cotton costume with trousers that reach down to the ankle, except that in this case, the trousers have been rolled up to the knee, to allow them to run fast. Over the top part of the kameez, they wear long, quilted corduroy capes [chapans]. On their feet they wear sneakers, sandals, loafers, and boots. Some wear fatigue shirts. On their heads, they wear turbans or Pakul caps. And they all have gun belts and colorful sashes. Most of them have moustaches. They enjoy posing for pictures. . . .

To see those soldiers, among the best in the world when it came to guerilla warfare, so simply clad, so young, so shy yet fierce was a sight to behold.[1]

As the mujahideen grew bolder, Dostum himself continued to lead men like these in confronting the rebels. While the chief rebel in the north, Zabiullah Khan, had been killed in an intramujahideen dispute, the Tajik commander Ustad Atta had kept up the pressure on Dostum. In one of his bolder moves, Atta launched an attack on the Turkmen-dominated town of Akche between Mazar-e-Sharif and Shiberghan. Dostum was called away from home, where his wife was nine months pregnant with their fourth child, to suppress the rebels. Once again Dostum and his trusted second-in-command, Yar, led their troops in storming the town to push the mujahideen out.

On this occasion, however, the rebels had set up an ambush for Dostum. As he and Yar led their men forward, hundreds of Atta's men converged on their position in an attempt to kill him. Dostum's loyal fighters quickly fell back to their leader's side to defend him, but he again pushed them forward. The enemy smelled blood and fought back ferociously, firing RPG-7s and AK-47s with deadly effect. Scores of Dostum's men died in the fierce fighting, and the enemy appeared to be close to killing Dostum himself.

Seemingly unconcerned about his fate, Dostum stormed forward, firing his AK-47 and killing two rebels who appeared committed to a suicidal attack. Dostum ran over their bodies and straight into another ambush. As he headed down an alley, three rebels on the roof above rose up to kill him.

Caught dead in their sights, Dostum did not have a chance. But as the rebels fired on him at almost point-blank range, Dostum sensed a blur by his side and was knocked behind the corner of a mud-bricked house. While the enemy's bullets cut into the thick mud wall, Dostum rose to his feet to fire back.

At that moment he saw who had knocked him to the ground. His childhood friend Yar lay where Dostum had just been standing; he was riddled with bullets. As Dostum tried to crawl toward him, Yar's body was penetrated by another hail of bullets. Dostum fired upward toward his attackers and rushed to Yar's side, pulling him behind the wall.

When Dostum got him to safety, Yar's face was bleeding, and he had wounds on his torso and neck. Consumed by fear, Dostum began to drag his friend through the enemy gunfire back toward his own men. But he was impeded by Yar's massive size, and frequently had to stop to fire back on mujahideen who were closing in on them.

It was only when they were safely among his own men that Dostum stopped to speak to his friend. Soviet medics came running toward them, and Dostum frantically signaled for them to assist Yar. As the blond Russians gathered around, one of them somberly looked the Uzbek general in the face and spoke through his interpreter.

"Comrade, I'm afraid it is too late. Your man went into shock and has died from his wounds."

Dostum's head spun as he grasped the news that the friend he had known since childhood—almost as long as he had memory—had just died saving his life. As he looked down on the blood-spattered face of Yar, he was consumed with self-loathing. Yar, the jovial village lad, had joined the army only to be with Dostum, to protect him. If he had not done so, he would still be alive at this moment. After all these years, how could he lead his men without Yar by his side? Was his sacrifice worth it?

At that moment one of Dostum's soldiers came and gently placed a hand on his shoulder. "Pasha, we've defeated the rebels; they're in full retreat. Akche is ours again."

Dostum nodded, only half aware of the words being spoken, and tried to offer a word of encouragement. But he could not, so great was his misery.

A while later a second soldier came tentatively forward with another message. "My general, word has come from the hospital in Shiberghan. Your wife gave birth to a healthy boy this morning. We have communication with some soldiers there guarding the hospital. Would you like to send a message?"

Dostum's heart soared with the news, and it helped ease the pain of his best friend's death. Truly Allah gave even as he took away.

Closing Yar's eyes, Dostum rose slowly and stared at the soldier who was giving the news, trying to master his grief. "Yes, I have a message. Please send my love to my wife and tell her I have a name for our son."

Dostum paused and looked at the face of his childhood friend. "Tell her he is to be named for a hero who died here today. He is to be named Yar."[2]

13

CONSPIRACIES

"After the Soviets left Afghanistan, the war changed entirely.
It became a struggle for power and autonomy."

—GENERAL DOSTUM

AFGHANISTAN. 1989–92.

By 1988 it was obvious to all parties involved in the conflict that the new
Soviet leader Mikhail Gorbachev was going to withdraw his country's forces
from the unwinnable war in Afghanistan. The Soviets had lost thousands of
soldiers to a guerilla enemy that controlled most of the countryside. By the
beginning of 1989 the Soviets began their much-heralded withdrawal, and
on February 15 the last Soviet soldier crossed the Bridge of Friendship at
Termez into Uzbekistan. The Soviet bear had been worn down and defeated
by the indomitable mujahideen. As the Soviets pulled out, the American-
and Pakistani-backed mujahideen sensed that victory lay just around the
corner. On its own, President Najibullah's Afghan Communist Army could

not stand for long against the Tajik and Pashtun rebels operating in the south and east.

But the rebels clearly needed to gain control of a major city as their first interim capital. In the spring of 1989, the fundamentalist Pashtun commander Hekmatyar launched an all-out assault on the eastern city of Jalalabad, which lay near the Pakistani border. The mujahideen made the monumental decision to switch from guerilla tactics to frontal combat and even used Pakistani-supplied tanks in their attack. As thousands of Pashtun mujahideen stormed the city, the writing appeared to be on the wall for President Najibullah and the beleaguered Afghan Communist government in Kabul.

In desperation, Najibullah flew in Dostum's Jowzjani Uzbek division to bolster the disheartened Afghan Army defenders in Jalalabad and save the day. While the regular army tended to look down their noses at the tribal militias, when the fighting got tough they knew to stand back and let the Uzbeks do their thing.

This was to be the most costly battle of the entire war. Thousands died on both sides as the mujahideen stormed across mine fields, took the airport, and closed in on the town. With the rebels infiltrating the city's suburbs, small groups of Afghan Army soldiers began to defect in Afghan fashion to the mujahideen.

But this trickle of defection ended abruptly when a group of Arab mujahideen, led by a tall bearded Saudi known simply as the Sheikh, received a group of Afghan Army prisoners. The Arab fanatics fell on the Communist prisoners in fury. In a gory slaughter that sickened Massoud and the moderates among the Afghan mujahideen, the Arabs cut their screaming government prisoners into bloody pieces. Then, in a demonstration of just how poorly they understood the dynamics of the Afghan culture of defection, the Arabs sent the hacked body parts back to the besieged garrison in Jalalabad with a threatening note attached.[1]

With that message firmly beaten into the soldiers' minds, the government garrison defending Jalalabad fought back furiously. They were helped by the bombing runs of government MiG and Sukhoi fighter-bombers and by the fact that the government forces rained deadly Scud ballistic missiles down on the attacking mujahideen. Dostum's Uzbeks also made forays beyond the defensive parameters of Jalalabad, striking terror and inflicting severe damage against the volunteer Arab forces led by the Sheikh, Osama bin Laden.

By the summer of that year, against all odds, the rebels were beaten, and Jalalabad was saved. The Afghan Communists had not needed the Soviets to beat the mujahideen after all. Dostum's Uzbeks played a key role in saving the city and thus heartening Afghan government defenders across the land. Clearly, with the help of Dostum's Uzbeks, the war would go on for years even without the Soviets there to fight. The Najibullah government still had some fighting spirit left and meant to hold on to Afghanistan's cities and northern plains at all cost. The civil war that had been raging before the Soviets invaded would continue.

In their continuing efforts to keep the rebels out of Kabul, Jalalabad, Mazar-e-Sharif, Kandahar, Herat, Khost, Kunduz, and other cities, the government troops were helped by dissension in the ranks of the rebels themselves. As the mujahideen vultures began to circle over the corpse of the Afghan Communist government, the fragile sense of unity that had kept the Tajik and Pashtun mujahideen fighting against the common enemy began to fray. Without the Soviet infidels to fight against, could their struggle against fellow Afghan Muslims, who had not called themselves Communists since 1988, even be considered a jihad?

By 1990 the undertones of ethnic division in the war that had long been overlooked by the Americans began to rise to the surface. This was first seen when the Pashtun mujahideen leader Hekmatyar began to attack the troops of Massoud, the moderate Tajik leader. In response, Massoud hung several of Hekmatyar's men who had been found to be behind the campaign.

The rising ethnic tension also affected Najibullah's ex-Communist government. Thousands of Tajik ex-Communists began to defect from the government to Massoud's forces, while Pashtun ex-Communists defected to Hekmatyar. At this time Shahnawaz Tanai, the Pashtun defense minister who had earlier vowed to bring down Dostum and his *ghulams* (slave warriors), secretly began to reach out to the Pashtun rebel leader. His plan was to overthrow President Najibullah and put the Uzbeks, Turkmen, and Ismaili Hazaras back in their place. Tanai, at heart a Pashtun nationalist as much as a Communist, strongly disliked the fact that the former Communist government had empowered Dostum and his Uzbek slave warriors. Tanai seethed when he read combat reports of ethnic Uzbeks killing his fellow Pashtuns among the mujahideen in the south. He distrusted Dostum, who had become even more powerful since the withdrawal of the Soviets, and he secretly began a campaign to have the Uzbek general arrested.

While this move would probably weaken the Najibullah government, it would also put the Uzbek *ghulams* back in their place. Dostum's tanks, aircraft, artillery, and light weapons would be removed, and he and his men would be sent back to their backwater farms where they belonged. Then the Pashtun Communists and Pashtun mujahideen could put aside their differences and rebuild a government that kept their group at the top of the ethnic hierarchy.

To implement his plan, Defense Minister Tanai began a whisper campaign against Dostum. He began to suggest that Dostum was in league with the failed Uzbek mujahideen organizer Azad Beg. He sent fraudulent intelligence memos to President Najibullah, allegedly from spy sources, that spoke of Dostum's desire to split the plains of Afghan Turkistan off from the rest of Afghanistan.

At first President Najibullah did not believe that the apolitical Uzbek commander who appeared so eager to please could have developed such an elaborate political platform. Scheming with Uzbek mujahideen leaders in Pakistan? Making ambitious plans to break up Afghanistan and separate the Uzbek-dominated areas from the rest of the country? Those actions just didn't seem to fit the profile of the hard-fighting gas worker who loyally fought wherever he was told.

But as the government's Pashtun soldiers continued to defect to the ranks of the Pashtun rebels, Tanai warned Najibullah that Dostum and his Uzbeks had become a political liability. It was time to move against his powerful praetorian guardsman.

Reluctantly, Najibullah agreed to Tanai's plan to remove Dostum. It was true that Dostum had become too strong and enrolled too many Uzbeks and Turkmen on his payrolls. He and his tribal army had become a drain on the treasury. And Tanai had struck a nerve: despite their previous talk of the equality of Communism, in their hearts Communist Pashtuns had never been able to reconcile themselves to Uzbeks killing their own people among the mujahideen. Blood, not foreign political theories, came first in Afghanistan. For all of his loyalty, Dostum would have to be destroyed. But how?

Najibullah came up with several plans. First he sent Dostum to fight in Khost, a dangerous Pashtun tribal area where he would sustain heavy casualties and probably be defeated. While Dostum lost hundreds of his men trying to defend Khost, he himself escaped with only minor wounds.

Later, when Dostum and his men went to fight the rebels south of Jalalabad, Najibullah had KHAD agents poison their food. But this only made them sick; not enough poison was used. Then he ordered Dostum to fly from Mazar-e-Sharif to Kabul and planned to shoot down his plane en route. But the SAM-7 antiaircraft missile that was shot at his plane missed, and Dostum arrived safely to receive his new orders.

Finally, in late 1991, Najibullah secretly ordered the removal of Dostum's Uzbek subcommanders across the north and their replacement with ethnic Pashtuns. After his numerous failed attempts to take Dostum out directly, Najibullah planned to quietly whittle away Dostum's strength in a piecemeal fashion and then, before the general knew what had happened, have him arrested for treason.

But this move was what finally led to Dostum being alerted to the plots against him. Khadija had always told her husband to beware of the Pashtun Najibullah, but Dostum refused to accept that the man who had been his sponsor would turn against him. When she had insisted that the missile shot at his plane had not been fired by rebels, he refused to believe her. He even refused to believe that he had been poisoned in Jalalabad, claiming the sickness was merely due to food poisoning.

But then in late December 1991 he received a messenger from the muja-hideen. This was not unusual. Dostum routinely kept in contact with the various rebel leaders and even sent and received congratulations on vic-tories, weddings, and childbirths from the mujahideen. In the north the conflict between the mujahideen and the Communists had been moderated by Dostum's middle-of-the-road policies. What did surprise Dostum, how-ever, was the messenger's origins: he came from the most successful of all the mujahideen, the legendary Massoud—the Lion of Panjshir.

Dostum was intrigued and agreed to meet with the messenger. The Tajik mujahideen messenger told Dostum that Massoud had many spies in the ranks of the Communist government.

"Recently, my commander Massoud came upon some fascinating news that you will likely be interested in hearing. General, how are your relations with President Najibullah?"

Dostum paused before confidently replying, "They are well. Najib relies upon me to keep the rebels off the plains of the north and to clear and sweep mujahideen from the Pashtun areas in the south. Me and my men are respected and well paid for our services."

The messenger pushed ahead. "So it may appear," he said, "but Massoud has uncovered information that President Najibullah is moving against you. His aim is to gradually remove your commanders from their posts and place Pashtuns in their position. Once he has gained control of your troops, he will move against you personally. You are to be arrested soon and tried for treason. The charge will be that you have artificially inflated the number of men on your payroll in order to enrich yourself.

"There are powerful Pashtun elements in the government that are seek-ing rapprochement with the Pashtun mujahideen, and you are an impedi-ment. Your payback for all your services to Najibullah will be a one-way trip to Pul-e-Charkhi Prison. If you don't believe me, I have copies of some of the documents that were issued to Taj Muhammad, the head of KHAD in Mazar-e-Sharif, to begin an investigation against you."

Dostum asked the obvious question: "Why has your commander decided to share this information with me?"

"Massoud believes you are in your heart a moderate and pragmatist. You have always had good ties with the mujahideen, and many of your men are former mujahideen. You are not a Communist, and most importantly, you are not a Pashtun. The times are changing, General. It's time for you to put your finger to the wind, find out which way it's blowing, and make sure you come out on the winning side. The Soviet funds that have allowed Najibullah to pay you and your men are drying up, and the USSR itself is facing troubles. My master believes it is time for you to come over to the mujahideen, who will win this war. If you join Massoud, you can overthrow Najibullah and govern the north in conjunction with a mujahideen government. It's time for the northern races to make an alliance that will make sure we are never again oppressed by the Pasthuns."[2]

Dostum mulled over the messenger's words. They made sense and certainly vindicated Khadija's warnings that Najibullah was not to be trusted. But if he acted on Massoud's warning, he would be engaged in treason, a capital offense. How could he move against Najibullah without being arrested by the all-powerful KHAD?

Dostum thanked the messenger for the warning and vowed to get back to him soon. Clearly there was still plenty of time to decide, and he wanted to move with caution.

But then, on the following day, December 25, 1991, came extraordinary news from Moscow. Boris Yeltsin, the head of the Russian Republic, had disbanded the larger Soviet Union. The red hammer-and-sickle flag of Communism had been lowered over the Kremlin, and in its place the Russians had raised the tri-color flag of Russia. Yeltsin was now the leader of Russia, and he officially cut off all funds for Najibullah's government. Without funds to pay his troops, Najibullah was a dead man walking.

As these events were taking place, Dostum's subcommanders began to report that Pashtun replacements were arriving from Kabul to take over their posts. Massoud's claims had been borne out.[3] Khadija had been right—he and his men had never truly been equals. Najibullah had simply used them to fight the mujahideen. Now they were to be suppressed before Najibullah lost power.[4] He and his men had been nothing more than *ghulams*, Turkic slave warriors for the Pashtuns. All of the Communists' talk of modernity and ethnic equality had been a lie. Now that Najibullah's government appeared to be finished, it aimed to put Dostum and his Uzbeks back in their place and make peace with the Pashtun rebels.

But Dostum had previously sworn to the Russians that the Uzbeks and Turkmen would never be put down and mistreated as before.[5] It was now time to act in conjunction with Massoud to make sure that he and his men were not demobilized and forced back into servitude. The Uzbeks would rise up and reclaim the power that had once been theirs before it was too late.

With this decision, Najibullah's loyal praetorian guard went rogue and began to plot against his master, even as his master plotted against him.

The Revolt

MAZAR-E-SHARIF AND KABUL. JANUARY–APRIL 1992.

As always when confronted with complex decisions, Dostum retreated to his heavily guarded compound in Shiberghan to share the news of his betrayal with his most trusted counselor, his wife. Khadija was both vindicated and furious when she heard the news, but she cautioned her husband against acting precipitously out of anger. She suggested that Dostum could choose to beat both the mujahideen and the treacherous Najibullah by taking a third path.

Khadija advised Dostum not to jump ship and go over to the mujahideen entirely. "For all his help in giving you this news, it's clear that Massoud is no friend. With Najibullah gone, he'll move on you eventually," she predicted.

"Massoud is the most powerful of the mujahideen commanders, followed by Hekmatyar. He will eventually try to disarm you too; you are not an Islamist, after all. You must outwardly play his game for now, but secretly rally your own people and resist him if need be. If the Tajiks are fleeing from the government to Massoud and the Pashtuns fleeing to Hekmatyar, then surely Uzbeks and Turkmen mujahideen will rally around you. Everyone is rallying to their strongest ethnic leader now that the war is ending. You are the strongest Turkic military leader in the country. With the jihad coming to an end, you must bring the Uzbek mujahideen *and* Uzbek government forces together under your banner. If everyone else is fighting for their people, it's time for the Uzbeks to do the same. You'll be the one who unites us for the impending struggle."

Dostum was fascinated by the notion. After over a century of Pashtun dominance, now could be the time for the Uzbeks and their Turkmen little brothers to rise up and regain autonomy, if not outright independence. He had long walked a tightrope between the mujahideen and the Communists. Now it was time to come out and defend his people on their own platform.

Dostum began his preemptive conspiracy by sending messengers to the Uzbek, Tajik, and Turkmen mujahideen in the north, from Ustad Atta and Massoud's Tajiks to Ahmed Khan's Uzbeks. From the deserts of Andkhoy to the mountains of Darya Suf, his messengers spread the word that General Dostum and his army, forty thousand strong, were preparing to rise against Najibullah and tip the balance in favor of the rebels. He asked the various mujahideen leaders to attack Najibullah at the same time to distract him. If they chose not to join him, he asked them to stand aside and remain neutral.[6] Dostum, who had been described at the time as the only government commander "capable of aggressive offensive operations," was turning on his master.[7] All of those who received his electric message realized that this was the turning point in the long war that had begun back in 1978. If Dostum succeeded, it could be the end of both the government and the jihad.

After laying his plans, Dostum personally met with various Uzbek and Turkmen mujahideen commanders and told them of his second plan, which was to join with them and create a unified Turkic political party. Dostum spoke out on the historic mistreatment of their people at the hands of the Pashtuns and promised that he would protect them. Never again would the sons of the steppes be ground down as in the past. Dostum also swore to the various Turkmen and Uzbek rebels that he would not enforce Communist principles if they came over to his side. Like Babur the Tiger, the Moghul leader of old, he had changed his color. He was now a Turkic nationalist willing to make friends with his former enemies in the name of defending their joint tribes.

Much to his delight, Dostum was openly embraced by the most charismatic of all the Uzbek mujahideen rebel leaders, Ahmed Khan. Khan promised to join him in his rebellion against Najibullah and to unite with him on the basis of their shared Uzbek identity. The jihad was over, Ahmed Khan announced. It was now time for Uzbeks on both sides of the war to rally around the banner of Turkic unity, lest they be destroyed by their common enemy, the Pashtuns.

Having shored up his alliance with the Uzbek mujahideen and built the foundations for a separate Turkic resistance, Dostum sent his agents to the pro-government Ismaili Hazara leader, Sayid Mansur Naderi. Naderi was the charismatic *pir* (holy man) who led a thirteen-thousand-man pro-government militia that controlled territory south of Dostum's lands. It had been Naderi's job to protect the government convoys bringing aid and ammunition from the Soviet Union to Kabul. Dostum warned Naderi that Najibullah was moving against the non-Pashtun ethnic militias like his own. Dostum also warned Naderi that Najibullah would soon disarm him and his Hazara fighters in the interest of reempowering the Pashtuns. It was time to act.

When Naderi heard that Dostum had drawn Massoud, Ahmed Khan, and even the Tajik commander Ustad Atta to his side, he quickly agreed to join the mutiny against Najibullah. The Ismaili Hazaras, like the Uzbeks and Turkmen, had been horribly repressed by the Pashtuns over the last century. They were no more willing than the Uzbeks to be disarmed and forced back into submission. When the time came, they too would rise up and join Dostum and Massoud's combined forces, the Northern Alliance.

And so Dostum began to plot, while Najibullah dispatched a Pashtun "chauvinist" named Juma Asak to replace Dostum's commanders with loyal Pashtuns.[8] Asak planned to put his men in charge of all the non-Pashtun militias in the north, and then order them to turn their weapons in. After that he would move against their commanders and have them arrested before they knew what was happening.

Despite his feigned naivety, Dostum was forewarned, and accordingly, he cautioned the various non-Pashtun government commanders of the north in advance. When Asak came, they should be ready for him.

All the non-Pashtun commanders in the north fearfully awaited Asak's next move. As it turned out, his first step would be replacing a certain General Abdul Mumin, a Tajik government commander who controlled a large stockpile of weapons in the northern border town of Hairaton.

When Asak and his Pashtun troops began preparing to leave Mazar-e-Sharif to disarm and arrest Mumin, the Tajik commander urgently sent a secret message to Dostum asking for his support in resisting. This was precisely what Dostum had been waiting for, another government commander willing to start the mutiny.

The pieces were now in place for a rebellion of Uzbek, Turkmen, Hazara, and Tajik pro-government commanders in the north to rise up in conjunction with the local non-Pashtun mujahideen. It was time for the northern races to put aside their jihad or counter-jihad motivation and fight for their own rights. A successful revolt would bring down the Najibullah government before it could disband the various non-Pashtun militias of the north, making it impossible for the Pashtuns to put them back in their place. The race was on. Dostum knew he had to move first before it was too late.

The actual signal for the rebellion was a speech by President Najibullah given on March 18, 1992, announcing his decision to resign from his position and give power to an interim Pashtun-dominated government.[9]

Najibullah had revealed his weakness to all. The mutineers had to strike immediately and gain the momentum before Asak could disarm them.

On the following morning Dostum and Mumin moved together. They began their rebellion by sending Najibullah a joint message rejecting his policy of removing non-Pashtun commanders in the north. Then, in a bold move few could have foreseen, they moved against the Pashtun forces sent by Juma Asak to replace Mumin at Hairaton. Dostum personally led more than fifteen thousand Uzbek troops into Mazar-e-Sharif to surround Juma Asak's Eighteenth Division. Asak awoke to the surprise of his life as thousands of Uzbeks and Turkmen, many of them on tanks, surrounded his military base.

From their midst walked General Dostum, who threatened to annihilate Asak's division if it did not surrender immediately.[10] With dozens of tanks and Grad multiple rocket launchers aimed at his men, Asak knew that attempting a battle with Dostum's hardened troops would be suicidal.

Asak blanched with fury but knew he had to do as ordered. Dostum merely smiled at Asak's ranting and took in the sight of hundreds of Pashtun soldiers surrendering their weapons.

When Najibullah frantically radioed his "good friend" Dostum asking him to cease his rebellion, Dostum could not be dissuaded. He and his *ghulams* had been used and betrayed; now they were paying their Pashtun master back in kind.

Having gained control of Mazar-e-Sharif, Dostum fulfilled his end of the bargain to Massoud and allowed his Tajik mujahideen forces and those of his Tajik subcommander Ustad Atta to enter the city. Dostum then drove to the holy shrine of the Ali and there, within its gleaming marble premises, promised the people of the north that a new era had begun. As tens of thousands of Hazaras, Uzbeks, Turkmen, and Tajiks chanted his name, Dostum entered the world stage and openly declared himself in rebellion against Najibullah.

The symbolic importance of Dostum's seizure of the shrine of Mazar-e-Sharif was obvious to all. Abdur Rahman, the Iron Amir, and other Afghan rulers had seized the shrine on the way to gaining power. The Rowza shrine in Mazar-e-Sharif was one of Afghanistan's holiest places, and it imparted a certain mystique or mandate on its possessor. Now, for the first time in a century, an Uzbek was staking his claim to the power in the sacred confines of Mazar-e-Sharif.

While Massoud claimed to be the spokesman of the rebellion, Dostum's forces outnumbered his three to one and were armed with heavy weaponry, helicopters, and fighter-bombers.[11] There was no doubt who dominated the Northern Alliance; it was Dostum. Far from being passively disarmed, Dostum now had the mandate of Mazar-e-Sharif and would use it against Najibullah.

As predicted, the events in Mazar-e-Sharif triggered the takeover of government positions elsewhere. As Dostum seized Afghanistan's most important shrine, Massoud moved out of the Panjshir Valley and took Bagram Airfield north of Kabul. He did so with the help of defectors from the government forces who had heard the news from Mazar-e-Sharif. Dostum's defection appeared to have unhinged the base defenders, who went over to Massoud with all of their weapons rather than fight an alliance that had a mandate to rule. Their defection proved the first of many as the momentum switched overnight from Najibullah to the Hazara-Uzbek-Tajik alliance.

In the following weeks, government garrisons across the land began to lay down their weapons as well. In the west Tajik mujahideen commander Ismail Khan seized the great city of Herat, while in the south, Pashtun mujahideen seized Kandahar. In the east a coalition of Pashtun rebels seized Jalalabad, and in the central highlands Hazaras seized Bamiyan. Now that Mazar-e-Sharif had fallen, the writing was on the wall; and no one, it seemed, was willing to fight to defend a doomed regime.

But even as a host of local mujahideen commanders seized power in the Pashtun south, all eyes looked to see what the powerful northerners would do. By early April, Dostum and Naderi the Hazara controlled the Salang Pass and most of the plains territory north of the Hindu Kush. Massoud controlled the mountains of the northeast and the Shomali Plain. The way to Kabul was now open for Dostum and Massoud to march on the capital and seize power.

Leading the joint army was the thirty-seven-year-old Uzbek commander from the backwater village of Khoja Doko who had been promoted precisely because he had been seen as a trustworthy member of a despised Afghan subrace. But as Dostum's tanks made their way over the Salang Pass and down toward Kabul, it became clear to all that he and his men were slave warriors no more. As many Pashtuns had feared, the *ghulams* had awoken, and their leader was now the most powerful man in the land. In April 1992, the fate of Afghanistan lay in the palm of the peasant commander known to most simply as the Pasha.

14

THE WARLORD

"Men of action, when they lose all belief,
believe only in action."

—William Butler Yeats

MAZAR-E-SHARIF AND KABUL. 1992.

With the fall of Mazar-e-Sharif, the various factions vying for control of Afghanistan knew it was only a matter of time before Kabul fell as well. And it was in Kabul, the *tahkt* (throne), that the reigns of secular power lay. Controlling Kabul was key to controlling Afghanistan, for it gave its possessor legitimacy. As President Najibullah's forces melted away that spring, the question on everyone's mind was who or what was going to replace his government in the capital.

It soon became clear, however, that the Northern Alliance of Naderi, Massoud, and Dostum was not the only contender for power. Another leader claimed the throne for himself. That man was Hekmatyar, the fanatical Pashtun mujahideen commander who had allied himself to Arab jihadi volunteers and the Pakistani Inter-Services Intelligence. As Massoud seized Bagram and Dostum seized the north, Hekmatyar made it clear that he, and he alone, had the right to Kabul. Afghanistan was a Pashtun state, and only a Pashtun had the right to claim it. Although both Massoud and Dostum were reluctant to seize the capital, Hekmatyar had no such qualms and began a march on Kabul, accompanied by much fanfare.

While the other mujahideen parties based in Peshawar dawdled and tried to create an interim government to replace that of overthrown president Najibullah, Hekmatyar planned to pull off a coup. His actions forced Massoud and Dostum to act. To prevent Hekmatyar's forces, dubbed the Army of Sacrifice, from capturing the capital, Massoud requested that Dostum fly in reinforcements to help him seize Kabul first. Once again Massoud was forced to rely upon the indispensable Dostum to achieve his own goals, which seemed to draw the Uzbeks and Tajiks even closer.[1] As always, Dostum seemed to relish the fact that he and his Uzbeks were needed and respected.

Dostum, who had an abundance of heavy weapons and troops already stationed in Kabul, agreed to help Massoud in any way he could. By mid-April he had begun to fly additional troops into Kabul in his Russian-built Antonov transport planes. These troops united with other Uzbek troops sent over the Salang Pass and prepared to move on the capital.

As fate would have it, at the very moment that Dostum's men flew into Kabul's airport they found President Najibullah attempting to flee the country. Surrounding the president's convoy, the Uzbeks famously refused to let him travel to India to join his family in exile. According to popular legend, the Uzbek lieutenant who halted Najibullah's car told the president, "You started the fires in Afghanistan. Now it's time for you to cook in them."[2] Frustrated in his attempt to flee, Najibullah made his way to the UN compound in Kabul and stayed there until he was eventually captured years later by a new force that would later emerge on the scene—the Taliban.

Having seized Kabul International Airport and the Bala Hissar fortress, a medieval castle that overlooks Kabul, Dostum's heavily armed

Uzbeks fanned out over central Kabul and began to push Hekmatyar's advancing men out. With plenty of bad blood between them going back to Dostum's days as a counterinsurgent, this was a task his Jowzjanis relished. By the end of April, Dostum's armor had retaken Kabul from Hekmatyar after several intense engagements.[3] This allowed Massoud and the other mujahideen parties to enter the city. Dostum subsequently claimed, "When Massoud's troops entered Kabul, they did so on my tanks and in my planes. It was me that made the almost bloodless takeover of Kabul by the mujahideen possible."[4]

With his forces overlooking Kabul and in control of several key government installations and the airport, Dostum effectively controlled much of the capital. At that moment in late April 1992, his power reached its zenith. With control over an area in northern Afghanistan that was slightly smaller than England and with mastery of an army that had swollen to sixty thousand men, Dostum was a force to be reckoned with.[5]

By this time he commanded three infantry divisions and one armored brigade.[6] According to one military analysis, Dostum also had sixty MiG-21 and Su-22 fighter-bombers, sixty helicopters, two hundred T-55 and T-62 tanks, dozens of Scud B ballistic missiles and "plenty" of artillery, making his army "the best-ever equipped and armed militia under the control of any warlord ever."[7] To compound matters, the area he controlled in the north contained approximately 80 percent of Afghanistan's mineral and gas wealth and 60 percent of its agricultural resources.

This wealth and weaponry were much appreciated by Massoud and the newly established Afghan mujahideen government—especially when the fanatical Pashtun leader Hekmatyar responded to his previous setback by doing what no one could have expected. Expelled from Kabul by Dostum, Hekmatyar set up his artillery on the southern hills of the city to rain shells on the civilian-packed capital. Without warning, he began to slaughter and maim the innocent people of Kabul, who had been largely spared such destruction thus far. If he could not possess the city, then he would destroy it block by block. Hekmatyar—who had accepted thousands of Pashtun

Communists into his army—claimed to be attacking Kabul because he was unhappy with the presence of Dostum's Uzbek "Communists" in the city.

Tens of thousands of Kabulis fled the city in panic as shells crashed down on their homes, and the death toll rose into the thousands. The only indication civilians had that an artillery shell was headed toward them was the eerie whistling sound it made seconds before impact. This wasn't war—it was slaughter.

In desperation, Massoud and his political master, the mujahideen president, Burhanuddin Rabbani, called on Dostum to use his air force to bomb Hekmatyar. Everyone remembered Dostum's role in saving Kabul back in the 1980s when Rasul Sayyaf's mujahideen had put his artillery within firing range of the city just as Hekmatyar was doing all these years later. Once again Dostum did as requested and used his MiG and Sukhoi fighter-bombers to bomb and strafe Hekmatyar's positions at Charyasab.

Deprived of the capital, Hekmatyar moved his headquarters further afield to avoid Dostum and sulked. And he was not the only one. In the ranks of his army were hundreds of Arab volunteers who had triumphantly marched to Kabul with him. Their goal was to establish a strict Muslim theocracy and bring in jihadis from across the Middle East for training. But they too had seen their ambitions thwarted by Dostum and Massoud. Among these disgruntled Arabs was Osama bin Laden, who never forgave the northern commanders for depriving him of his chance to help build a fundamentalist government in Kabul. In a rage, he and his Arab followers abandoned Afghanistan and eventually migrated to Sudan, where they briefly established their al-Qaeda base. But bin Laden promised he would one day return to a land that had been sanctified by the blood of Arab "martyrs."

In the meantime, the quarrelling mujahideen parties in Peshawar, Pakistan, hoped Rabbani—their chosen leader and Massoud's political master—could bring peace to the Afghan capital during his limited four-month term as interim president.

Dostum, who had spent his time shuffling between his troops in Kabul and Mazar-e-Sharif, was also eager for an official role in the new government. As the man with the largest army in Afghanistan, he and his men harbored great expectations that were perhaps only natural. Dostum anticipated that his rank as general in the new government would be confirmed and he would be given an important ministry.

But not everyone was supportive of Dostum. While he had made the hajj pilgrimage to Mecca and been given the honorary title of mujahideen for his role in bringing Najibullah down, many mujahideen (including his supposed ally, Massoud) could not forgive him for having fought against them during the great jihad. President Rabbani, an extreme fundamentalist, listened to these voices. When it came down to the final dispensation of power, Rabbani granted the minister of defense post to Massoud, named Hekmatyar prime minister (in an effort to win over his support), and gave other posts to Tajiks and Pashtuns, but deliberately overlooked Dostum.

Dostum, who had so eagerly sought a role as a mediator between the mujahideen and the former Communists, was left out in the cold, and he took the news badly.[8] According to various sources, he and his men felt "betrayed" and "outraged" at this blatant sign of disrespect.[9] It appeared they had been used yet again, this time by the Tajik president Rabbani and his defense minister Massoud, who "never recognized [him] as full partner."[10] For all their high-sounding words, Massoud and his master Rabbani saw the Uzbeks not as equal allies but as *ghulams* who did not deserve their share of the power.

To appease Hekmatyar and prevent him from shelling the capital, President Rabbani even ordered Dostum and his men to leave the city by the end of 1992.[11] And if that was not enough, the new mujahideen government passed a series of fundamentalist laws that infuriated Dostum, a confirmed secularist. Many of these laws, such as those closing cinemas, banning women from appearing in public without headscarves, and outlawing alcohol, presaged the strict Sharia laws of the Taliban. Dostum, who had developed a healthy appreciation for everything from fine whiskey to emancipated women, was infuriated. As the Islamist mujahideen made it abundantly clear that they were not willing to moderate their fundamentalism or include Uzbeks in their power-sharing agreement, Dostum seethed with fury.

In early 1993, Dostum finally responded to these developments publicly. He threatened to create a "secular democratic republic" in the north if the "rabid mullahs in Kabul did not change their line."[12] Dostum was in effect defending hundreds of thousands of secular Kabulis who had more liberal views of life than the bearded jihadi fundamentalists from the provinces did.

As Dostum threatened to secede from the increasingly fundamentalist Islamic State of Afghanistan, Massoud and Ismail Khan, the Tajik commander of Herat who belonged to the same party, decided to move against him. This would usher in the continuation of the Afghan civil war that had begun with Hekmatyar's attack on Kabul.

The Tajik mujahideen leaders started the second stage of the war by launching attacks on Dostum's troops on the eastern and western borders of his de facto autonomous region, which was made up of six northern provinces. These attacks demonstrated all too clearly that Dostum would never be accepted by the new Islamist government. Even though the jihad was over, many of the mujahideen clearly saw Dostum's secular realm in the north as unfinished business. The Uzbeks and Tajik mujahideen were allies no more.

To compound matters, President Rabbani, who had been chosen to serve as interim president for just four months, refused to stand down when his term was up. He produced a stream of excuses to stay in power and began to abuse his authority to oppress other groups—and no group more so than the Shiite Hazaras, who had already been horribly repressed by the Pasthuns. While Dostum was able to come between the Massoud-Rabbani partnership and the Hazaras and keep the peace for most of 1992, in 1993 Massoud and his ally, the fundamentalist Rasul Sayyaf, launched an attack on the Hazaras of Kabul. In what became known as the Afshar massacre, as many as eight hundred Hazaras were hunted down and slaughtered by

Sayyaf and Massoud's men.[13] Tens of thousands would eventually die in Kabul during this Tajik-on-Hazara violence.

Massoud's master Rabbani, who was subsequently described as being "as ruthless and autocratic as his opponents," carried out "acts of brutality and barbarism as bad as those of the later Taliban were committed."[14] Clearly the Tajiks meant to replace the Pashtuns with their own ethnic monopoly on power.

By the end of 1993 Dostum had reached his limits. His newly established Turkic political grouping, the Jumbesh Party, had been excluded from the Afghan government. His vital assistance in overthrowing Najibullah and pushing Hekmatyar out of Kabul had been ignored. His realm had been attacked by a mujahideen government that was too fundamentalist and Tajik-dominated for his taste. For all his efforts to be included in the new political order, he had been deliberately sidelined and treated as a pariah. Dostum was convinced this had more to do with his Turkic ethnic origins than his pro-Communist background, since all of the mujahideen parties had warmly embraced Communist defectors from their own ethnic groups. It was clear that Dostum needed to respond in some fashion, but how?

Before he made his move, Dostum decided to return from Kabul to Shiberghan to see Khadija and get advice. She always had the ability to calm him down, help him see through the issues that confronted him, and craft an approach that oftentimes was more nuanced than what he would have chosen. As a man of action, Dostum liked blunt responses; but Khadija cooled him off and helped him plan more sophisticated action. It was also his intention to catch up with his children, who were growing up.

At Kabul airport Dostum boarded one of his Antonov transport planes, flew out of the capital, and made his way over the Hindu Kush. After an hour of flying, the mountains began to peter out, and the vast plains of Turkistan appeared below. Home, his children and Khadija, beckoned him. It was time for the warrior to put aside his struggle for power and be with those who were closest to him.

Catalyst

SHIBERGHAN, MAZAR-E-SHARIF, AND KABUL, ISLAMIC STATE
OF AFGHANISTAN. WINTER 1993–1994.

While the word "warlord" is a relatively recent addition to the English language, based on the German word *Kriegsherr*, the concept itself is not new.
It essentially refers to a substate political ruler whose claim to legitimacy is
based on his control of military forces. Afghanistan had long known warlords, and it was not until Abdur Rahman, the Iron Amir, that the Afghan
rulers became more than just the strongest warlords in the land.

Dostum's journey to becoming a warlord was largely shaped by greater
Afghan events. First he was betrayed by the Najibullah government; then
he was rejected by the Tajik mujahideen government. These twin events
pushed him into working increasingly as an independent actor on behalf of
his ethnic community and his secular beliefs.

But it was developments at his home as much as these external events
that catalyzed Dostum's transformation from a general into a warlord.
These little-reported developments further embittered the Uzbek commander from Khoja Doko and pushed him to seize power in the six provinces of Afghan Turkistan.

As Dostum flew into Mazar-e-Sharif in the winter of 1993, he was a man
disillusioned but not necessarily obsessed with acquiring power. The secular
system he had fought so hard to protect was being dismantled by the mujahideen. Kabul, the epicenter of the world that Dostum hoped to expand to the
rest of Afghanistan, had been devastated by Hekmatyar. And he and his Uzbek
people had once again been used and marginalized, this time by the Tajiks.

To make matters worse, his own commanders chafed under his rule
and sought to strike back at those who marginalized them. They clam-
ored to use their vast stores of weapons and power to carve out a space for
themselves and gain power in Kabul. Several of his Uzbek commanders,
especially the Pahlawan (wrestler) brothers who ruled over the province
of Faryab, were semi-independent feudal commanders who had their own

troops. While they were fellow Uzbeks, they were also hotheaded, so Dostum did not trust them any more than he did Massoud and Rabbani.

So it was with a heart weighed down by many burdens that General Dostum made the ninety-minute journey by car from Mazar-e-Sharif to his home in Shiberghan. He had told Khadija and the children in advance that he was coming, setting off a commotion at his home, as always, as they cleaned and prepared for his visit. Although Khadija was a modern woman whose greatest joy was working with female students, she had a domestic side as well. She took great pride in her household and wanted to make sure that all was in order before her husband arrived. Bright and early that morning she woke and ground the flour to make her husband's favorite *manti* meat pastries. With her two trusted servants by her side, she then cleaned their compound from top to bottom.

Afghans of all ethnic backgrounds strongly believe in the concept of kismet, and it was while Khadija was cleaning the house that her and Dostum's fates were changed forever. According to General Dostum, even as he drove toward her, Khadija had begun to clean the kitchen from her morning's work making *manti* and soup for her husband. As she did so, she cleaned behind the refrigerator that her husband had brought her from Uzbekistan. Sticking her broom behind the refrigerator, she felt it catch on something and assumed it was one of the coils protruding from the rear. But as she pulled, she saw that it was something else: one of the guns her husband kept around the house to protect his family. Having twice had his compound attacked by Arab jihadis who did not recognize the sanctity of home, he had hidden several of these automatic weapons to be used in case of an attack.

As the gun caught on her broom and fell sideways toward her, Dostum explained later, a coil behind the refrigerator set off the trigger on the deadly automatic weapon, shooting off several rounds and causing Khadija and her servants to scream in panic.

Khadija jumped away but was shot in the chest. Even as her servants ran to her side, the woman who had been both the mother of Dostum's children and a major influence in his life slowly began to bleed to death.

Later in the day the wailing servants heard cars arriving in the driveway and the sound of approaching voices. Moments later Dostum walked into the house and instantly knew something was wrong when he heard the sounds of ritualistic wailing. With a pounding heart he ran to the back kitchen, expecting an enemy attack.

There, according to Dostum's subsequent account, he found his wife lying on the floor with two bullet holes in her chest. Having spent years fighting on the battlefield, he knew the wounds were fatal and that they had been delivered by his own weapon.

Even as Dostum's brain told him that Khadija was dead, his heart told him she could not be; she was his wife, the mother of his children, his closest friend, and his counselor. As the two realities collided, Dostum silently walked to his wife and ordered the servants to leave the room. The last thing the servants saw was Dostum alone in the room, crying and cradling the body of his dead wife.

15

THE COUP

"The Mujahideen government was too fundamentalist
for me and my people."

—General Abdul Rashid Dostum

KABUL AND NORTHERN AFGHANISTAN, ISLAMIC STATE OF
AFGHANISTAN AND AUTONOMOUS NORTHERN ZONE. 1994.

Those who knew Dostum, including Lal Muhammad, the man who would
become his most trusted commander after Yar's death, claim that he never
recovered from the loss of his wife. After her death, Dostum's dark black
hair, which he continued to keep in a prickly military crew cut, turned gray
almost overnight. While he shared his grief with Lal Muhammad and his
family, he kept up a strong facade to the outer world. From the day he had
gotten into the fight with the village lads in Khoja Doko, he had known
that he could not display weakness to others. And he did not do so after
Khadija's death. While he spent a few weeks with his family in Khoja Doko

and turned his children over to Lal Muhammad's family for safekeeping, by all outward appearances he appeared to be unscathed by the loss of his wife.

But Dostum was not the man he had once been. His jovial nature was replaced by a deeper sense of purpose and determination. No longer did he ride with his troops, play buzkashi, or drink with his officers. While Dostum had always been gruff and conscious of his military charisma, he now appeared to be purposefully projecting a message of unbridled strength and determination as a counterweight to his sorrow. There was no room for human weaknesses in Dostum's life, and he became a man driven. It was as if he was consciously trying to compensate for the loss of his wife by making himself impervious to harm. He seemed to be showing the world that he had a heart that could not be damaged. Tellingly, after Khadija's death he moved out of their house and set up his home and headquarters in the Qala-e-Jangi (Fortress of War), a nineteenth-century castle built by the Iron Amir just to the west of Mazar-e-Sharif.

After a period of inward mourning, Dostum closed the door on his pain and threw himself into the business of running what had in effect become his own substate in the plains of northern Afghanistan. He turned to the protection of this sprawling fiefdom to block out the painful memories of Khadija.

It was obvious to him that, unless he fought back, he would never be left alone by the Tajik-dominated mujahideen government that controlled Kabul. Dostum understood one rule all too clearly: in Afghanistan, one had to constantly demonstrate one's strength to keep enemies at bay.

He also knew he had to keep the respect of his own semifeudal army. Rasul Pahlawan, the Uzbek commander of Faryab Province, had made it clear that he found Dostum's lack of response to Massoud and Ismail Khan's attacks to be a sign of weakness. He suggested that perhaps the Pasha was not up to the task of defending his people from their enemies.

Most alarmingly, word also spread to the north that Massoud and President Rabbani had their eyes on the shrine of Mazar-e-Sharif.[1] Using the local Tajik commander Ustad Atta as their proxy, they meant to foment a rebellion against Dostum and seize the holy shrine. That was something that Dostum could not allow. It was time to act decisively.

As word of Dostum's growing frustration with Massoud and President Rabbani spread, messengers came once again from an unexpected source proposing an alliance. On this occasion they represented the fanatic Pashtun leader, Hekmatyar, who had been described by Massoud as a "madman" for shelling the capital in 1992.[2] Operating under the principle that "the enemy of my enemy is my friend," Hekmatyar's messengers suggested that their master and Dostum put aside their feud and attack their common enemy, Massoud and the Tajik government.

Dostum knew that Khadija would never have countenanced such an unholy alliance with Hekmatyar. But she was dead, and Dostum was filled with an uncontrollable rage. And so he agreed to launch a joint attack on the Tajik-dominated government in Kabul alongside his allies-of-the-day, Hekmatyar and the long-suffering Hazaras, who could not forget the Afshar Massacre. The allies' aim was to carry out a coup similar to the one that had brought Najibullah down and overthrow the new president, Rabbani.

The whole plan was kept secret lest Massoud be alerted. Then, on the morning of January 1, 1994, the allies commenced their joint attack on Massoud's government positions in Kabul. As they did so, Dostum announced, "We launched an attack because we want to change the political system and make it accessible to all national minorities. As to Rabbani, he rules the country only in Tajik interests."[3]

But things went wrong right from the start. The cloudy and rainy weather prevented Dostum's Sukhoi and MiG fighter-bombers from attacking Massoud's positions. To compound matters, as Dostum's troops attacked the government-controlled television station overlooking the city, they found Massoud's troops waiting for them. A spy in their own army had warned Massoud in advance.[4] While there were some early successes—Dostum's loyal commander General Rauf Beg, for example, took the airport—these proved to be fleeting. Massoud's troops rallied their own tanks and, after a bloody battle, retook the airport.

As the skies momentarily cleared, Dostum's planes bombed the presidential palace, the Ministry of Defense, and the radio and television station. In return, Massoud's MiGs bombed Dostum's positions in the Bala Hissar fortress. The skies above Kabul were soon covered by a pall of smoke as the two factions' planes bombed one another.

As all this was going on, Hekmatyar launched his most devastating bombardment to date.[5] Hundreds of rockets poured down on the city, wreaking havoc in the southern neighborhoods. While these created panic and caused tens of thousands to flee the city, they were of limited military value to Dostum's men. In fact, neither Hekmatyar nor the Hazaras proved to be useful as allies. Both seemed to be unwilling to take on Massoud in combat, and the greater portion of the fighting was left to Dostum's men.

While the conflict went on for several days, it was obvious by the end of the week that the coup had failed. Massoud had more troops in the city than Dostum and had been forewarned of the allies' plans.

Massoud and Rabbani had survived, and they had learned an important lesson. Dostum was still the strongest man in Afghanistan. If he was not given respect, he could bring the war to Kabul with deadly consequences.

From then on, Dostum was essentially left alone by Massoud and Rabbani. But for Kabulis, his name would forever be linked with Hekmatyar's deadly bombardment. As many as eight hundred people had been killed in Hekmatyar's shelling and the related fighting between Massoud and Dostum.[6] The inhabitants of Kabul, who had previously praised Dostum for saving them from the attacks of Sayyaf in the 1980s and Hekmatyar in 1992, now cursed him and ranked him alongside Hekmatyar as a *jang salar*, a bloody warlord.

But not everyone cursed his name. In fact, many of the refugees who had fled Kabul when the mujahideen fundamentalists began to enforce their strict Sharia Islamic laws made their way north to Mazar-e-Sharif in search of freedom.

And they were not the only ones. In spite of his undisputed role in wreaking the havoc on Kabul that ultimately took the lives of some twenty-five thousand of its inhabitants from 1992 to 1996, Dostum's role in protecting Mazar-e-Sharif's inhabitants helped salvage his reputation. (It should be noted that most of the destruction in Kabul during that time had been at the hands of Hekmatyar, who left to Dostum the fighting against Massoud during their joint coup attempt, even as he continued to shell the city's neighborhoods.) For Dostum, protecting Mazar-e-Sharif and its shrine was a means of redemption for his sins, the most important of which was his role in the death of his wife.

Sanctuary

MAZAR-E-SHARIF, THE AFGHAN NORTHERN ZONE. 1992–96.

Since the time of Shaybani Khan, the shrine town of Mazar-e-Sharif had been a Central Asian trade hub and a meeting point for Shiites and Sunnis and all of the region's various peoples. Over the centuries, the blue-domed shrine had attracted pilgrims in times of both war and peace. While many regional centers such as Kabul, Kandahar, Jalalabad, and Herat suffered heavily from fighting during the Soviet invasion and subsequent civil war, Mazar-e-Sharif was spared such devastation. This stemmed, in part, from the fact that Dostum and his men kept the mujahideen out of the city and prevented it from becoming a battleground in the 1980s. Thus the blue-domed Shrine of Ali was spared the damage that destroyed other monuments throughout the country.

When Dostum seized the city from Najibullah in the spring of 1992, he vowed to keep it free from the sort of mujahideen brigandage and plundering that had begun to plague the Pashtun towns of the south. While the southern city of Kandahar slipped into darkness as the Pashtun mujahideen whipped unveiled women on the streets, fought one another for control of neighborhoods, and set up checkpoints on the roads in order to rape and pillage, Mazar-e-Sharif became a beacon of hope for tens of thousands who migrated there after the Soviet withdrawal. The great city was described by one author as the "glittering jewel in Afghanistan's battered crown."[7]

It became a matter of pride for Dostum to keep the city that became known as his capital functioning as a safety bubble, much like Kabul during the Communist period. When the mujahideen captured Kabul and outlawed unveiled women, cinemas, and alcohol, Dostum let it be known that he would permit such things in his realm. To enforce security, Dostum and his bodyguards were known to travel incognito across the land looking for bandits and those running illegal checkpoints.

Consequently, women who cherished the freedom formerly granted them by the Communists began to migrate to Mazar-e-Sharif as bands of fundamentalist mujahideen swarmed into Kabul and other cities. In addition, thousands of former Communists, liberals, schoolteachers, modernists, and women's activists migrated to Mazar-e-Sharif. There they found a bustling regional capital that thrived on trade with neighboring Uzbekistan and served as the de facto seat of power for Dostum's substate.

The freedoms that Dostum offered in his bastion of secularism infuriated many of the fundamentalists among the mujahideen. The existence of Dostum's realm drove both Rabbani and Hekmatyar to define him at various times as their number-one enemy.

Eyewitness accounts of Dostum's mini-state paint a picture of stability and prosperity. Clearly Dostum saw himself in the classic sense as the protector of the shrine of Mazar-e-Sharif and all those who lived in its vicinity. Dostum proudly proclaimed that he would keep the shrine functioning peacefully and spent considerable money to repair and update it. Like the Uzbek Khans of old, he validated his rule by presenting himself as the defender of the shrine.

Such activities won Dostum the support of people of all ethnic, religious, and political backgrounds in his self-declared Autonomous Northern Zone. Hazaras, Pashtuns, Tajiks, Turkmen, Aimaqs, and Uzbeks all benefited from his benevolent rule. Dostum kept the peace by distributing money he earned from his control of Hairaton, Afghanistan's main port with ex-Soviet Central Asia, to various subcommanders, who acted as his feudal lieges.[8] This prevented them from preying upon the common people for cash, as many mujahideen commanders did in the south.

By Afghan standards of the 1990s, Dostum's realm was a true sanctuary from the fundamentalism and warfare that had swept over much of the country. With financial and military support coming from neighboring Uzbekistan, Dostum's fiefdom thrived. Dostum ran his own airlines, protected the only university in Afghanistan that women could still attend, and accepted the establishment of diplomatic consuls from the UN, Iran, Turkey, Pakistan, and Saudi Arabia in Mazar-e-Sharif.

Eyewitness accounts from the time paint a picture of a protected enclave teeming with freedom, prosperity, and security. Tom Cole, a rare American writer to visit Mazar-e-Sharif, wrote of his trip to Dostum's capital:

> Women walked freely in Mazar, either in full *chador* or completely unveiled, as they had been doing for many years. Unveiled students from Balkh University strolled the dusty streets chatting, holding hands and laughing as young girls do everywhere, I walked around this great city, brandishing my camera and feeling perfectly relaxed.[9]

Another interview with some residents of Mazar-e-Sharif captured the liberal spirit of the town at the time:

> "It was a normal life. I studied in Balkh University. We had female teachers. There was a medical college where we had female doctors. There were no restrictions on women. You could do your own thing."
>
> "Life did not change even after the fall of the communist government. We had freedom even under the rule of General Dostum." . . .
>
> "It is true that the different ethnicities in Afghanistan have been at loggerheads with each other. But we lived comfortably in Mazar-e-Sharif. Some of my best friends were Pashtoons and Tajiks."[10]

A *New York Times* article entitled "Afghan Fights Islamic Tide as Savior or Conqueror?," published during a slightly later period when the Taliban began to emerge, paints a similar picture of Dostum's rule:

> General Dostum is widely popular here in Mazar-i-Sharif, the dusty city of two million people where he makes his headquarters. . . . For many others, it is the freedoms here, fast disappearing in areas under Taliban control, that make him an icon.
>
> "I think he is a good leader, because people here can live as they want," said Latifa Hamidi, 18, who is in her first year of medical studies at Balkh University, an institution financed by General Dostum. . . . She has nightmares about what would happen if the Taliban defeated the general and took control here. "I want knowledge, and I want a useful life," she said. "I don't want to be forced to stay at home."[11]

A British guest captured a little more of Dostum's personality in this account of his meeting with the Pasha:

> At his over large house in his stronghold, Shebergan, west of Mazar-i-Sharif, he was happier talking about horses than conflict. . . . He said he hated being called a warlord, although it is hard to think of anyone better suited to the description, and gave us the ridiculously expensive "Blue Label" Johnnie Walker, affordable only by dictators, oil sheikhs and footballers, as fairy lights lit up plaster deer nestling in the plastic undergrowth fringing his pool.
>
> The air hostesses he used to import from Essex (England) to sit around the pool when he briefly ran his own airline had gone now, but a few days spent with Dostam in the north were a glimpse of another Afghanistan—outward looking and Central Asian; Islamic but not enclosed. He took us on a tour of a medical school, walking purposefully through the girls' dormitory to shrieks of consternation, and arranged a meeting of the Shiberghan women's committee.[12]

One Pakistani general reported of Dostum's rule:

The shops in his domain are full of imported goods from Dubai. Local cinemas show Indian films, and Russian vodka and German beer are available. [But] he is not as popular as is made out by his followers. . . .

Although every shop carries his photograph and every official building displays his portrait, behind the scenes he is accused of corruption, nepotism and leading a lifestyle far beyond what even the northern provinces could afford.[13]

But even as Dostum kept the peace in the north, the southern parts of the country fell into mujahideen anarchy. It became unsafe for the Pashtuns of Kandahar and neighboring regions to travel on the roads. Bands of mujahideen-turned-criminals roamed the land killing, raping, and plundering at will.

Things came to a head when a family traveling from Herat was attacked by mujahideen at a checkpoint in the Pashtun village of Sangesar in 1994. As they had done on many occasions before, the predatory Pashtun mujahideen pulled the terrified family from their car, molested the boys, shaved the heads of the women and girls and raped them. Then, in a demonstration of their power, they killed several members of the family and burned their bodies.

Sickened by the news of the attack on an innocent family, a local Pashtun mullah named Omar gathered thirty to fifty Talibs (religious students) from his mud-walled religious school and attacked the mujahideen checkpoint. In the ensuing gunfight the mujahideen were defeated and their commander was hung by a noose from the barrel of his tank to shouts of "Allahu Akbar!" (God is great). The surviving girls were released by the Talibs, and thus was born the messianic fundamentalist movement known as the Taliban (plural of Talib).

This strange new clerical movement would reconfigure the playing field and ultimately confront Dostum with his greatest challenge. The story of the Taliban's conquest of the quarreling Afghan warlords is the story of a fanatical movement the likes of which had not been seen since the invasions of the sixteenth-century Kizil Bashi Red Turbans.

The Taliban

AFGHANISTAN. 1994–97.

From the village of Sangesar, the Pashtun Taliban gathered new members and began to move from district to district like a rolling snowball, gathering size and momentum. It became obvious that this new band of austere religious students was unlike the previous mujahideen, who had become a byword for rape, licentiousness, and murder. And the Taliban had no compunction against taking on even the most powerful of the mujahideen. By the end of the year the Taliban were even attacking their fellow Pashtun fundamentalist leader, Hekmatyar.

With Pakistani help, the Taliban gained access to weapons depots in the south, gathered thousands of Pashtun fighters who were drawn to the austere new brotherhood, and moved on Kandahar, the spiritual capital of the Pashtun heartlands. They took the city in November 1994, and with it gained access to MiG-21 fighter-bombers, tanks, and artillery. The Taliban were now the strongest force in the Pashtun heartlands.

From there they conquered the remaining Pashtun provinces of the south, bringing peace—but at a cost. While the checkpoints and predatory mujahideen bandits were removed, the people were forced to follow a strict form of Islam the likes of which not even the Saudis enforced.

But the Taliban were not content with ruling the Pashtun belt of the south. By 1995 they had begun to move on the territory of the great Tajik mujahideen commander of the western town of Herat, Ismail Khan. In a series of extraordinary seesaw battles, the Taliban shocked the nation by conquering this warlord's western domain. In response, Ismail Khan and his men fled across the Iranian border to the town of Meshed.

Once they conquered the cosmopolitan Tajik-dominated city of Herat, the Taliban repressed the Tajik locals and brought in Pashtun tribesmen from the south to rule over them. Then they turned on their fellow Pashtun, Hekmatyar, who was still continuing his on-again off-again siege of Kabul.

Around this time Massoud and Dostum offered to help Mullah Omar's forces, and Dostum sent technicians to help the Taliban get their small fleet of MiG-21s air-worthy. Even the Shiite Hazaras proved to be willing to work with this strange new movement, which seemed intent on attacking their common enemy, Hekmatyar.

But the Tajiks, Hazaras, and Uzbeks soon found that they were playing with fire. They learned the real nature of the Taliban when the mysterious Mullah Omar signaled his intent to reconquer the Uzbek, Hazara, and Tajik lands of the north. In April 1996, all hopes for a modus vivendi with the new religious movement ended with one symbolic gesture. For the first time in recent history Mullah Omar had a holy relic, the *khirqa* (cloak) of the Prophet Muhammad given by the eighteenth-century Uzbek ruler of Bukhara to the Pashtun amir, removed from its sacred mosque in Kandahar. There he donned it before crowds of teary-eyed Kandaharis who chanted his name and had himself declared "commander of the faithful," a title given only to the great caliphs who had ruled the medieval Arab Empire.

The symbolism for Dostum was clear. The cloak signified the Pashtuns' right to rule over the plains of Afghan Turkistan in the name of Islam. It meant that, despite Dostum's efforts to remain on the good side of the new Pashtun religious movement, sooner or later the Taliban would be coming for him.

But first, the Taliban moved on Massoud and his forces in Kabul. By the fall of 1996 they had entered the battle for control of the capital. In response to the threat to both the government and his own forces, Hekmatyar buried his axe with Massoud, ceased bombarding his capital, and belatedly accepted a post as prime minister in the Rabbani government.

But it was too little too late. Both Massoud and Hekmatyar had been weakened by their years of fighting each other for Kabul. The Taliban also appeared to have both the momentum and the support of thousands of Pashtun volunteers from the madrassas in Pakistan. By early September, Hekmatyar's positions had been overrun and he was forced to flee to Iran. As the seemingly unstoppable Taliban army swarmed onward toward the capital, Massoud decided to retreat to the northeast and fight a defensive war from the Tajik-dominated mountains there. In one fell swoop the Taliban gained control of Kabul and staked their claim to rule the entire state of Afghanistan.

As their troops poured into the capital the black-turbaned Taliban began to drive women, many of them widows and the only breadwinners for their families, out of their jobs and to enforce draconian laws that were harsher than even those of the mujahideen. But it was their treatment of former president Najibullah, who had been hiding out at the UN compound ever since Dostum's men had prevented him from leaving the country, that caused the most revulsion. The Taliban captured Najibullah and his brother, beat them savagely, and then castrated them and drove around while dragging the screaming men behind their trucks. Finally they shot the ex-president and his brother and hung them from a lamppost in the center of Kabul for all to see.

When Dostum heard the news of his former mentor's grisly death, he reportedly broke down in tears and cried.[14] Despite the fact that Najibullah had ultimately turned against him, Dostum still held a debt of gratitude toward him. He was furious that the Taliban had broken all codes of Afghan sanctuary and civility and killed the man who for years had been his patron. The symbolism to Dostum, whom the Taliban subsequently began to describe as an infidel, was clear. They would be coming for him next.

Lest this message be lost, the Taliban supreme council soon thereafter put out a death warrant for its enemies. High on that list were Massoud and Dostum.[15] In the words of a journalist who was there at the time, "Dostum was everything that the Taliban despised," and sooner or later, he would have to fight to defend his autonomous realm.[16]

With the fall of Kabul, it became obvious to Dostum that he would have to end his feud with Massoud and create an alliance against their common enemy. In October 1996, Dostum, Massoud, and the Hazara leader Karim Khalili signed a pact uniting the Uzbeks, Tajiks, and Hazaras in a revived Northern Alliance.

On October 18, the allies launched a joint military offensive, with Dostum's air force providing bombing cover for Massoud's troops. Dostum's soldiers also formed the backbone of the offensive and included hundreds of tanks, fighter-bombers, and attack helicopters.[17] As the allies rolled the Taliban back, they discovered a disturbing sign of things to come. Moving toward Kabul, they approached a newly established camp for Taliban-allied Arab jihadi volunteers known as Najm al-Jihad (Star of Holy War). But the four hundred armed Arabs who lived there remembered the damage inflicted on their forces by Dostum during the 1989 siege of Jalalabad and fled for their lives.[18]

Around this time Dostum learned that an eccentric Saudi leader of the Arabs, Osama bin Laden, had returned to the country from Sudan to seek sanctuary with the Taliban. Among bin Laden's first moves had been organizing the Arab volunteer support army from among his old Arab mujahideen volunteer comrades. This unit, known as the 055 Ansar Brigade, was soon fighting alongside the Taliban, who shared their worldview. This was a challenge that Dostum, who blamed the Arabs for attacking his house and thus inadvertently leading to his wife's death, was more than willing to answer. He ordered his troops to show as much mercy to the foreign fanatics as those fanatics had extended to the defecting Communist soldiers they had cut to pieces at Jalalabad back in 1989.

The Taliban, however, soon found another way to deal with the combined Northern Alliance offensive. With Pakistani support, they had gradually evolved from a group of provincial students into an army of forty thousand and now had the means to attack across Afghanistan. In an effort to divert Dostum, the Taliban launched a distractionary raid on his realm from the recently captured western town of Herat. The attack on Dostum's southwestern frontier caught him by surprise and forced him to divert troops to a second front in the province of Badghis. The Taliban had checked his move, and Dostum was now on the defensive.

In a search for allies to help him fight in the west, Dostum airlifted the former Tajik commander of Herat, Ismail Khan, from exile in Iran to bolster his western front. Proving the Afghan axiom that yesterday's foe is today's friend, Ismail Khan arrived with two thousand of his men and promptly helped his former Uzbek enemy fight the Taliban.[19] Together the allies halted the Taliban at Faryab Province after losing Badghis to the enemy.

But it had been a close battle, and the Taliban let Dostum know that there would be no rest for his forces. They began the new year of 1997 by announcing on their newly established Radio Sharia that "soon the forces of the Islamic State of Afghanistan will cross the Hindu Kush ranges to uproot Dostum."[20]

But with a battle-hardened, professional army that still swelled to forty thousand men, Dostum would be a hard nut to crack. As the storm clouds swirled south of the Hindu Kush, Dostum claimed to be unworried by the enemies' approach, proclaiming that the Taliban "do not play buzkashi."[21]

A reporter from the Australian Broadcasting Corporation visited Dostum's isolated northern realm beyond the Hindu Kush at this time and filmed a vivid television report entitled "Dostum the Kingmaker," which was later posted on YouTube.com, where it can still be found. This revealing report gives some insight into Dostum's confident frame of mind as the Taliban moved ever closer to his realm. It begins with a survey of the military situation in Afghanistan:

> To the south the Islamic warriors of the Taliban are fighting a full-scale war with the ousted government army. But these [Uzbek] soldiers fight for a different master, and they feel no fear of the Taliban.

General Dostum returns to the embattled lands of the Tajik Northern Alliance in April 2001 to fight a lonely battle against the Taliban. Here he is greeted by throngs of cheering Tajks in Badakhshan Province. Courtesy of General Dostum

Dostum, far left, confers with Massoud, the Tajik Lion of Panjshir, as the two warlords plot their joint offensive against the Taliban in April 2001.
Courtesy of General Dostum

Dostum gives a speech to his Tajik allies and swears to die fighting against the Taliban or be buried in his *chapan* (riding coat), April 2001. Courtesy of General Dostum

Having been infiltrated into the Hindu Kush by Massoud, Dostum rallies his outnumbered Uzbek *cheriks* (raiders) to fight against the Taliban. Courtesy of General Dostum

Dostum riding on his horse Surkun wearing his famous green *chapan* to lead his riders in waging a hit-and-run war against the Taliban from the mountains, May 2001.

Courtesy of General Dostum

In a timeless scene as old as the Uzbek nomads, Dostum's horsemen gather in the mountains for a war council, May 2001. Courtesy of General Dostum

Dostum issuing orders to his number two in command, Lal Muhammad, in the barren peaks of the Hindu Kush, May 2001. Courtesy of General Dostum

Dostum leading his Uzbek horsemen out of the mountains in a raid on Taliban positions, May 2001. Courtesy of General Dostum

Dostum, on far left, holds a war council with his cavalry commanders. Courtesy of
General Dostum

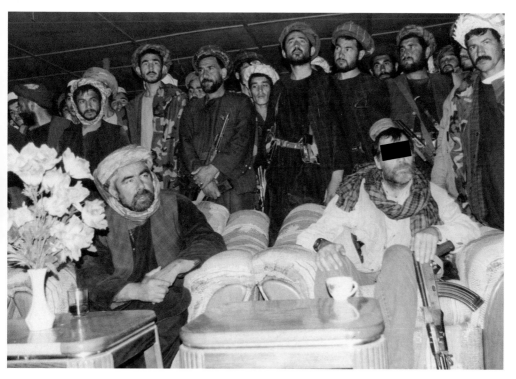

After the September 11 attacks the CIA sent experienced field operative R.J.
to plan a joint US-Uzbek offensive against the Taliban; R.J. is at right with an
AK-47. Courtesy of General Dostum

Dostum (now wearing US camouflage) informs his men that the Americans will be sending an elite special force team to help them fight their common Taliban foe. Courtesy of General Dostum

On October 20 the elite Green Beret team Operational Detachment Alpha 595 (Codenamed Tiger 02) is infiltrated by helicopter into the mountains to help Dostum's riders fight the Taliban. Team commander Captain Mark Nutsch is at the bottom right of the picture in black with goatee. Courtesy of General Dostum

General Dostum confers with CIA agent Johnny Micheal Spann (in black at left), who was subsequently killed by the Taliban, thus becoming America's very first casualty in the war on terror. Courtesy of General Dostum

America's unsung allies in the war on the Taliban, a group of Uzbek fighters led by Ahmed Khan's nephew Hikmet, prepare to mount a raid on the Taliban.
Courtesy of Commander Hikmet

Uzbek horsemen armed with an RPG prepare to go into combat against the **Taliban.** Courtesy of Commander Hikmet

US Air Force close air support specialist Master Sergeant Bart Decker riding with Dostum's horsemen in the background in the famous photograph that was released to the press by Secretary of Defense Donald Rumsfeld in the early days of Operation Enduring Freedom. This picture now hangs in the Smithsonian. Author's collection

Dostum watches bombs being guided onto distant Taliban targets by Bart Decker.
Courtesy of General Dostum

Bart Decker and two unidentified members of his team calling in bombs on
Taliban positions with a SOFLAM (laser target designator) on the ground below
them. Author's collection

Dostum riding with several Uzbeks and American Air Force special forces operatives whose faces have been obscured to protect their identity.

Author's collection

General Dostum on his horse Surkun with his red Turkmen carpet behind him.

Author's collection

Several members of Operational Detachment Command 53 (the Air Force close air support team that called in bombs on the Taliban for Dostum's men) with Dostum. Author's collection

US Air Force special operators mount up to ride to the front to call in air strikes.
Author's collection

This statue of a US horse-mounted Green Beret entitled *De Oppresso Liber* ("Free the Oppressed") honors the A Teams of Afghanistan. It is located in Two World Trade Center and was dedicated by Vice President Joe Biden in November 2012. Courtesy of Colonel Edwin "Andy" Anderson

Taliban prisoners of war captured by Dostum. Author's collection

As Dostum and his men gather momentum they capture several Taliban tanks in the plains. Courtesy of General Dostum

Dostum is greeted by thousands of cheering townsmen as he and his men liberate the city of Mazar-e-Sharif from the Taliban. Courtesy of General Dostum

Dostum holds a ceremony and places US special forces in a place of honor by his side. Courtesy of General Dostum

General Dostum is thanked for his role in helping defeat the Taliban by General Tommy Franks, the head of Central Command. Courtesy of General Dostum

Dostum and Ahmed Khan (seated on Dostum's left) say goodbye to the Green Berets of Tiger 02 in an outdoor ceremony. Courtesy of General Dostum

The author with General Dostum and his horses in Shiberghan, his headquarters in the northern plains. Courtesy of General Dostum

Dostum with horse Surkun. Courtesy of the author

Dostum poses with a Sig pistol given to him by General Tommy Franks. Courtesy of the author

The author and his wife, Feyza, meet with Dostum in his compound in Shiberghan during the author's second visit to northern Afghanistan, in 2005. Courtesy of the author

This is the army of Afghanistan's great survivor, the warlord general Abdul Rashid Dostum. He doesn't serve the central government, but he has long used his fighting force to determine who the central government will be. As leader of the Jumbesh faction, General Dostum controls six northern provinces with the power of an absolute monarch. His people even call him Pasha, the King.

Dostum's provinces are a blatant barrier to the Taliban dream of one Afghanistan under ultra-Islamic law. In the south many welcomed the Taliban advance for ending the fighting and corruption of rival mujahideen. But here in the north they already had peace under General Dostum's rule.

[The televised images feature turbaned Uzbek soldiers getting out of Russian jeeps and stores packed with television sets.]

By Afghan standards they also have prosperity with thriving trade and vast reserves of gas. Most are prepared to fight for their independence and freedom.

In Dostum's capital, Mazar i Sharif, people have reacted in horror to Taliban rules banning music and smoking. They now know that even their children would be in breach of Taliban law; in Kabul they banned kites for distracting children from their scriptures. But the greatest affront to the Taliban is that women here live normal lives in public.

General Dostum is a master at picking sides and emerging the winner. . . . At the very least General Dostum has now ended the Taliban threat to his kingdom. . . . The big unknown is whether his new power will be a harbinger of years more fighting or a chance to make lasting peace. That too may depend on the next move of this master of the art of Afghan war.[22]

Later that year, Dostum, who was at that moment leading his cavalry against the Taliban from the western hills of Faryab Province, welcomed a BBC reporter. His report provides a fascinating view of Dostum's role as a front-line commander:

Far away, across a plain, a column of armed horsemen was making its way down a hillside. They hit the flat ground and broke into a canter. This was Uzbek cavalry, perhaps 100-strong, surging towards us, dust rising from the pounding hooves. And there at the centre of the line—on a white charger—rode General Dostum himself.

As the riders reached us they reined in hard. There was a great neighing of horses and stamping of hooves. We were engulfed in dust, and the gathered soldiers roared in salute of their commander-in-chief.

The General dismounted and strode towards me, a huge man in a turban, his Uzbek jacket reaching down to his riding boots, and in his hand he carried a whip.

In his deep, booming voice he joked with his troops and gave a running commentary as he strode down a line of captured Taleban vehicles. The General glowered briefly at a forlorn group of six Taleban prisoners of war. He lined up his senior officers and introduced them to me one-by-one.

Next a string of jeeps took us rocketing up a hillside. At the summit, arrangements had been made for a picnic like no other. There were carpets and cushions spread on the grass, and there was chicken and rice and fruit and nuts. The guns on the frontline were silent, and as we ate and drank we gazed at the hills that turned blue in the distance as they rose and fell towards Iran. The General talked of politics and war, and at one stage he pointed with a chicken bone at a peak off to the left and said, "See that mountain—the one with the snow on it? Well I captured it three days ago."[23]

Those who visited Dostum found a strongman who was hospitable, loyal to his men, charismatic, gruff, naively friendly, and eager to impress. Dostum was also someone you did not want to cross. He seemed to take great pride in his troops and their fighting prowess and did not appear to be fazed by the prospect of a full-scale war with the Taliban. He was convinced that, when push came to shove, his army—which was equal in size to that of the Taliban and more professional—would be able to defend his bastion of liberalism on the steppes of Turkistan. It was inconceivable that the black-turbaned fundamentalist Pashtun student militias from the south could overrun the core lands of his Uzbek-dominated substate.

But not all of Dostum's time was spent focused on war. At roughly this time Dostum was approached by a delegation of white-bearded elders from Jowzjan. While Dostum had tremendous power, he still had to work through the traditional social structures that dominated the north, so he made time to hear what they had to say. But nothing had prepared Dostum for their message.

A spokesman from the delegation began by telling the Pasha that he had forgotten his Muslim duty to get married following the death of Khadija. The delegation claimed to have found him a suitable wife, a Pashtun from the Popalzai clan whose family had been settled in the north. Her name was Zuya, and by marrying her Dostum could make an alliance with the Pashtuns living in the northern plains of Turkistan.[24]

At first Dostum was tempted to resist the elders, but he knew that their support was crucial. What they said also made cold, logical sense. After giving it much thought, he finally agreed to the elders' suggestion. It was strange in Afghan culture for a successful man to be unmarried, and in truth he did need someone to take care of him.

Within a month he was married to a beautiful young Pashtun woman whom he had never laid eyes on before. While Dostum found himself attracted to Zuya, he found she could not replace Khadija no matter how hard she tried to please him. Sadly, his relationship with her gradually came to resemble that of other Afghan men and their wives. He began to live a life that was largely separate from her.

They were, however, drawn closer by the fact that Zuya bore five children: Mustafa Kemal (named for Mustafa Kemal Ataturk, the founder of the secular republic of Turkey), Babur (named for the Turko-Mongol figure Dostum admired), Reshide, Hushbu, and Sultan. These children and their mother lived in a separate compound from Khadija's children in Shiberghan.

Later in the year the white-bearded elders again came to Dostum and told him that they wanted him to take a second wife. While Dostum was a modernist who did not believe in the old tradition of rich men taking up to four wives, he was moved by their story. It so happened that one of his earliest Jowzjani followers from his very first assignment to Darya Suf had been killed in recent fighting with the Taliban, as had his younger brother. His family was impoverished and could not take care of his wife. The elders asked if Dostum would marry her and take her into his household. In a decision that had more to do with following ancient traditions than with love, Dostum decided to take her as his second wife. The woman, whose name was Zubeyda, was subsequently given a house, servants, and a healthy stipend, but Dostum rarely visited her and never had any children with her.

To all outward appearances, Dostum and his realm appeared to be stable and secure in the aftermath of his second and third marriages. His substate was flourishing with Uzbekistani, Russian, and Turkish support; the shrine was safe; and he was appreciated for having made it all possible.

But things are not always as they appear in Afghanistan; and for all of his outward appearances of strength, there were cracks of disunity in Dostum's realm. The truth was that Dostum's power was built much like that of Shaybani Khan—on the alliance of quarreling, semifeudal subcommanders. Not all of them walked in lockstep with the Pasha.

These inherent divisions would ultimately destroy Dostum's kingdom and allow the Taliban to gain control of the symbolically important Shrine of Ali in Mazar-e-Sharif.

16

MALIK

"No one among the Uzbeks or Turkmen could ever forgive Malik for his betrayal. He was the cause of our suffering."

—Seracettin Mahdum, Turkmen political leader
and son of the Kizil Ayak Sheikh

THE PLAINS OF NORTHERN AFGHANISTAN. SPRING 1997.

As the de facto khan of Afghan Turkistan, Dostum had several great Uzbek commanders below him, each with his own private army. The most powerful of these feudal lords were Rasul and his seven brothers and half-brothers, known as the Pahlawans (translation: "wrestlers").[1] The Pahlawans had formerly been mujahideen but had come over to the government with their fighters at Dostum's behest. Their seat of power was in Faryab Province, which lay west of Jowzjan. Rasul Pahlawan's army of four thousand fighters was tasked with fighting in the southwest against the Taliban who were approaching from Herat.

But Rasul was no Dostum. He carried out his military tasks in return for a certain independence in his feudal domain, which he ruled with an iron fist. He was known for assassinating his enemies, including one whom he had invited for a peace conference and then had killed.[2] He was also known for his cruelty and had a reputation for taking local girls and making them his concubines.[3] On several occasions Dostum tried to rein in his nominal Uzbek subordinate but had to walk delicately in light of Rasul's power.

Rasul's cruelty may have ultimately come back to haunt him. In 1996 he was gunned down in Mazar-e-Sharif by one of his own bodyguards, Abdul Samed, who sought to avenge an insult. The Pahlawan brothers subsequently had Samed's entire family massacred in revenge; in addition, they killed over a hundred people believed to have been in on the plot.[4]

With Rasul's death, his younger stepbrother Malik took over as head of the clan. Unlike his older brother, Malik was not a military leader; he was an intellectual. He had finished high school and gone on to college by the time the Soviets invaded. In recognition of his talents and to placate his powerful family, Dostum made Malik his foreign representative after Rasul's death.

But as the Taliban continued to mount offensive operations on Faryab Province, Dostum's intelligence officers began to provide him with disturbing reports of Malik's activities. The reports mentioned the comings and goings of Pakistani Inter-Services Intelligence (ISI) operatives in Malik's headquarters.[5] Since it was well known that the ISI was in bed with the Taliban, this was alarming news indeed—especially when it was later discovered that Malik's mother was actually a Pashtun. While this fact did not in and of itself mean he was a traitor, it was cause for concern—particularly after Dostum's agents told him that Malik had grown tired of living in Dostum's shadow. Malik had even told the Pakistanis that he felt Dostum stood in the way of unity and that the Taliban could be negotiated with.

Malik was also in favor of uniting with the Taliban and attacking Massoud, for whom he and his brothers had a deep-seated hatred.[6] If this were not enough, at the end of February 1997, Dostum's agents foiled a plot by Malik to shoot down Dostum's helicopter with a surface-to-air missile.[7]

But Dostum was loath to move against Malik when his troops were fighting on the crucial western front against the Taliban. In the interest of maintaining unity, Dostum publicly forgave Malik the attempt on his life. The word *Uzbek* meant "self-master" after all, and it was perhaps natural that Malik would try to challenge him for power. Having just received a shipment of fifty T-62 and T-72 tanks from Russia, Dostum was determined to use them to push the Taliban out of Badghis Province, and he needed Malik's local troops to do so. Dostum was also working with the Tajik leader Ismail Khan to foment a rebellion in the Taliban-occupied province of Ghor. The last thing he could afford on the eve of battle was infighting with Malik's 511th Division.

Desperately trying to shore up his fragile unity, Dostum waited for the snows that covered the mountains and plains of Afghan Turkistan to melt so they could begin. In early May the conflict began anew when the Taliban commenced their much-anticipated spring offensive in the southwest. At the same time they also attempted to come over the Hindu Kush via the Salang Pass. It was clear that the Taliban were focusing all of their resources on conquering Turkistan and the shrine of Mazar-e-Sharif. They were confident that, if they could acquire this symbolic city, all Afghans would recognize them as the official government of Afghanistan.

In the end, however, Massoud's Tajiks held the Taliban off in the mountains while Dostum led his men in repulsing the Taliban in the west. But hundreds of Uzbeks lost their lives in the fighting. Thanks to Pakistani aid and the assistance of bin Laden's Arab jihadis, the Taliban were getting better. Bin Laden had never forgiven Dostum and Massoud for pushing his men out of Kabul in 1992, and he burned for revenge. For bin Laden, Massoud was a hated moderate rival, and Dostum was the epitome of the secularist Sufi tradition he loathed. To defeat them, bin Laden sent out word to thousands of Arab fanatics to come to Afghanistan for one last battle with the two warlords. For the first time Bin Laden's 055 Ansar fighters began to appear on the battlefield, and they quickly established a reputation for unparalleled fanaticism.

Curiously, many in the Northern Alliance also suspected that the United States was helping the Taliban so that the Americans could build gas and oil pipelines across their territory. Dostum himself had been wooed by the American oil firm Unocal and invited for a brief trip to the United States to meet with their officials in 1996. He was fascinated by the wealthy country whose efforts to support the fundamentalist mujahideen in the 1980s had set back his own dream of a secular Afghanistan. But nothing came of his visit, and Dostum continued to get the majority of his support from the Russians, Turks, and Uzbekistanis, who were more concerned about the threat of militant Islamists than the distant Americans.

As Dostum continued to lead his men from the front, in mid-May a message came to him from Mazar-e-Sharif that a Malik supporter, Mullah Abdul Rahman Haqqani, had been gunned down. Dostum quickly sent word to Malik that he would have the police investigate the murder. The timing could not have been worse. Dostum suspected the perpetrators were Taliban sympathizers trying to sow dissension between him and Malik.

But Malik used the assassination as a pretext to begin openly speaking out against Dostum, whom he accused of being behind the murder. Almost a year after the death of his brother Rasul, Malik also began to claim that Dostum had been involved in that plot as well.[8] Clearly Malik was on the edge, and Dostum hoped his Pahlawan brothers could control him as the Taliban launched another major assault on May 19, 1997.

But Dostum had no idea how far things had gone by that time. As the Taliban forces commenced their operations, Malik requested a meeting with Ismail Khan, whose two-thousand-man Tajik force was helping him fight the Taliban. Offering traditional Afghan hospitality, Malik then provided meals to Khan and his soldiers. But as their guests ate, Malik's men suddenly pulled their guns on Khan's Tajiks and ordered them to disarm. More than seven hundred of Khan's men were arrested by Malik's Faryabi Uzbeks that day.

When Ismail Khan furiously demanded to know why he and his men were being arrested, Malik calmly led several Taliban commanders into the room. Outside, hundreds of their black-turbaned companions waited to take possession of their captives.

After several weeks of secret negotiations and a bribe of $200,000, Malik had finally cut a deal with the Taliban. In return for being offered the position of governor of a semiautonomous region to be known as Turkistan, he was handing the Taliban their first major mujahideen war-lord as a gift. Ismail Khan, the man known as the Amir of Herat, was subsequently placed in chains and taken triumphantly to a Taliban prison in Kandahar.

Malik did not, however, stop with Khan and his troops. He and his Faryabi Uzbeks then surrounded and disarmed hundreds of Dostum's men. By afternoon, Malik's troops had captured scores of Dostum loyalists; having surprised and disarmed them, he felt confident enough to raise the white flag of the Taliban over Maimana, the capital of the strategic Faryab Province. He and his men were now openly in rebellion and their first move was to let the Taliban into their province.

Dostum found out about the mutiny when some of his troops radioed him urgently to tell him that they were being surrounded by Malik's men. They also reported that Malik's troops had Taliban soldiers with them.

At first Dostum did not believe it. Uzbeks uniting with the Taliban? It seemed inconceivable. But then the reports began to filter in from across Faryab. The Taliban were on the move, and Malik and his brother Gul Mohammad Pahlawan were radioing all Uzbek commanders, telling them to lay down their weapons.[9] Dostum himself radioed Malik and spoke to him and his brothers directly. He offered to step down as head of the north if they would only break their ties with the Taliban.

When they refused, a furious Dostum predicted, "Your victory will be built on the misery of the people of the north," and slammed down his radio.[10] It was now time for Dostum to fight to defend his realm, even if it meant killing fellow Uzbeks.

As the Taliban and Malik's traitorous Uzbek troops swarmed into his home province of Jowzjan, Dostum flew to Khoja Doko to make a stand. From the hill above his home village he watched through binoculars as the enemy surged across the Dasht-e-Leili plain toward his positions. Only then did he realize the magnitude of the joint Malik-Taliban offensive. As the enemy's pickup trucks stormed toward him in a wall of dust, Dostum ordered his tanks to shell them from afar and then commanded his gunners to open fire on them at will.

But the enemy proved to be resilient and kept coming, even after sustaining heavy losses. As the Taliban and Malik's troops surged forward, Dostum's younger brother Abdul Kadir pleaded with him to flee. Having fought so hard to build his secular state, Dostum initially refused and contemplated going down fighting. But at the last minute he reluctantly conceded to Abdul Kadir's reasoning and boarded one of his awaiting helicopters. Dostum's helicopter took him above the battlefield, giving him his first overview of the Taliban-Malik offensive. Staring in awe at the approaching Taliban-made dust storm, Dostum prayed for his brother and commanders and flew to Mazar-e-Sharif.

Less than an hour after Dostum left, the enemy overran Khoja Doko, and Lal and Abdul Kadir made a fighting retreat to Shiberghan. By the following day Shiberghan, the capital of Jowzjan Province, had fallen, and the enemy continued to surge toward the ultimate prize, Mazar-e-Sharif. There Dostum planned to draw a line in the sand and fight off the enemy with Tajik and Hazara reinforcements.

But at that moment terrible news came from the troops guarding the strategic Salang Pass. Massoud's commander in charge of the pass, Bashir Salangi, had also been bribed by the Taliban. He and his men had defected to the Taliban and opened the southern gateway into Turkistan for the enemy. Thousands of Taliban troops were pouring over the mountains of the south as well, and the enemy was now set to launch a pincer assault on Dostum's crumbling state. The Pasha would be facing Taliban troops from the front and the rear.

As Dostum weighed the odds of beating off Taliban attacks from the west and the southeast, he had to accept that the most important ingredient for victory in any Afghan battle—momentum—now lay with the enemy. He could stand and turn Mazar-e-Sharif, the city he had fought so hard to protect, into an urban battlefield. But this would doubtless lead to thousands of civilian deaths and damage the Shrine of Ali. This was something he could not allow.

And so Dostum, the man who a few days earlier had been the most powerful person in all of Afghanistan, ordered thousands of his troops to melt into the countryside. Only a small elite group led by Lal was ordered to retreat into the mountain valley of Darya Suf to regroup.

For Dostum, who had worked so hard to keep both the mujahideen government and the Taliban out of Mazar-e-Sharif, it was heartbreaking to see the overthrow of everything he had fought for. The time had come for the fanatical Taliban to assume control of the Shrine of Ali and use it to legitimize their cause.

Overwhelmed with fury and despair, Dostum gathered 135 of his officers and on May 24 drove seventy miles across the barren desert north of Mazar-e-Sharif to the border of Uzbekistan. At the border, under a billboard with his picture on it, Dostum crossed over the Bridge of Friendship into Uzbekistan, seeking sanctuary.

But the Uzbekistani government, fearing Taliban attacks on its southern border, told him he had to leave within twenty-four hours. Dostum was now a man without a country. Fortunately, Turkey, which had always considered the Turkic groups of Central Asia to be its *kucuk kardesler* (little brothers), acted to save Dostum out of Turkic solidarity. Turkey sent a Boeing 727 to pick up the general and several of his followers and family in the Uzbekistani capital of Tashkent and then flew them into exile in Ankara, Turkey.[11]

As the plane departed Tashkent, Dostum, who had been forced to abandon everything in his desperate escape from Mazar-e-Sharif, seemed a broken man. His long journey from being a peasant in Khoja Doko to the most powerful man in his homeland had ended with one act of betrayal.

Nine Wells

MAZAR-E-SHARIF. MAY 1997.

Dostum arrived in Ankara, Turkey, and was overwhelmed by reporters. At first he seemed to be stunned and withdrawn, refusing to speak to the journalists. But when they followed him to a compound where he was being temporarily housed by the Turkish authorities, he finally agreed to give an interview. He spoke with rage of the betrayal by Malik. He claimed that he could have easily held off the Taliban had Malik not stabbed him in the back. Dostum thanked the Turks for their hospitality.[12] He vowed never to forget the sanctuary offered to him and his children.

Dostum pointedly refused to accept permanent asylum in Turkey, however, and made it clear that he would be returning to his homeland to fight his people's enemy. He was sure that the easygoing Uzbek Sufi Muslims would not be able to live with their new Taliban masters. Sooner or later, he would be recalled to deliver his people from their enemies.

But as Dostum listened to the reports from his supporters in Mazar-e-Sharif, he initially received little grounds for hope. After his departure the Taliban and Malik's men had divided the plains of Turkistan among themselves. On May 20, Malik and his men poured into Dostum's well-preserved capital of Mazar-e-Sharif and went on a looting spree. The following morning, to the horror of its citizens, especially those who had fled there seeking sanctuary from mujahideen and Taliban fanaticism, hundreds of Taliban pickup trucks roared into the city. They carried black-turbaned, bearded men manning heavy machine guns. At their head was a dreaded commander named Abdul Razaq, the very Taliban general who had ordered the brutal castration and killing of President Najibullah one year earlier. Once again the message could not have been clearer: Razaq was there to weed out the last of Afghanistan's Communists.

By the end of the day over three thousand Taliban soldiers had poured into the town, sending its people into a panic. Mullah Razaq and his men promptly called for a public meeting in the marble courtyard of the Shrine of Ali. As the nervous citizens gathered before the glowering Taliban gunmen, Razaq delivered a chilling speech into his microphone. He told the people that the Taliban had come to the north to solve the region's problems. First among those problems were women who were breaking God's law by attending Balkh University and leaving the house without burqas. All education for women was to cease immediately, and women who were caught without burqas on would be arrested and beaten. Those who engaged in more serious crimes like adultery would be summarily executed. Men who did not attend mosque would be beaten and arrested. Kite flying, marble playing, movies, singing, buzkashi, dancing, dog fighting, televisions, secular education, and men without beards were also outlawed.

As the stunned citizens of the great city fearfully went to their homes, the Taliban soldiers fanned out throughout the town to break television sets, beat men who did not have full beards, and arrest women in school or without burqas. Once-liberal Mazar-e-Sharif was transformed into a grim religious Taliban prison camp. Across the north billboards featuring Dostum's face were symbolically burnt to demonstrate that the era of the secular warlord was over.

But these were not the only pictures being burnt. The Taliban, who believed that any portrayal of human images was un-Islamic, also began to burn the billboards honoring Malik's slain brother, Rasul Pahlawan. And thus begun the trouble between the Taliban and their traitorous Uzbek allies from Faryab.

Misunderstandings between the Taliban and Malik's men increased after the Taliban paid a visit to Malik's home on their second day in Mazar-e-Sharif. At Malik's house they found a picture depicting the great Persian poet Omar Khayyam and a woman offering him wine from a goblet. In fury the Taliban iconoclasts destroyed the picture and then bayoneted Malik's sixty-inch television set. Malik wisely chose not to confront his heavily armed visitors at that moment, but it became clear that the Taliban were going to be difficult to get along with.[13]

Despite these outrages, however, Malik still seemed to believe the alliance would work and that he would be made governor of an autonomous Turkistan. For this reason he was totally unprepared for what happened on the following day. Pakistan, Saudi Arabia, and the United Arab Emirates recognized the Taliban as the official government of Afghanistan. Their seizure of the shrine of Mazar-e-Sharif signified that they, not President Rabbani, had the mandate to rule the land.

But there was no mention of an autonomous northern zone to be run by Malik. Instead the Taliban gave him the largely symbolic post of deputy minister of foreign affairs and ordered him to travel to Kabul to take up his new job.

Then, to compound matters, the Taliban began to disarm the troops of Malik's brother Gul Mohammad Pahlawan.[14] Soon reports came in that the Taliban had begun to beat and disarm Malik's own men.[15] Some reports indicated that the Taliban had even gunned down some of his men.

Having turned on their new Uzbek ally, the Taliban then began to disarm Dostum's Hazara allies as well. As the Taliban moved into the Hazaras' neighborhood to take their prized weapons, the Hazaras fearfully recalled the fate of their great leader, Abdul Mazari. In 1996, Mazari had similarly laid down his weapons and gone to the Taliban to try to arrange a treaty. At first the Taliban accepted him as a guest, but then they turned on him and beat him savagely. After torturing him, they took him up in a helicopter—and then threw him out to his death. The grieving Hazaras later found his body and took it to the shrine of Mazar-e-Sharif for a burial.

Now, having conquered Mazar-e-Sharif, the first thing the Taliban did was to desecrate Mazari's grave at the Shrine of Ali. Such sacrilege at the holy shrine shocked the great city's people, who had always gotten along despite their Sunni-Shiite differences. Clearly the Shiite Hazaras could expect no mercy from the Sunni Taliban. One journalist in Mazar-e-Sharif reported on the tension in the air, claiming the Malik-Taliban alliance was "one bullet away from disintegrating."[16]

It was in a poor Hazara neighborhood near the Shrine of Ali that the bullets that shattered the fragile alliance were fired. Hazaras who refused to be disarmed shot and killed eight Taliban, and the people of Mazar-e-Sharif shuddered at what was to come. Unused to such resistance in a conquered town, the Taliban furiously vowed revenge and stormed the offending neighborhood.

But instead of fearful civilians, they found a heavily armed population that had turned the alleys and warrens of their community into an ambush zone. Hundreds of Taliban were slaughtered, picked off by Hazaras who rained down bullets from windows, rooftops, and side allies. When the gun smoke cleared, 350 Taliban lay dead in the streets.[17]

But it did not end there. Groups of Taliban who were unaware of the mounting resistance were gunned down as the revolt spread outward from the shrine. A BBC reporter in Mazar-e-Sharif at the time witnessed the following scene:

> About forty Taleban soldiers were sauntering down the road. Their weapons were not raised at the ready and some were talking to each other. I only had a moment to take in how strangely unaware they seemed to be of the danger before they started dying. From the windows and doors around them, local people opened fire. And many of the Taleban stood still as their friends were being spun about by bullets.[18]

Sensing that the tide was beginning to turn against the Taliban, Malik frantically called his commanders to find out what was going on. As reports of further Hazara attacks on the Taliban came in, Malik calculated the odds. Momentum appeared to have shifted against the Taliban; and in the finest of Afghan traditions, it was to time jettison his new allies.[19] He turned on the Taliban and joined the resistance.

Malik ordered his men to fire on the Taliban, who had overconfidently dispersed their forces throughout the maze of Mazar-e-Sharif. Hundreds of Taliban, who were unfamiliar with the town, were gunned down by Malik's vengeful Uzbeks, who fought alongside the Hazaras. In the ensuing slaughter, the Taliban commander Abdul Razaq tried to flee but was captured. The murderer of Najibullah expected no mercy, and none was given. He was brutally executed along with the Taliban foreign minister, who had just flown into the city with a group of Pakistanis to celebrate Mazar-e-Sharif's conquest.

By the next day it was over. With the bodies of over six hundred of their comrades lying dead in the streets, as many as 2,500 surviving Taliban surrendered to Malik to save their lives. This was to be their final mistake.

Malik's Faryabi Uzbeks were known to be in an unforgiving mood. They quickly disarmed their erstwhile Taliban allies, who had been gloating just the day before. Then they silently drove them out in convoys past Shiberghan to a spot in the Dasht-e-Leili desert known as Nine Wells. There the Taliban prisoners were lined up in the hot sun to await their fate. As they fearfully said their prayers, the Uzbeks opened fire on them at point-blank range with heavy PK machine guns while Malik watched. Hundreds of unarmed Taliban prisoners were gunned down in cold blood without mercy in the unforgiving desert.

And these were the lucky ones.

Others were thrown alive into the nearby wells. As the screaming prisoners began to pile on top of one another in the suffocating darkness, Malik's men put them out of their misery by throwing hand grenades in on top of them. It was a cruel fate for the Taliban, who themselves had gone to such lengths to enforce their harsh brand of Islam on the people of the north.[20] When it was over as many as two thousand Taliban lay dead in the wells, which were then bulldozed and booby-trapped with hand grenades.

To compound matters, the attacking Taliban force that had come over the Salang Pass was subsequently trapped by Massoud, who blew up a key tunnel in the mountains. The trapped Taliban retreated to Kunduz and decided to hold out in this city on the eastern plains of Turkistan, which had a mixed Tajik, Uzbek, and Pashtun population. There these surviving Taliban fighters in the north prepared to make their last stand. For a religious movement that had days earlier been recognized as the government of

Afghanistan by Pakistan, the United Arab Emirates, and Saudi Arabia, this setback was nothing short of catastrophic. Even by fluid Afghan standards, the turn of events was stunning.

Dostum followed the events from afar with keen interest, although he heard no word of Malik's massacre, which was initially kept hidden from the world. By all accounts, he grew restless upon hearing that Malik was attempting to reunify the Tajik-Hazara-Uzbek alliance to push the remaining Taliban out of Kunduz.

But this proved easier said than done over the summer of 1997, for Malik was no Dostum. Notwithstanding his skill as a traitor, Malik proved to be an incapable warleader. In many ways, he had sown the seeds for his own destruction. The massacre of so many Taliban infuriated the local Pashtun population in the north, which had already been collaborating with the invaders. As the war devolved into even more of an ethnic struggle, the local Pashtuns stepped up to aid the Taliban fighters trapped in Kunduz. This proved to be decisive in enabling them to hold the strategic city. By mid-summer this force in Kunduz was joined by thousands more Taliban airlifted in from Kabul.[21] Having acquired a strategic foothold in the north, the Taliban meant to use it to take Malik down.

In August the Taliban also launched a mass assault on Faryab Province in the west, a conflict that drew most of Malik's men to the western front. As his men fought and died against a Taliban enemy that by now was sure its missing men had been massacred, Malik desperately tried to prevent the Pashtuns at his rear from aiding the enemy. But in late August the Taliban force broke out of Kunduz with local Pashtun support and began to move on Mazar-e-Sharif from the east. In September this army overwhelmed the forces of Ahmed Khan, the Uzbek mujahideen commander who had been linked to Dostum, and began a second march on the capital of the north.

As they approached the city it became obvious to everyone that Malik was not the man to lead the Uzbek army in its hour of need. Riots broke out in Mazar-e-Sharif as the inhabitants chanted Dostum's name and waved placards with his face on it. As the discontent spread, troops who were loyal to Dostum began to clash with those tied to Malik. With the vengeful Taliban army fast approaching their city, many inhabitants prayed at the Shrine of Ali for the return of their former master, Dostum.

Then, on September 11 a rumor began to circulate in the streets that Dostum had come back and was making his way from the border town of Hairaton to reclaim his throne. According to the rumor, the Pasha had returned and was vowing vengeance against both Malik and the Taliban.

Afghan Phoenix

MAZAR-E-SHARIF. 1997–1998.

On September 12, Dostum and thousands of his supporters arrived in Mazar-e-Sharif. He was given a hero's welcome, and his men swarmed to his side. They were not the only ones. Key Malik commanders, such as Majid Rowzi, defected and came back over to Dostum as soon as he arrived. Across the north the big question was how Dostum would treat the man who had betrayed him.

As the resurgent Taliban approached Mazar-e-Sharif, Dostum surprised everyone by sending a message to Malik telling him that he once again forgave him. He asked Malik to join him in resisting the common enemy. With the Taliban at the gates, Dostum made it clear that he wanted to put aside their differences and present a united front. In public, at least, he stressed that he had only returned to help organize the resistance to the Taliban, not to reclaim his power.

In mid-September Dostum held a war council in his fortress at Qala-e-Jangi and vowed to resist the Taliban, who were now a mere day's march from Mazar-e-Sharif. He publicly forgave all the Uzbek troops from Faryab who had betrayed him and offered to lead them once more against the enemy. To Malik's dismay, thousands of his own men flocked to Dostum, who warmly embraced them. With his army galvanized by their leader's presence and the enemy fast approaching, Dostum prepared to lead them into battle to save Mazar-e-Sharif from the vengeful Taliban army.

As the Taliban moved into Mazar-e-Sharif's suburbs, they were met by thousands of Uzbek horsemen who had covering fire from tanks and MiG fighter-bombers. At their front was Dostum, and by his side were his Tajik and Hazara allies. To confuse the enemy, Dostum divided his force and launched a two-pronged counterattack on the invading force. The Taliban fought back ferociously on both fronts but could not stop Dostum's momentum. Whenever his army stalled, Dostum was there in person to drive them onward. By nightfall, the Taliban were in full retreat, leaving the bodies of hundreds of their men sprawled out on the plains south of Mazar-e-Sharif.

On their retreat back to Kunduz, the Taliban took their vengeance on the local Uzbek, Hazara, and Tajik populations and slaughtered hundreds of them in the villages of Kizilabad and Kul Mohammad. Tellingly, local Pashtun villagers joined in the massacres as the interethnic harmony that Dostum had so assiduously built began to disintegrate.

As Dostum victoriously returned to his base at the Qala-e-Jangi fortress to plan his next move, he sent a message to Malik telling him he wanted to meet him in person to iron out their differences and shore up Uzbek unity. By this time Malik had been abandoned by all but his most loyal supporters. Fearing a meeting with the powerful man whom he had betrayed, Malik instead decided to retreat to Faryab Province. There he and his brothers frantically tried to salvage their situation.

But as even his closest followers rushed to join Dostum, Malik could see that neither time nor momentum was on his side. In November he and his brothers suddenly decided to withdraw from their feud with Dostum. As vengeful Dostum supporters poured into his regional capital of Maimana and arrested his men, Malik and his brothers burnt their compounds, destroyed their extensive weapons caches, and then boarded Mil Mi-8 helicopters with their wives and children to fly across the border to Turkmenistan.[22] From there they made their way to Iran and then on to exile in Turkey.

Malik and the troublesome Pahlawan brothers were now out of the picture, but the damage they had done in just a few months of misrule was incalculable. Before leaving, Malik and his brothers had spitefully destroyed vast quantities of ammunition and weapons in Faryab Province that could have been used to confront the Taliban. Malik had even destroyed several Scud missiles that Dostum had planned to use should the enemy achieve a breakthrough.

The greatest damage, however, was done to the fragile multiethnic alliance that Dostum had so carefully constructed. Although his military and government were dominated by Uzbeks, they were not ethnically exclusive. Dostum had made a point of appointing ex-Pashtun Communists, Tajiks, Hazaras, and Turkmen to positions in his Jumbesh Party and in his military. As always, he had tried to walk a middle road, bringing diverse groups together much as his Uzbek ancestors had done.

But the ethnic balance had been disturbed by Malik's betrayal. As soon as the Taliban entered the land, the northern Pashtuns had gone over to them. The Uzbeks were no longer unified, and the Tajiks, Turkmen, and Hazaras no longer trusted their Uzbek allies. Only Dostum had possessed the charisma and farsightedness to bring this diverse coalition together.

Dostum spent the winter of 1997 through 1998 desperately trying to patch up his tattered alliance and re-equip his men for the Taliban's upcoming summer campaign. In the midst of this effort, he made a frightening discovery in the Dasht-e-Leili desert at the spot known as Nine Wells. His men uncovered twenty mass graves filled with as many as two thousand rotting Taliban corpses, men slaughtered by Majik's forces months earlier. Stunned by this evidence of the systematic murder of unarmed men, Dostum quickly called the International Red Cross and helped them uncover the scene of the slaughter.[23]

International investigators who arrived at the scene found evidence of a horrific war crime. One wrote, "The air in the barren desert is poisoned with the smell of rotting flesh. One corpse, partially decomposed and partially torn apart by scavenging animals, was wrapped in a distinctively striped cotton-stuffed hospital mattress. The needle from an intravenous drip was still lodged in his decayed arm."[24]

Dostum was clearly upset by Malik's killing of the Taliban prisoners of war, which he felt was un-Afghan. The massacre reminded him of the Arabs' treatment of captured government troops during the 1989 siege of Jalalabad. Dostum also found six hundred Taliban in the prison in Shiberghan and, in a goodwill gesture to the Taliban, publicly released them.[25]

The Taliban were not mollified by Dostum's apologies on behalf of Malik, however. They burned for revenge and plotted to overthrow his weakened realm in the summer of 1998. The Taliban began their offensive in May by attacking Malik's home base of Faryab. As they stormed into the province they entered the town of Kaysar and dragged over six hundred of its Uzbek inhabitants out into the town square.[26] There they raped the women and then gunned them down, along with the town's men, in cold blood.

Dostum personally led an assault that pushed the Taliban out of the devastated village, but he was too late to save its civilian inhabitants. To his disgust he found the bodies of naked women and girls and the corpses of slain children and the elderly scattered throughout the burning village. The relative civility of the previous war between his Jowzjani militia and the mujahideen seemed a thing of the past.

As the war became more vicious, Dostum continued to lead his men from the front, putting himself at considerable risk. During one Taliban assault he received serious shrapnel wounds and had to be airlifted to Uzbekistan for emergency medical treatment. Demonstrating just how important he was to his army, many of his men began to abandon their trenches when they heard that he had departed from the battlefield. Dostum, who was having bits of metal removed from his ear, back, legs, and neck, was forced to return from the hospital before he had healed in order to rally his dispirited troops.

Then, having pushed the Taliban back to Badghis Province, Dostum returned to Mazar-e-Sharif expecting to be congratulated by his allies. Instead he found that the Hazaras had seized control of the city and the Tajik commander Ustad Atta had attacked his troops in the nearby town of Tashkurgan. The alliance was terribly weakened, and the trust of the previous period seemed impossible to reproduce. As Dostum desperately tried to keep up the defense in the west, his Tajik and Hazara allies undermined him from behind.

When Dostum's lines began to waver under a particularly brutal Taliban offensive on Faryab Province, he desperately sent a message to Massoud asking for reinforcements. But the reinforcements never arrived, and in mid-July Dostum's weakened lines finally broke. The victorious Taliban then poured through Faryab and once again overwhelmed Dostum's defensive lines in Jowzjan Province. As the Taliban stormed forward they captured eight hundred Uzbek soldiers and, in a sign of things to come, massacred them all. The Taliban then overwhelmed a Hazara force stationed to the west of the city and massacred those men as well.

As his western lines collapsed, Dostum suddenly found himself attacked from behind as the local Pashtun population of Balkh rose up against him. With his supply lines cut, his allies ignoring his pleas for help, and a Pashtun fifth column waging war at his rear, Dostum retreated eastward toward Samangan Province and once again surrendered Mazar-e-Sharif to the enemy.

This decision was to have catastrophic results for the population of the city that had been the epicenter of the grassroots revolt against the Taliban just a year before. The Taliban could not forget the death of hundreds of their comrades at the hands of the people of Mazar-e-Sharif. Now, with Dostum on the retreat, the great city—a symbol of the very tolerance and moderation that the Taliban despised—lay open before the fanatics.

On August 8, the vengeful Taliban poured into Mazar-e-Sharif in hundreds of pickup trucks and began to gun down men, women, children, and even animals unfortunate enough to be caught out in the open. Then they herded the fleeing populace toward the great Shrine of Ali. As the panicked crowds stampeded toward the tomb, the Taliban soldiers gunned down those who ran too slowly. Once at the shrine, the Taliban massacred four hundred more people who had gathered there desperately trying to find sanctuary on its holy grounds.[27] The Taliban then planted explosives in the nearby tomb of the Hazara leader Mazari and blew it up with civilians trapped inside.

While the Taliban were apparently targeting anyone with Mongol features—they had been ambushed and defeated by Mongol Uzbeks and Hazaras in the previous year—they seemed to especially focus on Shiite Hazara "apostates." The Taliban went from house to house dragging Hazara women and children out and ritualistically slitting their throats.[28] The men were shot in the testicles and left to bleed to death.

But Hazaras were not the only Shiites to die in the carnage. As it transpired, the Iranians had been supporting their fellow Shiites, the Hazaras, and their fellow Persians, the Tajiks, with supplies from their consul in Mazar-e-Sharif. When the Taliban broke into the city, they broke all diplomatic protocol and stormed the consul. Once inside, they dragged eleven Iranian diplomats downstairs to the basement and shot them all in cold blood.

Their countrymen quickly found out about the massacre. Furious citizens in Tehran began to chant "Death to the Taliban!" as seventy thousand Iranian troops mobilized on the Afghanistan-Iran border. A full-blown war between Iran and the Taliban was averted only when the Taliban apologized for the diplomatic breach and returned the bodies of the slain diplomats.

But there were no apologies for the Hazaras, who cowered in fear in their homes, waiting for the Taliban to kick in their doors. With their fighting men killed in the Taliban assault, they were defenseless. The Taliban went from door to door killing Hazaras for two days straight. The bodies of the dead rotted in the streets and were eaten by dogs as the Taliban forbade anyone to bury them.[29] Thousands of Mazar-e-Sharif's inhabitants fled to mountains in the south to escape the carnage, but their refugee columns were deliberately shelled by Taliban artillery and strafed by Taliban MiGs. When it was over, as many eight thousand had been killed, and a deep sense of dread swept over the town. After years of warfare, the Taliban finally controlled the most important shrine in the land. Afghanistan, for all intents and purposes, was now theirs.

Among the Taliban's first moves upon reseizing the town was to ban worship at the Shrine of Ali. The fanatical Pakistanis and Arabs in the Taliban army even called for the destruction of the shrine, which they considered a Sufi abomination. For the time being, however, the Taliban leadership resisted this urge.

But the Arabs were aiming at other targets as well, for not all of the foreign fanatics were engaged in combat in Afghanistan. On the day the Taliban began their second breakthrough into Mazar-e-Sharif, al-Qaeda terrorists stunned the world by blowing up the US embassies in Kenya and Tanzania, killing hundreds. Al-Qaeda's fateful war with the United States had begun.

US president Bill Clinton responded to the attacks by launching a wave of cruise missile strikes on al-Qaeda training facilities in the Pashtun south. But bin Laden, the mastermind behind the embassy attacks, was not in the camps at the time and thus escaped injury. Bin Laden's survival of the widely televised attack by the American superpower made him an icon for many Arabs who hated the Americans. In subsequent years, Arab recruits flocked to his Afghan camps in droves to train for terrorism against the United States. Ironically, Clinton's retaliatory attack on the sovereign territory of the Islamic Emirate of Afghanistan also drew the Taliban leader Mullah Omar closer to bin Laden as the Taliban swore to protect their Arab guest at all costs.

In the meantime, a retreating Dostum fought the Taliban alongside his loyal friend Ahmed Khan until their positions in Samangan Province were overrun in September 1998. As the Taliban swept over Samangan, the two Uzbek commanders fled south into the Hindu Kush to the Hazara town of Bamiyan.

But their refuge was to be short-lived, for no sooner had they arrived in Bamiyan than the Taliban broke through the Hazara lines to the east. The Taliban then forced their way over the Shibar Pass and broke into the Hazara highlands. It was as if a dam had burst. Tens of thousands of Taliban troops poured across the Hazarajat plateau, burning and slaughtering everything in their path.

With the Taliban rapidly moving on Bamiyan, Dostum once again prepared to flee the country. Because the Taliban fundamentalists considered him a high-level infidel enemy, he could expect no mercy from them. Mere hours before the Taliban reached Bamiyan, a bitter Dostum boarded a helicopter and flew to Iran to seek sanctuary.

As Dostum was greeted by Iranian officials, who saw him as a counterweight to the Sunni Taliban, he promised them he would not be staying for long. Stunned by the speed with which the Taliban had overwhelmed the Hazara lands and the plains of Turkistan, Dostum vowed to return to fight the enemy as soon as the moment was ripe. At the time, he had no idea that it would be three long years before he would be able to return to his homeland.

Redemption

TURKEY AND IRAN. SEPTEMBER 1998–APRIL 2001.

Once again Dostum's world had collapsed, and this time there seemed to be little chance of redeeming the situation. The Taliban army had now swollen to fifty thousand men, largely due to recruitment of Pakistani Pashtuns from the madrassas across the border. Mullah Omar's power over almost 90 percent of Afghanistan was nearly unchallenged. From Mazar-e-Sharif to Herat and Bamiyan to Kabul to Kandahar, the Taliban ruled supreme. Only Massoud's fragile Tajik enclave based in the Panjshir Valley and the mountains of the northeast remained independent.

Having been twice defeated by the Taliban, Dostum was despondent; for a while he gave up hope of ever freeing his people and regaining power. But then word came from four of his most trusted commanders—Lal, Abdul Cherik, Hakim, and Ahmed Khan. In the chaos of the Taliban conquest of Mazar-e-Sharif, they had managed to sneak hundreds of men and weapons into the upper reaches of the remote Darya Suf Valley. They promised to carry out pinprick attacks on the Taliban from their mountain hideout and await Dostum's return. For now, however, they warned Dostum that it was too dangerous for him to come back. He should instead spend his time getting treatment for his wounds and trying to gather support from foreign powers for an anti-Taliban alliance.

So Dostum spent the rest of 1998 and beginning of 1999 shuttling between his exile homes in Ankara and Tehran trying to gather money for the Northern Alliance rebels and receiving treatment for his wounds. He also spent considerable time with his children and found that this was the one benefit to his exile.

Dostum also found time to be with his second wife, Zuya. She proved to be faithful and supportive of her husband during this time, but she could not calm the storms that raged in him. He felt as if he were living in a gilded cage in Ankara, and on many restless nights he walked outside, staring at the stars and wondering what was happening in his homeland. The reports that came in from the Darya Suf were not heartening. The Taliban had pushed Lal and his men further up the valley, and the Uzbek raiders were hard-pressed. In addition, in the spring of 2000, Massoud's capital at Taloqan was overwhelmed by a Taliban army that had been reinforced with Arab Ansar fighters. Many Uzbeks fighting alongside Massoud's forces were killed in the assault.

Desperate to do something to help the resistance, Dostum flew to Moscow to meet with Russian officials. The Russians were furious at the Taliban government's words of support for Chechen highlander rebels who were fighting for independence from Russia. While the Russians promised to help out their old Uzbek ally should he return to Afghanistan, they could not offer him the sort of military support they had provided in the past. Dostum left Moscow with promises of help but little in the way of funds or weapons.

In a demonstration of the sort of pragmatism that Babur had once displayed, Dostum similarly visited the Iranians to ask for assistance. The Iranians told him that they would provide him with transport and modest funds to return to Afghanistan to fight their common Taliban foe should the time come.

By 2001 Dostum had done all he could to gather support from international actors, and he began to think that the time was approaching for him to return to Afghanistan. Massoud's lines appeared to be wavering, and the small bands of Uzbek raiders fighting from the mountains near Darya Suf had almost been pushed out of the valley. Dostum was in satellite phone contact with one of his men, Abdul Cherik, when his position was overrun by a Taliban force. The line suddenly went dead, and Dostum was later given the sad news that Abdul Cherik had been shot in the chest by the Taliban. The death of the famed raider, who had fought alongside Dostum since their time in the Afghan army, came as a blow.

Dostum received more bad news when word came from his home village of Khoja Doko from his older brother Mohammad Omar. When the Taliban conquered the village, Mohammad Omar had hidden in a well, escaping the fate of village elders who were hung by the Taliban. Dostum's parents had also escaped the Taliban's wrath and lived undisturbed for the most part. But in the spring of 2001 Dostum's mother died—some said of a broken heart from being separated from her son and grandchildren. While the Taliban police chief in the village allowed her to be buried, he did not allow anyone—not even her husband—to attend the funeral.

These events caused Dostum tremendous grief. As a man of action, he felt helpless in exile in Turkey and longed to make the Taliban pay. He also longed to see his father, who had taken the death of his mother badly.

All these events conspired to push Dostum to the edge. He could no longer sleep, and he seemed incapable of focusing on the world around him. He was living in a limbo of exile that he swore would kill him.

But at that moment he received a fateful phone call that was to change the course of history. When Dostum picked up the phone, he knew by the tone that the call had to be coming from afar. A voice spoke in Dari.

"Dostum, it's time you returned to Afghanistan. Your country needs you, your people need you, and I for one could use your help in my hour of need."

Dostum instantly recognized Massoud's voice. For Dostum, the peasant from Khoja Doko who had for so long yearned to be accepted and appreciated by his peers in the Afghan government, these were the words he had waited years to hear. Dostum and his men were needed; they were not *ghulams* to be used and dispensed with. Considering Dostum's state of mind, he did not hesitate. He quickly promised to return to Afghanistan to help fight the all-powerful Taliban, even though the odds were against them.

With those words, Dostum's mood changed. Overnight, he seemed to recover from the depression that had begun to consume him. He was again alive. Various exiled commanders came by his compound to plan with him and plot their return to Afghanistan. Everyone understood that time was of the essence. The Taliban were promising a massive 2001 spring offensive against Massoud's embattled enclave in the northeast. It would probably begin in May, as soon as the snows melted. Dostum needed to return to the Darya Suf and lead his men in creating a new front before that date. While his children and his wife Zuya pleaded with him not to return, he had rediscovered his sense of purpose, and nothing could stop him. It was time for him to return to command his people.

But there was a deeper impulse driving Dostum as well. Prior to his second exile, he had had little time for reflection. Life had been a tumultuous series of battles that never seemed to end. His exile had given him time to search his soul and look back upon his past. When he recalled the eight hundred civilians who had lost their lives in the 1992 battle between his forces, Rabbani, and Hekmatyar for control of Kabul, he blamed himself.

Dostum increasingly came to see that his salvation lay in returning to the land and fighting against the odds to free the Shrine of Ali in Mazar-e-Sharif. While he did not place any faith in his chances of winning the struggle—the odds were that it would be a one-way journey to his death—he had no choice. It was his kismet.

So in the first week of April 2001, Dostum boarded a plane for Iran and flew to Tehran. There he and twenty-five of his exiled followers prepared to make one last journey to Afghanistan to fight the Taliban. Dostum's spirits were high, despite the dangers, and his enthusiasm proved to be contagious. As their prop plane made the two-hour journey from Tehran to Tajikistan, where they would meet Massoud's liaison team, Dostum galvanized his followers for combat. For better or worse, they were Uzbeks, and exile did not sit well with them. Now, at least, they had a chance to shape their future.

The Last Mission

PANJSHIR, DARYA SUF VALLEY, AND BALKHAB PROVINCE. APRIL 2001–SEPTEMBER 2001.

Dostum and his men did not know what to expect when they arrived in Tajikistan, but there they were warmly greeted by Massoud's representatives. If there was any memory of bad blood between their peoples, it did not show. The urgency of getting Dostum into the field took precedence over any lingering ill will.

From Tajikistan, Dostum and his men boarded rickety Mil Mi-8 helicopters and were finally flown back to their homeland. As they crossed over into Afghanistan, Dostum led his men in an impromptu prayer for success.

On April 6, 2001, Dostum and his men touched down in the Tajik-dominated province of Badakhshan, the largest territory still controlled by Massoud's Northern Alliance faction. There they were warmly greeted by Massoud himself. Dostum had not seen Massoud in more than three years, and the Lion of Panjshir seemed to have aged under the pressure of fighting the Taliban alone. But he also appeared heartened by Dostum's return and asked him to give a speech to his people to bolster their spirits.

As Dostum prepared to speak before an assembled crowd, a young Tajik girl came to the podium with flowers in her hand and boldly spoke before the people who had gathered to catch a glimpse of the legendary Dostum. She said, "Oh leaders, if the hand of the Pakistanis falls upon us, I will blame you on judgment day in this world as well as the next!"[30]

Dostum was moved by the girl's words and promised the gathered crowd that his *chapan* would either be his death shroud or his victory garment. But he did not spend much time in Badakhsan. On April 9, he was flown down to the Panjshir to meet with more Tajik commanders. Finally, on April 12 he and his men boarded Massoud's helicopters and prepared to fly over enemy territory to an isolated mountain base between Darya Suf and Bamiyan known as Balkhab. Everyone held their breath as their helicopter took off from the Panjshir Valley at sunset and began the dangerous journey through Taliban airspace to their destination. If their slow-moving helicopter was caught out in the open, they would be a sitting target for the Taliban MiGs.

Fortunately the *hizir* travel spirits protected them, and they arrived at Balkhab undetected. On the following day, Dostum's semifeudal troops began to arrive in waves from the surrounding provinces. Within a week he had gathered the kernel of a two-thousand-man fighting force and named Lal, Ahmed Khan, Kamal, and Fakir as his subcommanders. These men were then tasked with leading their units in raiding Taliban territory in the foothills.

Dostum and his men soon made their presence felt in the mountains by launching several bold assaults on Taliban positions. As exposed Taliban garrisons were attacked and overrun, it did not take the enemy long to discover that the Pasha had returned. The mountain bards were soon singing his praises.

While the Taliban initially tried to counter Dostum by placing more soldiers at key checkpoints, his riders simply rode around these posts and continued to raid down into the plains of Turkistan. In May 2001, just as the Taliban were preparing for their great offensive against Massoud, Dostum launched his first major military operation. Hundreds of his men overrode the isolated Taliban garrison in Zari Province and sent the Taliban fleeing. This proved to be the straw that broke the camel's back. In fury, the Taliban sent thousands of troops up into the mountains to take the province back from Dostum's *cheriks*. Dostum's men fought back ferociously, but when the assaults became too costly, retreated back up into the mountain heights to fight another day.

This diversion of resources hurt the Taliban just as they launched their assault on Massoud's lines. Massoud's men fought back with renewed vigor against the depleted Taliban force, knowing that they were no longer alone in their struggle.

Around this time another old rival and ally of Dostum's, Ismail Khan, also returned to the fray. The last time Dostum had heard from Khan, he and seven hundred of his men had been treacherously arrested by Malik during his 1997 mutiny. Khan had been thrown into chains and dragged off to a cell in Kandahar, where he remained until 1999. Then one day, one of his Taliban guards took pity on him as a great leader of the mujahideen resistance and decided to release him. On the designated night, the guard came to his cell when his fellow guards were sleeping and ushered Khan out of the prison and into a waiting SUV.

Then, in an adventure that could only happen in Afghanistan, Ismail Khan and the guard sped out into the desert toward the Iranian border. The Taliban promptly sent trucks to track Khan down, and the race was on. But just before Khan and the guard reached the border, their truck hit a land mine and blew up. Both Khan and the guard who was driving each broke a leg, and their escape seemed doomed. But before the Taliban caught up with them, some local villagers found them and delivered them safely to the Iranian border.

Once in Iran, Ismail Khan, like Dostum, chafed at the inactivity and asked to be let back into the fray. In early May 2001, Khan and his men were granted their wish and were flown into Badakhshan to meet with Massoud. Massoud quickly dispatched Khan to the isolated province of Ghor in the western Hindu Kush. There he and his followers began to raid Taliban positions, much as Dostum was doing. Now the Taliban were putting out guerilla brush fires on two fronts.

Massoud was also assisted by Dostum's old Tajik rival, Ustad Atta, who began to attack Taliban positions in the Balkh Valley in conjunction with the Hazara forces of Mohammad Mohaqeq. These diversions hurt the Taliban but did not represent an existential threat to their control of the Afghan north. By the end of the summer of 2001, the Taliban had pushed the Northern Alliance guerillas back up their valleys, and the Taliban forces were moving deeper into the mountains to isolate them.

Then on September 8, 2001, the Taliban and al-Qaeda moved to eradicate their two greatest opponents. The day began with a MiG bombing run
on the Darya Suf village where Dostum and his second-in-command Lal
were reported to be resting. As luck would have it, however, Dostum and his
riders left the village just before it was bombed, and he was spared. Dostum
watched the burning village from nearby heights and cursed his own lack of
aircraft, but he was grateful that he had at least survived the airborne assassination attempt by the Taliban.

But Massoud was not so lucky. On the next day the Lion of Panjshir was
killed by al-Qaeda suicide bombers in his headquarters at Khoja Bahauddin. His army barely survived the Taliban onslaught that followed in the
ensuing days, and the Northern Alliance seemed to be on its last legs.

When Dostum heard the news of Massoud's death, he knew that his
quixotic rebellion against the all-powerful Taliban would probably be even
more short-lived than he had planned. He and his *cherik* raiders had made
no contingency plans for an escape from the Taliban-encircled mountains.
They had only one option: to go down fighting.

The impending defeat of the Northern Alliance also meant Dostum
would never be able to see his elderly father again or visit the graves of his
mother or Khadija. His lonely battle against the fanatics would, in all likeli-
hood, end in the bleak mountains of the Hindu Kush. This was to be his fate
and his punishment for his sin of arrogance in joining the bloody fight for
control of Kabul back in 1994.

For Dostum the morning of September 11, 2001, was a grim one as he
prepared for his final struggle with an enemy that seemed stronger than
ever. He and his *cheriks* would fight to the death as the Taliban closed in on
them and die as Uzbek warriors. They would let Afghanistan know that the
fighting spirit of Shaybani Khan was not dead in the hearts of the Uzbeks.

Then, on September 12, came astonishing news via his representatives
in Uzbekistan and Panjshir: al-Qaeda had carried out a horrific attack on
the United States of America the previous day. When he heard the news
that the magnificent towers of steel and glass he had seen during his 1996

visit to Manhattan had been brought down by his al-Qaeda enemies, Dostum became pensive. As his men excitedly gathered around him to see what the news meant for their lonely campaign, their commander seemed to be lost in thought. After several minutes of quiet reflection, he looked up at his men with a thoughtful expression. Gazing out over the brown, rolling mountains of the Hindu Kush, he spoke slowly.

"I do not know the Americans well, but what I do know of them tells me one thing. They will want revenge, and they will not rest until they get it. The Americans will be coming to Afghanistan. When they do we must be prepared. . . . We might all be making a pilgrimage to the Shrine of Ali after all!"[31]

17

THE AMERICANS

"You are America's avenging angels."

—US Senior Operations Commander to US Special Forces
being deployed to Afghanistan, October 2001[1]

KARSHI, UZBEKISTAN. DARYA SUF VALLEY, NORTHERN AFGHANISTAN. OCTOBER–NOVEMBER 2001.

In the stunned days after 9/11, the American president, George W. Bush, made his demands for Mullah Omar to turn over bin Laden and his al-Qaeda terrorists, but was contemptuously rejected by the Taliban. Instead the Taliban leader Mullah Omar seemed to be daring the Americans to come to Afghanistan and share the fate of the Soviets.

In response, the Americans began to formulate a bold plan to destroy not only al-Qaeda but the Taliban host regime as well. The White House, Langley, and the Pentagon's Central Command took several weeks to rally the support of surrounding countries and deploy Special Operations Forces and CIA agents to neighboring Uzbekistan.

During this period, warfare continued to surge across the battlefields of Afghanistan as the Taliban and Northern Alliance sought to discern the Americans' intentions. Some in al-Qaeda gleefully predicted an ineffectual bombardment of al-Qaeda camps with cruise missiles like the ones launched by Bill Clinton back in 1998 after the US embassy bombings in Africa. Others foresaw a full-scale Soviet-style invasion and quagmire. Both were wrong.

By late September rumors began to spread that small groups of US special operators had been inserted into Northern Alliance territory in Afghanistan. The Americans had arrived and were now operating on soil claimed by the Taliban Amirate of Afghanistan.

While few knew it at the time, on September 27, America had arrived in the forgotten Cold War battlefield of Afghanistan in the form of a CIA Special Activities Division team led by Gary Schroen. This team, known as Jawbreaker, followed in Dostum's footsteps and covertly flew to the Panjshir Valley from Tajikistan in a CIA-owned Russian Mil transport helicopter.

Once in theater the team began to furiously work with Massoud's relatively unknown successor, Fahim Khan, to create a plan to bring down the Taliban regime. This subtle approach was in fulfillment of the secret Blue Sky Memo written by Counterterrorism chief Richard Clarke. The Americans' aim was to build upon Massoud's brushfire strategy and see if they could use small bands of US Special Forces raiders to act as force magnifiers for the outgunned pockets of Northern Alliance fighters. This might lead to the proxy overthrow of the Taliban, thus preventing the United States from having to launch a full-scale winter invasion of Afghanistan. If that did not work, US CENTCOM would launch a full-scale invasion in spring 2002.

Jawbreaker's team leader, Gary Schroen, broached the subject of backing the mysterious Uzbek commander Dostum as well as General Fahim's own Tajik fighters. Dostum had contacted the Americans via sources in Uzbekistan after 9/11 and offered an audacious plan that the Pentagon seemed to like.

The Uzbek commander's strategy called for his horsemen to launch a charge down the Darya Suf Valley in coordination with the US Air Force. Dostum had promised that if the United States could send horse feed, bullets, and bombers to help him, he and his small band would seize the holy shrine of Mazar-e-Sharif before December. He boldly predicted that this move would deprive the Taliban of the mandate to rule Afghanistan, and bring the regime crashing down in a matter of months or even weeks. It would be a replay of the collapse of Najibullah's Communist regime in 1992, when Dostum had first seized the shrine. This would prevent the United States from having to launch a full-scale invasion of the land referred to as the "graveyard of empires."

While the Americans did not fully grasp the symbolic importance of the ancient shrine of Mazar-e-Sharif to the Afghans, they instantly grasped the tactical importance of seizing a foothold in northern Afghanistan. If Dostum could acquire Mazar-e-Sharif, it would give the Americans a beachhead to wage war against the Taliban. The United States was already flying troops from the Tenth Mountain Division into neighboring Uzbekistan in case an invasion was called for. Mazar-e-Sharif was close to the Uzbekistani border and had two airports, which would allow the Americans to airlift troops onto Afghan soil.

But the CIA team was shocked when Fahim Khan, the new Tajik leader, outright rejected the notion of supporting Dostum and his Uzbeks.[2] In a display of the very sort of pettiness and Turkophobia that Dostum had long chafed against, Fahim Khan furiously told the Americans not to trust Dostum the "Communist." Instead he insisted on having the Americans send a support team to fellow Tajik rebel Ustad Atta, who was operating in the Balkh Valley to the west of Dostum.

The CIA was, however, leery of putting all their eggs in one Tajik basket. They opted to go with Dostum, whose secular credentials made him seem more reliable than Rabbani and Fahim Khan, both of whom had close ties to Iran.[3] At the end of the day, the Americans felt there was not much difference between the fundamentalist mujahideen Rabbani and the fundamentalist Taliban. Dostum's secularism, aggressive attitude, and willingness to strike against the Taliban without even waiting for US support appealed to the Central Command head General Tommy Franks.[4] Franks liked Dostum's strategy of trying to topple the Taliban before Christmas. It was exactly the sort of bold plan that he could sell to President Bush, who was demanding quick results.

The men chosen for the mission were six Special Activities Division members to be directed by the CIA's Counterterrorism Center. The identities of three of the men have become known. The first was R.J., an experienced CIA hand who had worked in the 1980s in Pakistan to arm the mujahideen. The fifty-something R.J. spoke fluent Farsi/Dari, which was not only the language of the Tajiks but a lingua franca for all ethnic groups in Afghanistan. R.J. was also an ex-Ranger who had spent considerable time riding horses in his home state of New Mexico. Those who met the blue-eyed, academic-looking agent, a cultural anthropologist by training, recognized his skills as someone who could "go native" in the part of the world that he knew so well.[5]

The second CIA agent was David Tyson, a forty-year-old ex-army specialist in Uzbek and Turkish who had picked up the languages in Indiana University's Central Eurasian Studies program in the 1980s. Like R.J., he was a man who had spent considerable time in the field and was more than capable of serving as a CIA paramilitary.[6] In fact, Tyson had perfected his Uzbek while working at the US embassy in Tashkent, Uzbekistan, and had been making regular, secretive forays into Afghanistan to liaise with Uzbek and Tajik rebels for some time. It was Tyson who had communicated directly with Dostum after 9/11 and told him that a small group of Americans would be coming to his remote mountain base to meet with him.

The third agent was Johnny Micheal Spann, an ex-Marine captain from Winfield, Alabama, who had joined the CIA's Special Activities Group in 1999. He was a specialist in calling in and directing close air support who had previously served with the elite Second Air Naval Gunfire Liaison Company.

The agents' job was to liaise with the mysterious Dostum and find out more about the symbolic importance of the shrine of Mazar-e-Sharif. Then they were to find out what Dostum and his men needed to achieve their objectives and lay the groundwork for the subsequent arrival of an elite Special Forces A-Team.

It was a dangerous mission, and the sense of urgency was palpable in light of the fury in America over the 9/11 attacks. The CIA agents' orders regarding what to do if they encountered al-Qaeda were specific. Cofer Black, the CIA's Counterterrorism Center chief, reportedly said, "I want their heads up on pikes."[7]

By mid-October the six agents had arrived at the windswept, ex-Soviet airfield at Karshi, Uzbekistan, to await their infiltration into the depths of Afghanistan's Hindu Kush. For two days they talked with General Dostum via satellite phone trying to establish a safe landing zone where they would not run the risk of being ambushed by the Taliban. The Taliban had heard the rumors of American agents being inserted into their country and were desperate to capture them.

Finally, on October 16, Dostum gave the CIA team a green light to come. By this time the Taliban air force had been completely destroyed on the ground by US and NATO bombings that had begun on October 7. Operation Enduring Freedom had begun with an air assault that cleared the skies of Taliban MiGs. This allowed Dostum and his horse-mounted rebels to establish a relatively safe base in the upper reaches of the Darya Suf, 110 kilometers (68 miles) south of Mazar-e-Sharif. Dostum provided the Americans with the coordinates of his position and told them he and his men would be awaiting them in the high mountains. They promised to have the perimeter well protected and let it be known that they were, after a decade of fighting *against* the CIA-funded mujahideen, delighted to finally have the legendary CIA on their side.

On the night of October 16, R.J., Micheal Spann, Dave Tyson, and the other three agents boarded a Black Hawk helicopter flown by the 160th Special Operations Aviation Regiment and prepared to be inserted into "Indian territory." Just before midnight the helicopter took off into the starry night and began its two-and-a-half-hour flight from the US base at Karshi into Afghanistan. Its journey would take the CIA team over the surrounding Uzbekistani mountains, across the northern plains of Afghan Turkistan, and into the Hindu Kush to the remote Darya Suf Valley.

As the CIA agents left the ex-Soviet republic of Uzbekistan and crossed into the Taliban Amirate of Afghanistan, they noticed that there were no city lights below; they had entered a country that was as dark as the Middle Ages. Crossing the barren plains of Afghan Turkistan, their helicopter was buffeted by strong winds and cold air. Halfway into their long journey the helicopter began to run out of gas and needed to be refueled. A dangerous in-air refueling, the first by a Black Hawk on a combat mission in Afghanistan, was carried out so the helicopter could continue its mission.

After half an hour flying over the open plains of Turkistan, a black wall of mountains loomed up ahead of them. Their helicopter was now entering the Hindu Kush, and this put them at greater risk. For the next half-hour their helicopter swerved and maneuvered up the dark valleys as everyone on board held their breath. Several times they noticed tracer fire being shot into the air as Taliban on the ground fired blindly into the night at the sound of passing American helicopters. The threat of being hit by ground fire was compounded by the fact that their helicopter was moving sluggishly due to the high altitude.

Finally, after winding their way up one ravine after another, the agents' Black Hawk approached a lit-up HLZ (helicopter landing zone) in the middle of a dark valley. In a whirlwind of fine dust the helicopter slowly emerged out of the dark sky and descended into the center of the lighted area. The Black Hawk was quickly surrounded by smiling Uzbek soldiers who emerged from the dark carrying weapons. The CIA team known as Alpha had arrived safely on Afghan soil and was ready to work with the mysterious Uzbek warlord to seize the shrine of Mazar-e-Sharif. They had little with them at the time except their own weapons and cases of money to be distributed to local fighters. This money would be used to pay them to fight or would be distributed to the Taliban to encourage them to defect.

Two days later, a visibly excited Dostum emerged and offered the weary Americans shelter for the night behind the clay walls of a fort they nicknamed the Alamo. On the following day, as the sun rose, he offered to give the CIA agents a tour of the bleak mountaintop battleground. While hundreds of his curious men gathered around to gawk at the Americans, he told them that he and his men were bottled up in the upper reaches above the Darya Suf Valley. The Taliban occupied most of the villages in the valley below them, which led down to the Balkh Valley, and from there down to the objective of Mazar-e-Sharif.

Having familiarized his guests with the terrain, Dostum laid out his improbable plan. His strategy was simple and seemed to fit the incomplete profile the CIA analysts had developed of him since his initial phone call. He meant to punch his way through the Taliban defenses one after another and drive down the Darya Suf; then he would turn north and push his way down the larger Balkh Valley. From there he aimed to drive northward through a key pass known as the Tangi Gap and push his way out onto the plains around Mazar-e-Sharif. Then he planned to charge across the open plain and seize the holy shrine of Mazar-e-Sharif before the Taliban could react. He was confident that, after he had captured the shrine, the Taliban's morale would collapse—along with their northern army.

The only things standing in his way were tens of thousands of fanatical Taliban and al-Qaeda fighters armed with T-62 tanks, truck-mounted ZSU-23-4 antiaircraft guns, BM-21 multiple-rocket launchers, RPGs, and small arms led by the fierce leader Mullah Razzaq (not the same Razaq killed in Mazar-e-Sharif by the Hazaras in 1997).

Though R.J., David Tyson, and Micheal Spann appeared skeptical, they promised to do what they could to make Dostum's dream of seizing Mazar-e-Sharif come true. They also began to prepare for the arrival of a twelve-man Green Beret A-Team that was awaiting deployment orders in Karshi, Uzbekistan. But for all their military skills, the Green Berets were not specialists on Afghan languages and tribes and needed the CIA linguists to pave the way for them to come in and do the actual fighting.[8]

Two nights later, word came that the Special Forces team Operational Detachment Alpha (ODA) 595, code-named Tiger 02, was ready to deploy. This Green Beret team was part of the Fifth Special Forces Group (Airborne) based at Fort Campbell, Kentucky. ODA 595 was chosen to be the spearhead of Task Force Dagger because its members had previously been training Uzbekistani Spetsnaz special forces in peacekeeping tasks, small-unit tactics, and counterinsurgency. Its members were specialists in unconventional warfare.

The majority of the team had been together for two years and included key noncommissioned officer (NCO) members who had served together in ODA 595 and other Fifth Special Forces teams in the Gulf War, Yemen, Somalia, Panama, Bosnia, Kosovo, Africa, Central Asia, and Iraq. After being flown to Uzbekistan from their base at Fort Campbell, they had been placed in an isolation facility at the Karshi-Khanabad (K2) base to await their mission.

Then, on the night of October 19 and into the early hours of October 20, the team was given their orders; they were to "conduct unconventional warfare in support of General Dostum in order to render his operational area unsafe for the Taliban." They would journey into Afghanistan aboard helicopters flown by the 160th Special Operations Aviation Regiment (SOAR), known as the Night Stalkers.

Once again Dostum and his men lit up a helicopter landing zone between the villages of Darya Kamach and Dehi (110 kilometers or 68 miles south of Mazar) and waited with excitement for their American allies. America's elite Special Forces soldiers were now entering the Afghan graveyard of empires to wage war with the Taliban and their al-Qaeda allies.

But Tiger 02 was slightly delayed on its journey due to bad weather. The incoming A-Team's massive MH-47E Chinook helicopter encountered a blinding sandstorm crossing the deserts of Afghan Turkistan. Walls of flying sand buffeted the Chinook and the two MH-60L Black Hawk Direct Action Penetrator helicopters protecting it. The high winds and flying sand eventually forced the two Black Hawk escort helicopters to turn back to Karshi, but the Chinook carrying the Green Beret A-Team plowed onward toward its distant destination. The journey seemed to go on for a lifetime as blasts of cold air came in the open back door, which was manned by a gunner.

The delay extended the A-Team's arrival time but allowed them to go over the dossier on Dostum that they had been given prior to departure. Unfortunately the file on Dostum was wildly inaccurate and spoke volumes to the Defense Intelligence Agency's lack of involvement in Afghanistan pre-9/11. According to the file, Dostum was frail, had diabetes, was eighty-three years old, was missing an arm, and had a fierce hatred for Americans.[9] The team had also been warned about the possibility that the Afghans they encountered would betray them. The file included nothing about the historical importance of the semimythical shrine of Mazar-e-Sharif or Dostum's record as a secularist waging war against jihadi fundamentalists since the 1980s.

Still, it was with considerable confidence that Combined Joint Special Operations Task Force North commander Colonel John Mulholland sent the twelve members of ODA 595 into the mountains to meet the fierce Afghan warlord who was to be their ally. Their orders once they had met the "muj" (short for "mujahideen") leader were simple. Find Dostum and help him achieve his objectives, whatever they were, just so long as it meant fighting the Taliban.

Despite their grand-sounding words, US Central Command did not put a lot of faith in Tiger 02's mission. CENTCOM warned the team's young commander, Mark Nutsch, an experienced cattle rancher and rodeo rider from Alma, Kansas, that he and his men could be in theater for as long as a year. They were told to expect a long winter guerilla campaign like that George Washington experienced at Valley Forge. The members of ODA 595 were told they would probably be in the mountains with Dostum until spring, training the Uzbeks for offensive operations with the aim of seizing Mazar-e-Sharif.[10]

When they finally reached their destination at 2 AM on October 20, the members of ODA 595 were locked and loaded in a security posture just in case they were attacked by their mysterious Uzbek allies. After landing in brownout conditions, the Green Berets scrambled out of the back hatch of the helicopter using PVS-14 night-vision goggles to survey the alien terrain. As they came out of the dust, the eerie green glow from their goggles and the laser beams from their weapons' scopes giving them an otherworldly appearance, the waiting Uzbeks approached to greet them. Two members of the team later recalled what happened next:

> We came out of the helicopter through the dust and clouds. You saw the Afghans coming out to lead us. It was a tense time and very eerie, because they wore robes with AK 47s coming out of them. . . . It was like Sand People from *Star Wars* coming at you. Of course you can't see their faces because it's dark. And you're just looking up. And they've got their weapons. But they're greeting you.[11]

At the head of the turbaned Uzbeks were two bearded American CIA agents dressed in local *shalwar kameez*, Micheal Spann and Dave Tyson, who warmly greeted the tense Green Berets. The Special Forces were carrying heavy packs and their equipment, and with the agents' help these "seemed to float from the landing site under a procession of brown blankets and turbans."[12]

Dostum himself was not at the landing zone at the time of Tiger 02's arrival, but he rode up with thirty horsemen the next morning at 9 AM to warmly greet his American allies. When he arrived he met a "cautiously postured" team of twelve US soldiers dressed in light tan fatigues and wearing black wool jackets and woolen caps. Their nervousness was understandable; as US reporter Bob Woodward put it, "The CIA and Special Forces teams were out in some pretty tough places alone. They could be attacked, run over, slaughtered or kidnapped and held for hostage."[13]

The members of the Green Beret A-Team, all in their late twenties or early thirties (average age, thirty-two), were armed with an exotic array of American weapons, from M4 carbines with advanced combat optical gunsight telescopic sights and laser designators outfitted with grenade launchers to special purpose rifles with sniper scopes and M79 grenade launchers. Their leader, Captain Mark Nutsch, had sandy blond hair, blue eyes, and a blond goatee that made an impression on the local Uzbeks. Dostum could tell that Captain Nutsch and his team were still tense, and he quickly moved to reassure them. One of the members of Tiger 02 described their initial meeting with Dostum this way:

> Mid-morning the next day, General Dostum arrived at the compound. The compound was on the edge of a clearing. First, about 20 horsemen came galloping up. They're armed to the teeth, looking pretty rough. And, the heavy beards, RPGs. Your typical Soviet small arms is what they possessed—light machine guns, AK-47s, RPGs. And they come galloping up on horseback. And about ten minutes behind them, another 30 horsemen arrived with General Dostum. This was his main body of his personal body guards, coming there to meet us. . . . He jumped off the horse. He shook our hands. Thanked us for coming. Led us into his little base camp, and grabbed [Captain] Mark and I, went up to this little hill, threw out a map, said, "This is what I want to do today."[14]

The members of Tiger 02 noted that, far from being one-armed, frail, or anti-American, Dostum was "healthy as an ox" and had a "firm welcome handshake." He made a point of grinning and patting the Americans on the back to reassure them.[15] The CIA agents found Dostum to be "savvy, jovial, personable and a sharp military thinker."

Dostum, for his part, considered the Americans to be an answer to his prayers, although he was nervous that they would be withdrawn should they suffer any casualties. For this reason he was very protective of them and commented that he could lose five hundred of his own men but not one American.

Afghan etiquette demanded that Dostum welcome his valued guests before anything else. As a formality, he and his men took their red Turkmen roll carpets off their horses, spread them on the ground, and warmed up chai and naan for the Americans. In accordance with Afghan culture, this was done to assure the US soldiers that they were Dostum's guests. Having broken bread with the American soldiers, Dostum and his men were now obligated to protect them.

Formalities aside, Dostum then pulled out a large Russian map that had the details of the Darya Suf and neighboring Balkh Valley marked on it and, using an interpreter, showed the Americans what he wanted to do. The team commander, Mark Nutsch, the thirty-two-year-old Kansan who had spent considerable time riding horses on his parents' ranch, quickly established a rapport with the Uzbek leader. In his gruff, simple way Dostum easily won over the Green Berets, most of whom also came from hardscrabble working backgrounds where the military had provided the only route to get ahead in life. Like Dostum, the Americans were also driven by a deep hatred of al-Qaeda and the Taliban after 9/11. They wanted to move fast against the common enemy. When Dostum suddenly announced, "Now we will go and kill the Taliban; we leave in fifteen minutes," it was music to the Green Berets' ears.[16] Moving against those they held responsible for murdering thousands of their countrymen suited them just fine.

That afternoon Dostum decided to take Captain Nutsch and several members of Tiger 02/ODA 595 up into the barren mountain ridges overlooking the nearby Balkh Valley to get a view of the entrenched Taliban. Nutsch, or "Mark Commander" as he quickly became known to the Uzbeks, split up his twelve-man team and had half of them ride with him. This half became known as Alpha Team while the other half, known as Bravo Team and led by the team's chief warrant officer, rode south down the Darya Suf Valley to establish a drop zone for additional equipment.[17] To maximize their potential, these teams were subsequently broken down further into Charlie and Delta squads. Delta Team, led by Bill Bennett, began calling in air strikes within hours of arriving in its distant outpost, and Charlie Team soon followed suit. At times, as these four isolated teams crisscrossed the mountains calling in air strikes, they were separated by rides of up to twenty-four hours.

This splitting up of the teams was not an unusual step, since Special Forces A-teams are typically manned and equipped to operate in a split-team configuration. A-teams have two sergeants who specialize in communications, engineering, weapons, and medicine with additional function areas of operations and intelligence. ODA 595, being a team focused on unconventional warfare, had thoroughly cross-trained to operate in small decentralized cells of one to four men, each able to coordinate their activities as part of a larger effort. This increased the team's effectiveness as a force multiplier in advising their Afghan allies.

Besides Captain Nutsch, no other members of the A-Team had any significant riding experience, and they found the Uzbeks' small wooden saddles uncomfortable. While laughing Uzbek *cheriks* surrounded them, the Americans did their best not to fall off their horses as they were led up treacherous paths into the mountain heights above. Dostum worried that the untrained Americans might ride a horse off a cliff, but they proved to be incredibly adept at learning how to ride. This came as no surprise to their superiors; in Special Forces selection and training, students are taught to expect the unexpected and to adapt. In one case a Green Beret named Joe Jung suffered a broken back when his horse fell on him. But this did not break his will to fight. Jung, in his own words, simply took "two shots of morphine to relieve the pain, and got back on the horse. I would not allow myself to be the weak link."[18]

For the Americans who had been in the United States only days before, the transition to riding on horses in the high mountains of Afghanistan with turbaned Uzbek raiders who seemed to be from another era was nonetheless profound. As they rode past staring villagers who had never dreamed of meeting real-life Americans before, they realized that they had truly entered another world. While the Americans had lost three thousand of their people to the Taliban on 9/11, these isolated people had lost tens of thousands to the fanatics and had seen their homeland occupied by them for over three years.

When word came that Americans were riding through their villages, the locals poured out to greet them and stare. Sons, brothers, and fathers trickled in by the hundreds to join the swelling force once it became obvious that Dostum had Americans riding with him. Commenting on the villagers' primitive conditions, one member of Tiger 02 claimed, "It was like riding through Biblical Jerusalem."[19] The barren, sand dune–like mountain plateau above the Darya Suf and Balkh Valleys only added to the exoticism of the bleak, 6,500-foot-elevation setting.

After hours of riding along steep precipices, Dostum and Alpha Team finally arrived at his dangerously exposed forward headquarters overlooking Taliban positions in the Darya Suf Valley. For the first time Mark Nutsch and his men caught sight of their enemy. Through the distant haze they could see hundreds of Taliban manning defensive positions around a nondescript-looking village in the center of the valley. The Taliban's black turbans made them stand out against the chalky white mountains around them. The Americans could tell that the Taliban were better armed than the Uzbek *cheriks*, whose armament was limited to AK-47 assault rifles, RPGs, and a few PK machine guns.

The members of ODA 595 were among the first Americans to lay eyes on a foe that had given sanctuary to the mass murderers who had killed thousands of their fellow citizens on 9/11, and they relished the chance to make them pay. Each member of the team had been given a small piece of burnt metal from the World Trade Centers to be buried at the site of future battles as a way to commemorate their nation's dead. Now they had the chance to be the first to wage war against their people's enemy, and the men considered it an honor to play the role of America's avenging angels.

Something primordial in the Americans' hatred spoke to Dostum. It gratified him to know that he could rely upon the Americans' fury to help him and his men wage war against those who had also harmed his people. While such sentiments might have seemed laughably quaint to noncombatants in a more civilized setting, this was the Hindu Kush of Afghanistan mere weeks after the horrors of 9/11. Both sides had put aside the accoutrements of civilization to wage a brutal war in which many would die. For Dostum, who dreamed of liberating the shrine of Mazar-e-Sharif, and the vengeful Americans, this was nothing less than a Manichaean battle between good and evil. They instantly became comrades in arms despite the cultural and physical distances that separated Alma, Kansas, from Khoja Doko, Afghanistan.

Staring at the enemy through his binoculars, Dostum asked the Americans a simple question. What could they do to help him kill Taliban? Mark Nutsch clicked his tongue and stared at the Taliban who were dug in seven to ten kilometers north of the Darya Suf Valley. He and his half of the team were only six men; there was little they could personally do to destroy the enemy in the valley below. But they did have access to the one thing Dostum had craved the most ever since he lost his own air force of MiGs back in 1997: close air support.

Using his radio Nutsch gave the rough coordinates of the Taliban trenches to a US Air Force communication plane. He wanted slow-moving A-10 Warthogs, which were designed to attack ground positions, to strafe the Taliban, but he was told none were available. The Air Force did have a massive B-52 Stratofortress bomber, though, which was being sent to his location. It was time for him and his men to take cover; the B-52 carried a tremendous payload.

Some time later a small silvery dot with a white trail behind it appeared in the blue sky. Nutsch and Dostum eagerly looked to the skies as the dot began to make racetrack circles above the Taliban position.

Then it began. With each pass the plane dropped a bomb on the enemy lines. Nutsch and Dostum watched the bombs' impact in the valley below them with excitement. Plumes of brown smoke rose up with each bomb, and the sounds of explosions reverberated off the canyon walls.

But it soon became obvious that the bombs were missing their targets. After one errant bomb went off, Dostum watched through his binoculars as the curious Taliban even came out of their trenches to inspect a bomb crater on a nearby hill.

After several failed passes Nutsch called off the attack and returned with Dostum to their over-watch, disappointed. He felt he was too far from the target to accurately call in air strikes. Nutsch's disappointment in the imprecision of the bombings was also due to the fact that he did not yet have a laser designator to paint the target and guide the laser-bombs to it. For all their unique skill sets, the men of ODA 595 did not have the equipment for directing precision bombings at hand.

This disadvantage would quickly change. US Air Force MC-130H Combat Talons flying from Turkey would soon be dropping a variety of supplies for the A-Team and its Uzbek allies. Among the supplies were the horse feed to power Dostum's four-legged offensive vehicles, AK-47 bullets, light weapons, blankets, green camouflage jackets, and MREs (meals ready to eat) for the hungry men. In addition, the Americans promised to deploy Air Force Forward Air Controllers equipped with SOFLAMs (laser target designators) and Garmin Global Position Systems to call in precise bomb strikes on the enemy. But a SOFLAM arrived by parachute the night after the infiltration before the air force personnel arrived, along with a Satcom (satellite communications) radio. Soon the bombs would be falling exactly where Nutsch and his team directed them.

For his part Dostum was thrilled by the B-52 attack, regardless of its limited tactical effect. While there had been no physical impact on the Taliban, the sheer fact that he and his American allies had been able to call in a bomber to strike against the enemy would generate profound psychological results. Dostum knew all too well that in Afghanistan the perception of strength was all-important. This was a strategic development he meant to exploit to its fullest.

That evening Dostum called up the targeted Taliban army post on his battery-driven radio and began to play a psychological game with them. In the simplest of terms he boasted to the head of the Taliban force, Mullah Razzaq, "This is General Dostum. I am here, and I have brought the Americans with me."[20] The bombing was proof that Dostum's outgunned rebels had powerful friends. Dostum's demonstrative logic was, "If I demonstrate that I can kill you, you might not fight."[21] Momentum, he was sure, was finally coming around to his side. The skies were no longer filled with Taliban MiGs hunting his men; they were now dominated by powerful American bombers. Soon, he was sure, the American "beeping joe dos" (B-52s) would begin to wreak havoc on the Taliban, who only weeks before had been mocking him on their radios for having no air force.

18

THE OFFENSIVE BEGINS

"I want to get out of this valley. I want to take Mazar."

—General Dostum[1]

DARYA SUF VALLEY, NORTHERN AFGHANISTAN. OCTOBER 21–31, 2001.

Over the next few days Dostum and his Special Forces allies called in several more strikes on the enemy since Tiger 02 was trained in "putting metal on the target." All of the 595 Green Berets had conducted close air support missions in training, and the veterans of the Gulf War and the conflict in Somalia had employed it on previous combat missions. The team also had a knack for deploying mortars, often using them to support Uzbek raids or to mark targets for air support. They understood fire support as well as air support planning and coordination, having received additional training in these skills.

By October 22, ODA 595 had a SOFLAM laser target designator delivered and other supplies brought forward on horseback from the HLZ near the village of Dehi by the team's chief warrant officer. Over the next several weeks, Tiger 02 would employ all manner of aircraft to bomb the nearby Taliban. USAF fighters based in the Persian Gulf, US Navy, and Marine Corp fighter-bombers from off US Navy Carriers in the Arabian Gulf, heavy B-52 bombers from Diego Garcia in the Indian Ocean, and even $1.2 billion B-2 stealth Spirit bombers from Whiteman Air Force Base in Missouri made the transit around the world to drop their ordinance. (Dostum chuckled at the notion of a plane costing that much flying across the world to work in conjunction with local horses worth a few hundred dollars.) One Tiger 02 cell also utilized a newly developed remote control Predator drone aircraft for the first time to help them identify an enemy bunker and then strike it precisely.

Not all of the aircraft "stacked" above the Darya Suf got to drop their ordinance right away, as it was initially often challenging for the pilots to see their targets before the SOFLAM laser target designators were in use. Some pilots got upset, but rules of engagement required the United States to have eyes on the targets, which meant some missions were called off.

All of the pilots were extremely cautious about clearly identifying their targets, as were the members of ODA 595. In addition, Dostum's number two, Lal, rendered tremendous help in verifying the good guys from the bad guys (identifying them in Uzbek as "*dost,*" for friend, or "*dushman,*" for enemy).

Meanwhile, ODA 595 and Dostum's Uzbeks tried to avoid direct confrontation with the larger Taliban forces that were actively looking for them. Their aim was to locate the Taliban from an undetected position and then call in air strikes to degrade the Taliban's strength and morale before directly confronting them.

Each night, the Tiger 02 team met in their recon base at Dehi, Çobaki, or elsewhere and discussed what had gone right and what had to be improved, adapting to the situation as they went along. In so doing they became deadlier as they perfected the use of communications equipment and the SOFLAM to guide aircraft that were stacked above them in various flight patterns to their targets. Dostum's network of local village spies, who were equipped with hand-held radios, also provided timely targeting information. Calls were made to Dostum whenever Taliban convoys passed through their villages or stopped for the night.[2]

But even as ODA 595 honed its skills, Combined Air Operations Center experienced frustrations. On several occasions aircraft with bombs were diverted from bombing other targets in Afghanistan (mainly on the Shomali Plain to help Fahim Khan's stalled Tajiks) to assist ODA 595 and were forced to return to base with their payloads unused because they could not acquire their targets.[3]

Meanwhile, on the second front, Bravo Team was soon involved in direct combat and began making headway north of the Darya Suf Valley. Fighting on horseback with their Uzbek allies, Bravo Team pushed its way through the Taliban in the villages of Bishqab, Beshcam, Chaptal, and Oimetan from October 21 to 25 in an effort to clear a way to the larger Balkh Valley.[4] From their recon base at Çobaki they also called in strikes on Taliban positions farther afield. The horse-mounted Americans of ODA 595 Bravo did not always fight from afar; despite the fact that Dostum was afraid of losing them in combat, they fought directly alongside their Uzbek allies the whole way.

Dostum's fears were not misplaced. In one instance the Americans and their allies were noticed on a distant hill by a larger Taliban unit. As the Taliban raced forward in their trucks to attack them, the American Special Forces calmly dismounted and began picking off the approaching Taliban with their M4 Carbines. Even CIA agent David Tyson joined in the sniping after one of the Green Berets gave him a weapon. As the approaching Taliban began to fall to the American marksmen, the Uzbeks gained courage and charged the enemy, firing their AK-47s. When it was over, dozens of Taliban lay dead on the valley floor while the survivors fled in the opposite direction.

This sort of skirmishing brought the Uzbeks and Americans farther down the Darya Suf Valley and closer to their secondary objective, the nearby Balkh Valley. But this movement was hardly the grandiose toppling of the Taliban that many back home in America were clamoring for. As the pressure on President Bush mounted, he and Secretary Rumsfeld in turn put pressure on Colonel John Mulholland, the overall commander of the Special Forces Fifth Group, to produce results. Mark Nutsch claimed that orders came from headquarters to "make something happen."[5]

By this time the scattered elements of ODA 595 had been fighting for over two weeks with very little sleep and at great risk. Their food consisted of a "handful of dirty rice and piece of goat meat," and they had no showers (although they did get soaked on a couple of occasions while wading with their horses across ice-cold rivers). Most members of the team had already lost ten to fifteen pounds and would lose even more in the upcoming frantic weeks spent in the cold mountains. At night they would collapse, exhausted, to sleep on the ground; in the morning they would wake, shaking frost off themselves.

As stateside frustration with the lack of progress trickled down to the men on the ground, a testy Captain Nutsch sent back his famous telegram to Central Command in Tampa, Florida, which explained his team's remarkable activity. In response to the stateside accusations that he and his team were, in his words, essentially "sitting on their asses," he explained:

> I am advising a man on how to best employ light infantry and horse cavalry in the attack against Taliban T-55s [tanks] and mortars, artillery, personnel carriers and machine guns—a tactic which I think became outdated with the introduction of the Gatling (machine) gun. [The Uzbeks] have done this every day we have been on the ground.
>
> We have witnessed the horse cavalry bounding over watch from spur to spur to attack Taliban strong points—the last several kilometers under mortar, artillery and PK fire. There is little medical care if injured, only a donkey ride to the aid station, which is a dirt hut. I think [the Uzbeks] are doing very well with what they have. They have killed over 125 Taliban while losing only eight.
>
> We couldn't do what we are (doing) without the close air support. Everywhere I go the civilians and Mujahideen soldiers are always telling

me they are glad the USA has come. They all speak of their hopes for a better Afghanistan once the Taliban are gone. Better go. The local commander [Dostum] is finishing his phone call with (someone back in the States).[6]

Nutsch later learned that his message had made it all the way to the desk of the president of the United States, who was eagerly reading the team's reports. Accounts of Dostum's military exploits with the Green Berets of Alpha Team captured the nature of his almost frantic drive to overrun the Taliban and move on Mazar-e-Sharif. While Fahim Khan's Tajiks in the Panjshir Valley and Shomali Plain refused to move against nearby Taliban lines, Dostum's actions provide insight into his high level of personal bravery. After one incident in which Dostum grabbed an AK-47 and personally led a charge up a hill toward the Taliban, one report states, "The [Green Beret] team was obviously growing fond of Dostum and couldn't help but admire his courage."[7]

Captain Nutsch further explained:

Tiger 02 would witness repeatedly incredible courage and leadership under fire displayed by Dostum and his Commanders Lal, Kamal, Fakir, Ahmed Khan, and Haji Chari as well as from the rank-and-file Afghan horsemen. Seeing them utilize small-unit cavalry tactics to assemble hidden from the Taliban until the last moment, then riding quickly towards the enemy positions, closing the distance through artillery, mortar and machine gun fire was a moving experience. [We saw them] move towards ZSU 23-2s [antiaircraft weapons used in ground combat] and tanks, outflanking them before they could get another round off or turn their turrets on the approaching horsemen, then closing the distance and killing the Taliban crews.[8]

Whenever Dostum's force encountered fierce opposition, the Special Forces called in bombs. Nutsch recalled:

We'd bomb the snot out of them in the morning right up until the ground forces [Dostum's cavalry] would move in to assault their positions around mid-morning and begin to engage the Taliban with direct fire. Their (the Uzbeks') technique can be described as the swarm. . . . They were at full gallop, firing their assault weapons, not accurately but it was scaring the hell out of the Taliban. And they would simply ride down any Taliban that attempted to resist them or refused to surrender.[9]

Dispatches of this nature painted a vivid picture of Dostum as a man on the move. He seemed to be driven by inner demons, and he meant to get to Mazar-e-Sharif despite the tremendous odds against him. When reports such as these arrived back in the United States, they thrilled important figures like Deputy Secretary of Defense Paul Wolfowitz, who declassified them and shared them with the media. Dostum's robust actions also won him the support of Central Command chief General Tommy Franks, who described him as "the best we've got."[10] The Americans believed that "Dostum on horseback was aggressive, a General Patton" who "rides 10 to 15 miles a day in windstorms and snowstorms with guys lacking a leg. They go blow up a Taliban outpost and take casualties knowing they have no medical assistance."[11] Donald Rumsfeld guesstimated that Dostum's men were outnumbered by the Taliban eight to one, but the Uzbek commander was going on the offensive.[12]

Such activity compared drastically to the inactivity of the other major component of the Northern Alliance, General Fahim's Tajiks, who were entrenched to the northeast of Kabul. Like Dostum, Khan and his army of twelve to fifteen thousand men had received a Special Forces A-Team known as Triple Nickel (ODA 555) and a CIA Special Activities Division team known as Jawbreaker. But Khan refused to budge. The Tajiks appeared to be casualty-phobic compared to Dostum and seemed to distrust their American allies as well. According to Gary Schroen, the CIA agent sent to head up the team fighting alongside the Tajiks, Fahim Khan was always complaining about a lack of money and bullets and "waiting for US bombers to do his work."[13] The CIA came to believe that the Tajiks were hoping that Dostum's small force would be wiped out attacking the larger Taliban force.

To compound matters, Fahim Khan's Tajik ally operating near Dostum in the Balkh Valley, Ustad Atta, threatened to attack the Uzbeks if he did not receive his own CIA operatives and A-Team. To placate his sensitive Tajik "allies," Dostum split up his CIA team and sent half of it to liaise with Atta and his Tajiks, who were a long, two-day horse ride to the west. By this time the CIA had infiltrated several other CIA operatives into the Darya Suf Valley. This mollified Atta and prevented what Central Command feared most, "red on red" infighting between the various factions of the Northern Alliance.

When he heard the news of Dostum's gracious decision to split up his CIA team and send a unit to work with Ustad Atta, CIA team leader Gary Schroen was thrilled. He later wrote:

> This was incredible news. I knew that Dostum was an intelligent field commander, but my impression had always been that he was more of a man of action than a wily political manipulator. His move to equally share the CIA supplies with Atta was brilliant. His agreement to let ALPHA split and send a small CIA team to Atta was equally farsighted. Dostum now had the high ground, leaving Atta little choice but to agree to cooperate with Dostum or risk being seen as petty spoilsport more interested in his own prestige and pride than defeating the Taliban. . . . If this worked out as I thought, I would owe a "tip of the turban" to General Dostum.[14]

Not surprisingly, dealing with his troublesome Tajik allies slowed down Dostum's momentum, as did the lack of precision bombing by his US allies. This lead to frustration among armchair quarterbacks back in the United States and mounting skepticism among a growing number of critics of the war. A scathing article that appeared in the *New York Times* on October 31, 2001, "A Military Quagmire Remembered: Afghanistan as Vietnam," described the liberal and conservative criticism of the sluggish war as follows:

> Like an unwelcome specter from an unhappy past, the ominous word "quagmire" has begun to haunt conversations among government officials and students of foreign policy, both here and abroad. Could Afghanistan

become another Vietnam? Today, for example, Defense Secretary Donald H. Rumsfeld disclosed for the first time that American military forces are operating in northern Afghanistan, providing liaison to "a limited number of the various opposition elements." Their role sounds suspiciously like that of the advisers sent to Vietnam in the early 1960s.

But unbeknownst to those critics back in the States, the Americans had decided to send in further Air Force air-controller teams to help Tiger 02 rain metal down on the Taliban.[15] The full might of the US air force would now be directed with unprecedented precision onto the Taliban and al-Qaeda forces blocking Dostum's movement out of the Darya Suf. The stalemate in the high valleys of the Hindu Kush was about to be broken as Dostum, Atta, and Moheqeq gathered their force for a push to the north.

Malaks

DARYA SUF AND BALKH VALLEYS. OCTOBER 31–NOVEMBER 5, 2001.

On the second of November, thirty-nine-year-old Master Sergeant Bart Decker and the other members of the Operational Detachment Command (ODC) 53 team of Air Force combat-controllers and noncommissioned officers led by Lieutenant Colonel Max Bowers received word to get their gear ready to be airlifted into Afghanistan. The weather had cleared, giving them a window for "infil." In response, the men rushed across the windswept tarmac and boarded their Chinook helicopter for the dangerous journey into Afghanistan.

Decker and his team had been among the first US personnel to arrive at the former Soviet airfield at Karshi, Uzbekistan, codenamed K2, on October 4. Their team, a component of the Air Force's elite Twenty-Third Special Tactics Squadron based at Hurlburt Field, Florida, was made up of trained combat controllers. Their primary job was to use GPS systems and laser SOFLAM designators to call in precision-guided air strikes.

This mission had become all the more crucial since the US Air Force had taken the majority of its non–laser-guided bombs and turned them into "smart bombs" by putting GPS systems on their tails. These formerly dumb bombs could, like their laser-guided equivalents, now be directed into the hatch of an enemy tank if given the proper GPS coordinates. The newly outfitted joint-direct-attack ammunition bombs, known as JDAMS, ranged from five-hundred-pounders to the massive two-thousand-pounders that could bring down buildings and devastate a battlefield.

Decker and his team's initial task had been to outfit the airfield at Karshi and make it suitable for the huge C-17 Globemaster transport planes that would be bringing in the personnel and equipment to wage a covert war against the Taliban. One of their members was subsequently attached to the first A-Team to be inserted into Afghanistan, ODA 555 (aka Triple Nickel), and helped its members direct bomb strikes onto Taliban positions in the Shomali Plain.

But ODA 595 had not initially been given an attached combat controller for their infiltration. On October 31, Staff Sergeant Matt Lienhard, the first member of what would become known as ODC 53, had been infiltrated into the Darya Suf to work with ODA 595/Tiger 02 to help hone the precision of their bombings. After two days of waiting in the village of Dehi for horses, he was able to ride to the front lines to assist the Green Berets. There he immediately made an impact. According to a CIA report by R.J., Matt had called in strikes by B-52 and B-1 bombers, hitting six key Taliban positions and killing more than three hundred Taliban and a senior commander.[16]

On November 2, the first combat controller received news that the rest of his team was arriving. They flew in on a moonlit night that was not optimal for an infiltration because it exposed their helicopter to the enemy fire, but they arrived without any serious mishap. As they emerged from their helicopter in a sandstorm, Master Sergeant Bart Decker said to himself, "This is it—this is the real deal. There's no going back now."[17]

Like the previous CIA and Special Forces teams, ODC 53 was quickly surrounded by smiling Uzbek fighters wearing turbans, *shalwar kameez*, and an odd mixture of boots and new green US Army camouflage jackets. The Uzbeks helped the Americans with their heavy equipment as Decker surveyed the dark mile-wide valley around him. That night Decker and his team slept fitfully in cold caves with horse manure plastered on the walls for insulation and awaited their meeting with Dostum.

Decker and his team members had only meager information on Dostum. They had in essence been told that he was an outcast, a rogue warlord from an Afghan subethnic group, but that he got things done. For the mission-focused Americans, who did not have Dostum's biographical details from his birth at Khoja Doko to his April 2001 return to Afghanistan from Turkey to help Massoud, that was enough. If the mysterious Dostum was willing to move against the Taliban and al-Qaeda and give them the force protection they needed to do their jobs, that was all they needed to know.

On the following day Dostum and Lal greeted Bart Decker and his team. They spoke to them via a translator named Laqat, who had the usual Uzbek uniform of a turban, *shalwar kameez*, green US army camo jacket, as well as a pair of Michael Jordan sneakers that he proudly showed off.

Dostum listened with excitement as Laqat told him about the new team's potential to bring down more bombs from both hunters (F-14 Tomcats, F-15 Strike Eagles, F-16 Fighting Falcons, and F-18 Hornets) and destroyers (B-52 Stratofortresses and B-1 Lancers). The hunters would operate from bases in the Middle East and offshore aircraft carriers, such as the *Kitty Hawk, Enterprise, Theodore Roosevelt,* and *John C. Stennis,* while the giant B-52s and B-1s flew in from the British-controlled island of Diego Garcia in the heart of the distant Indian Ocean.[18] Some of the bombers engaged in sorties over Afghanistan would fly over five thousand miles to carry out their missions.

The fact that Dostum had acquired the firepower of the US air armada impressed his men. Decker commented that Dostum's men seemed to be in awe of him, as did ODA 595. The larger-than-life Uzbek general was said to come alive in battle, and if the members of ODA 595 trusted him, then so did Bart Decker.

It was now time to rain bombs down on the Taliban blocking Dostum's charges in the Darya Suf Valley and see if they couldn't make his dream of liberating Mazar-e-Sharif come true. Decker and his team of combat controllers quickly began to work with ODA 595 and Dostum to coordinate bomb strikes on the stubborn enemy, which had taken to mocking the US bombing raids.

Decker recalled, "After our guys got on the ground, bombs were dropped with a 100 percent accuracy rate and the team began moving. The bombs being dropped were either laser guided or JDAMs, which is GPS derived."[19] The combat controllers directed the bombs by relaying the coordinates and elevation to aircraft sent from hundreds or thousands of miles away to make their bombing runs. They obtained this information by using range finders, maps, and mathematical triangulation to pinpoint the enemy's position. Then, from their overwatch in a trench dug into the high hills above the Darya Suf, Decker and his team watched the fireworks begin.

For the next three days the Taliban were pummeled by air strikes, and the enemy's mocking on the radio suddenly ceased as the bombs fell directly on their positions. Dostum and his men cheered every time a bomb hit the enemy bases in the valley below and patted Decker and his men on the back with glee. The might of the American air forces was now coming into play, taking place with a precision and impact that the Uzbeks, who were used to outdated MiGs, could not believe. Dostum's wistful dream of having an air force of his own had more than come true.

One of Dostum's men filmed much of the desperate combat, and the footage was later posted on a YouTube channel called "The Realm of the Warlord." The video depicts Uzbeks charging on horseback in an impossibly dry, mountain-desert surrounding. Some images show Dostum riding on horseback at the head of hundreds of his men and then suddenly having bearded American soldiers by his side. In one shot Dostum is sitting in a simple mud-walled home, poring over a large map with Mark Nutsch and CIA commander R.J. Other images show Decker's bombs landing on distant Taliban positions while Dostum and several Americans look on from a *qalat* (a dugout observation post). The footage becomes more graphic when it shows images of dozens of dead foreign al-Qaeda fighters, their bodies mangled after US bombings. Most of the bearded holy warriors appear to be Arabs with arms, legs, and bits of their heads missing. They are clear proof that the bombings, in conjunction with cavalry charges, were having an impact on the enemy.

As the campaign unfolded under the lens of Dostum's cameraman, the Pasha bragged to his men that he had harnessed the power of the *malaks*, the death angels of old. It would be like the miraculous sixteenth-century battle of Kul-i-Malik all over again—the angels were once again on the Uzbeks' side. Dostum warned the Taliban that the American *malaks* had brought death rays with them. His men were as awed by the seemingly supernatural success of the bombings as the enemy was frightened by it. Both sides came to have a superstitious dread of these American killer angels, who seemed to strike out of the blue with uncanny precision. On some occasions the men on the ground could not even see the high-flying planes that dropped the bombs and assumed that the lasers being pointed at the targets were destroying them. According to one account based on interviews with ODA 595, "Dostum loved the Death Ray. He loved even more calling the Taliban commanders on their radios and talking to them. 'I have the Americans with me here today. . . . Let me prove they are here.' . . . A short time later, Taliban bodies were flying through the air once again."[20]

Another account of the bombings at Darya Suf captures the proximity of the US Air Force combat controllers, who, through their scopes, could see the Taliban they were calling strikes on. Of Staff Sergeant Lienhard, the account says:

> With his scope, he spotted another enemy bunker where some of the men were reconvening, and he calculated new coordinates and waited for the planes again. Finally, one came. He heard the crackle on his radio and spoke to the pilot, and then he called out to the Green Beret team that a B-52 had arrived. It had laser-guided bombs, not satellite, so the Berets prepped their laser marker.

On cue, a sergeant stood tall in the trench, holding it with both hands, shining the laser beam through the front doors of the enemy bunker while the plane passed overhead, and soon a streak of bomb came pouring through at five hundred miles per hour, following the energy through the opening of the bunker, bursting into a massive flash, booming echoes across the valley and sending billows of black smoke and burned dirt into the sky.

He gritted his teeth in the mess of it. As the smoke began to clear, he could see the concave impression left on the mountainside where the bunker had collapsed. Fragments of blackened timber poked up from the crater, and enemy soldiers poured in from the hillsides to dig their wounded from the wreckage. He reached for his radio again. He was becoming a warrior fast. He called for a second strike on the same location. He watched the new explosion atomize the men digging for their friends.[21]

The US combat controllers used B-52s, F-18s, F-15s, and F-14s as precision artillery and roamed around the battlefield raining down devastation on an enemy that often did not know what was hitting them. Just days before, the Taliban had held the advantage over their Uzbek foes; now they were being pummeled mercilessly. In fact, on November 5, one of the strikes called in by the ODA 595 splinter team code-named Delta hit the command post of Mullah Razzak, the field commander in charge of the Taliban in the Darya Suf, and killed him, further eroding the enemies' morale.

Another after-action report by the air force forward combat controller Matt Lienhard captures some of the intensity of the battle as the Taliban furiously attempted to wipe out the US spotters who were calling air strikes in on them from their hidden outposts:

After that engagement we moved from our OP [outpost] via horseback to a more forward OP several km's closer to the dug in enemy positions. We set up on our new OP and began engaging enemy bunkers in the valley using F-18s and 14s w/ GBU-12s [Paveway laser guided bombs]. Once again we used the SOFLAM [laser target designator] to guide the bombs.

I basically gave them an estimated coord [coordinate] based on my range calc and then gave them a run in based off the laser safety fan. They would then pickle [laser direct] the bomb behind me and I'd guide it in.

The first couple tgts [targets] were engaged successfully but then suddenly we had a technical vehicle with a bed mounted ZSU-23mm [cannon] mounted in the back roll onto the battlefield. We attempted to engage it with a GBU-12 but it moved slightly behind a small noll just prior to impact and the SF [Special Force] guy running my SOFLAM for me couldn't maintain a spot on him.

This was about the same time that they [the Taliban] launched their counter attack. They began forming up from approx 1km away and began to fire and maneuver in a pretty coordinated manner onto our OP. They were using 7.62mm machine guns and RPGs. We attempted to return fire but they were just outside of effective range for our M-4's and my M203 [rifles]. By that time the RPG fire had begun to take its toll. They were able to lob them over our heads where they'd explode once they reached about 900m.

The northern alliance C2 [command] structure began to quickly erode and their discipline broke down and they began to retreat. I got on the radio and attempted to get more air support and was able to raise a B-52 who was only a few minutes out. I passed to him a grid that was about 800 meters in front of us and asked him to use that as a center point to drop a string of bombs parallel to our position. He came in and dropped his bombs in a long string in front of us effectively cutting the Taliban off and slowing down their advance. I then asked him for a second pass which he gave us.

By this time we were taking RPGs directly into the berm in front of us. I began packing up the SATCOM [satellite communication] while the SF guy quickly packed up the SOFLAM. We also returned fire with our M-4s and my M203 but it was too little too late and it became evident that it was time to depart or we'd be overrun.

By this time the northern alliance had completely fallen apart and fled. One commander rode up, grabbed my SOFLAM and left us. We began moving out as quickly as the terrain would allow, which wasn't very fast. I was still in communication with the B-52 and had him relay our situation and request for more air support.

He was able to contact an F-14 who checked on and was able to see the smoke remnants of the B-52 strike. He then quickly called tally on a group of taliban working their way up the terrain to our OP that we had just departed. He gave a good enough description that I felt comfortable clearing him to conduct 2 strafe runs on them. This in part, helped us work our way down into a valley where we were able to take cover in some rocks. That's where we linked back up with our northern alliance guys and they had horses for us. We moved out from there back to our first OP that we had worked from that morning. We got there just in time to see the Taliban overtake our previous location.

I then broke out the radio and SOFLAM and requested more air [support] which we got in the form of another B-52 with JDAMs [satellite-guided bombs]. Since we had just been there I simply had to just pull up the exact coords in my GPS and I passed a quick 9-line. He made a single pass and dropped 2x GBU-31s. One was an instant fuze and the second was a prox. It was an accurate strike and destroyed everything on the mountaintop which allowed the northern alliance to once again advance and over take that ground. This opened up the pass and allowed Dostum to move his forces through the valley for the next two days almost unopposed. We moved via horseback and truck for the next two days as Dostum's forces advanced and the Taliban continued to fall back.[22]

Matt Lienhard's account of the deadly role of the combat controllers describes the desperate mountain campaign:

The sun was still creeping up, turning from red to white as it rose, and he [the combat controller] rattled off a list of target coordinates, then watched as a torrent of thousand-pound MK-83 bombs made black plumes against the horizontal morning light. Soon a flight of F/A-18's materialized and joined the F-14's in battering his targets. Now, this was more like it, he thought. One pilot spotted a cluster of Soviet tanks a few hills away, and a deep tearing sound echoed through the valley as the armor blew apart. The Northern Alliance soldiers heard it and danced. It was still only dawn, and they were just waking up, but enemy bunkers were collapsing already, tanks exploding, trench lines filling with fallout. They had never imagined war like this. With each strike, Matt was taking out ten, twelve, twenty men. The Northern Alliance guys shouted and doubled over with laughter as the bombs fell.

He wanted to shout with them and shake their hands, but he had to stay focused. With each blast, the enemy reconfigured on the battlefield, and he had to track their movements. There was one ridgeline about two thousand meters to the west that caught his eye in particular. He had seen enemy soldiers running there for cover. How many he didn't know. Some had climbed to the top of the ridge and crouched in a bunker. Others hid in the trenches around it. He wanted to strike the whole area and move his men over there. From there, he would be able to spot a whole new set of targets and move closer to the mouth of the canyon.

But there was only a short window of time to make the move. He spoke with the Green Beret team leader, who spoke with the Northern Alliance sub commander, and the go-ahead was given: He landed a series of laser bombs on the bunker and the ridgeline, watched them burst and burn and collapse, then he gathered his equipment, threw it on the back of a horse, hopped in the saddle, and took off across the valley with his men.

Nothing about the valley was remarkable to him. It was the most desolate place he had ever seen. The mountains in the distance caught his eye briefly—they rocketed to the sky in sheer vertical leaps—but the valley floor itself was a dry, brown dustscape without a trace of vegetation. And yet he knew it was precious to the Afghans with him. It was the largest chunk of land they had taken in months, and to them, that's what this war was about. Land. They would never understand what it was to him, what he had felt in Kansas in September, the shock of it. These men were numb to that kind of shock, as he was numbing now.[23]

As Matt Lienhard called down a devastating rain of bombs on the Taliban positions in the Darya Suf Valley he was given the unique opportunity to observe the Uzbeks' fierce warlord commander up close. Lienhard would later describe this remarkable experience:

I think the second day I was there was when he rode up with his small group of commanders and bodyguards. He wasn't what I had expected. We were briefed that he was old and sick. This guy was definitely not old or sick. He was large and stood out among his entourage and he was obviously in good health, easily mounting and dismounting his horse.

When we received the intel brief on him back at K2 they painted a picture of him as one of the more brutal warlords the US would have to deal with. From that point until the fall of Mazar-e-Sharif I only saw him sporadically. I was split off with Paul (the team sergeant) and Mike Elmore (one of the weapon sergeants).

When I did see him he would show up, greet the Americans quickly, confer with his field commanders, and then be off again. He seemed extremely focused and not easily distracted. This stood out in sharp contrast to some of his junior commanders who, initially at least, didn't seem to share our sense of purpose or urgency. He obviously had the respect of his men. Some seemed in awe of him. His men didn't seem to fear him but they clearly feared the repercussions of failing or disappointing him. He didn't strike me as some Saddam Hussein–type of tyrant, but he clearly wasn't somebody you screwed around with in that part of Afghanistan.

I think that his reputation for violence was probably somewhat overblown, but not entirely. I don't want to come off as critical or judgmental though. I think he earned the fierce loyalty of his men through his charisma and his battlefield exploits, but I don't think he'd hesitate to resort to extreme measures if you crossed him or failed to carry out your duties while in his service. I think he was who he had to be to achieve his political and military goals in that part of the world.

Like Mark Nutsch has talked about, Dostum always dealt with us openly and honestly. He held up his end of things by giving us access to the Taliban's front lines and by continually putting us in a position to engage and destroy them. Had it not been for him, we would have been forced to introduce large maneuver elements into those valleys to root out the Taliban, which would have undoubtedly led to American casualties. I also think it would have taken months at a time when politicians and military commanders needed quick and decisive results.[24]

As the bombs began to explode on the Taliban defenses, a visibly thrilled Bart Decker sent back a photo of himself riding on horseback with Uzbek soldiers on a mountainside. Donald Rumsfeld later showed the photo to the press corp and the famous image was placed in the Smithsonian Museum in Washington, DC. The picture was proof that US soldiers were operating with indigenous Afghan allies on horseback to destroy their common enemy.[25]

And it was not only the Americans who were taking advantage of newfound synergy between medieval cavalry and twenty-first-century laser-guided bombs to gain a public relations victory. Dostum was in the forefront of the fighting and worked tirelessly to convince the opposing commanders to surrender to him and his *malaks*.

As the stunned Taliban gathered in the heavily defended village of Bai Beche to make a stand, Dostum recalled the Uzbeks' angel-assisted victory over the force of their Moghul enemy Babur at the Battle of Kul-i-Malik in 1512. Understanding that most Uzbeks knew the legend of the fiery sword-bearing angels who had appeared to help their ancestors in their hour of need, Dostum calculatingly applied the myth to their current situation. Outnumbered and outgunned by a fanatical enemy, Dostum proclaimed that the Uzbeks had once again received divine help from the shrine of Mazar-e-Sharif. Once again *malaks* were raining fire down upon their enemies and helping them carry out Allah's will. Bai Beche, Dostum promised, would be another Kul-i-Malik. It was time for the Uzbeks to sweep away their enemies as they had done centuries ago under Ubaidullah Khan.

For the superstitious Uzbeks, who believed in angels, the evil eye, and spirits, Dostum's explanation made as much sense as GPS, lasers, satellite-guided bombs, and fighter-bombers flying from aircraft carriers in a distant ocean they could not imagine. Lasers and JDAMs driven by satellites in space meant nothing to illiterate Uzbek horsemen, but their world was filled with evil jinn and protective angels that touched the lives of ordinary men. It was now the Uzbeks' destiny to do as Ubaidullah Khan had done at Kul-i-Malik and charge against a larger enemy with the help of divine assistance.

Dostum's calls for his riders to rally and carry out another glorious charge against a superior enemy began to resonate with his men, who had been so despondent just weeks earlier. To further impress his *cheriks* and inspire them to charge into Taliban machine gun fire, Dostum requested a spectacular display of precision-guided air power from his allies. This would serve to show the Taliban that momentum had switched the Uzbeks. The ancient legends could work with the new technology to get his men moving and give the Americans and Dostum the victory they both desperately desired.

CIA agent R.J., who became known as "Baba Jan" (the equivalent of Uncle Bob) because of his scruffy, white-streaked beard, promised Dostum he would do what he could and put in a request to CENTCOM for a particularly heavy bombardment. CENTCOM agreed to send bombers to pummel the Taliban's elaborate, Soviet-era trenchworks at Bai Beche. On November 3 and 4, Nutsch and Decker and his team called in a two-day bombing raid on the stubborn Taliban village that was key to controlling the Darya Suf.[26]

But Bai Beche was not the only village being bombed. Farther west toward the Balkh Valley the United States decided to wage psychological warfare against the Taliban by deploying a weapon of mass destruction known as the Daisy Cutter. The Daisy Cutter, so named because it cuts the heads off "daisies" (humans) like a scythe, had a reputation as the largest nonnuclear bomb in the world. It was so large (about the size of a minivan) that it could not be dropped by a conventional bomber. It had to be flown to its target in a specially modified MC-130 Talon cargo plane. The massive bomb, with a parachute attached, was then disgorged out of the rear cargo door of the slow-moving propeller plane. The parachute slowed the descent of the behemoth bomb, thus allowing the delivery plane to escape the atom bomb–like explosion that followed.

And what an explosion. As the parachuting megabomb approached the ground, a sensor on its conical nose detected the earth a few feet before impact and set off the device at head level. In a nanosecond a slurry of highly explosive ammonium nitrate, aluminum powder, and polystyrene coursed out from ground zero, cutting down everything in its path. The resulting explosion was lethal for a nine-hundred-foot radius. It sent shock waves over an area the size of several football fields and blew out the eardrums of those far from the actual detonation zone. The mighty bomb was even said to have caused earthquakes. It was precisely what Dostum and his allies needed to prove that Azrael the death angel was on the side of the Northern Alliance.

As the Northern Alliance troops under the overall command of Dostum prepared to attack the nearby village of Bai Beche, R.J. once again had a front-row seat to history. Watching from a mountain perch a safe distance away, he and a colleague were knocked back by the concussion of one of two Daisy Cutter explosions.[27]

But even after the horrific Daisy Cutter bombing in the nearby hills and direct bombings of their positions, the Taliban and fanatical al-Qaeda fighters in Bai Beche remained defiant. Their elaborate trenchworks were hard to spot from above and the forward combat controllers could not get proper coordinates. The Taliban would have to be flushed out the old-fashioned way, with boots (or at least hooves) on the ground. Thus was born the greatest cavalry action of Operation Enduring Freedom, the November 5 charge on Bai Beche. It was to be as close to a reenactment of the legendary Battle of Kul-i-Malik as could be carried out in modern warfare.

Dostum decided to begin the battle with two frontal charges of 250 Uzbek horsemen riding straight into the enemies' hardened positions. Dostum asked the Americans to soften up the enemy's lines with one last bombing. The men and horses were nervous as the final bombing took place and echoed up the valley. Then, as clouds of smoke and dust rose from the enemy position, Dostum gave the order for the charge, and the men and horses leapt into action. The valley rumbled with the sound of a thousand hooves as the Uzbek cavalry charged 1,500 meters toward the Taliban and al-Qaeda 055 fighters.

Bart Decker watched the fateful charge from the heights with Dostum, who spoke by radio to Lal, the commander leading the attack. At the time Decker thought to himself, *We're witnessing a cavalry charge!*[28]

According to Decker, the Uzbeks rode like men driven, and there can be no doubt that they believed they were acting in fulfillment of the ancient legends of old. Just like their sixteenth-century ancestors, they charged forward into a rain of enemy projectiles while shooting their own weapons from the saddle. It was a magnificent sight that few of the Americans ever expected to see in their lives. Decker and the other members of ODC 53 and Nutsch's Tiger 02 held their breath as the mounted daredevils rode straight into the teeth of Taliban RPG and machine gun fire. It was in many ways a reenactment not only of the battle of Kul-i-Malik but of Dostum's first youthful charge against the mujahideen in the town of Darya Suf.

Only on this occasion the horsemen's momentum was not enough. Dozens of men and horses were mowed down by the intense enemy fire. While the Uzbek riders overrode the first two enemy lines, they could not force their way through the third line. As the enemy mercilessly lashed them with RPG and machine gunfire, the Uzbeks broke and retreated, leaving the bodies of men and horses on the field. In a matter of minutes scores of riders and their horses had been cut down. The battlefield echoed with the sound of dying men and horses who lay strewn across the open terrain. That and the sound of Taliban cheering as the momentum switched to their side.

But Dostum had not come this far to be beaten. He truly felt that he would only have one chance to break the enemy and fulfill his dream of liberating his people and the shrine of Mazar-e-Sharif, and this was it. Roaring for the second wave of horsemen to come forward he did not give his men time to think about their losses. He was determined to take Bai Beche at any cost and called for another US air strike, this time right in advance of his second wave of horsemen.

This was an incredibly risky decision when one considers that Dostum was trying to coordinate five-hundred-pound bombs being dropped from high-flying planes with men charging on horseback into enemy lines. The potential for catastrophe was high. If the bombs landed on Dostum's troops, they would kill them all, momentum would be lost, and his small army would be beaten. The Mazar-e-Sharif campaign would fail. It was a do-or-die gamble, and everything depended on the air strike and cavalry charge. Dostum breathed deep and then gave the sign for the bombing run to take place. An eyewitness account of this charge by members of ODA 595 vividly tells what happened next:

> Commander Lahl [Lal] Mohammad, one of Dostum's cavalry commanders, had 250 men moving to an assault position, preparing to attack the enemy at full speed. The Taliban they were facing were fully dug in with interlocking machine-gun fire and scores of rocket-propelled grenades. While TIGER 02 was waiting for aircraft and bombers to arrive on station, Commander Mohammed was supposed to hold in place until ordered to attack. Mohammad jumped the gun and took off early without permission. . . .
>
> It was almost dark and, as the bombs closed, the Green Berets could see Taliban machine guns tearing into the formation as Dostum's horses began to fall. The TIGER 02 team was certain that the cavalry charge was too close to the enemy trench line. . . .
>
> Three bombs landed directly in front of the assaulting line and in the center of the enemy defense, stunning the Taliban. Al-Qaida and Taliban soldiers were sent flying in a dozen directions; the shock wave smashed their skulls, bursting their eardrums and exploding the capillaries in their retinas. The cavalry flew into the disoriented enemy just seconds after they were hit by the shock of the concussion and blast, and annihilated the remaining Taliban with what they later named "US Cavalry Close Quarter Combat."
>
> "I can see our horses blasting through them in the dust clouds!" Sergeant Will Summers radioed back.[29]

Dostum's commanders Lal, Kamal, and Ahmed Khan led their men in surging through the enemy lines, mowing down the Taliban until none were left standing. As his cheering men swept behind the enemy lines gunning down Taliban and al-Qaeda fighters, Dostum allowed himself a smile. With the sun setting over the battlefield, the Pasha and his American allies rode into the town of Bai Beche and inspected the carnage. Very few Taliban or al-Qaeda fighters had escaped the devastation, and their corpses lay scattered across the battlefield.

As the sun set over the scene, Dostum and the impetuous Lal said a prayer of thanks for their ability to pull victory from the jaws of defeat. They then quickly buried the bodies of their dead and prepared to fight another day. It was now time to move out of the Darya Suf and strike northward toward the prize of the north, Mazar-e-Sharif.

The Drive on Mazar-e-Sharif

BALKH VALLEY. NOVEMBER 5–8, 2001.

Soon after the extraordinary cavalry victory, Henry Crumpton, the CIA commander back home directing the whole operation, described it to President Bush and his team. For a White House that had been desperate for a sign of cracks in the surprisingly resilient Taliban, this was welcome news indeed. When President Bush heard that Dostum's men, whom the CIA estimated were outnumbered three to one, had won the battle with a horse-mounted charge, he was astounded to hear that horsemen were engaging the Taliban.[30] Donald Rumsfeld, ever the showman, subsequently went to press with a "poetic" account of the battle that inserted Americans into the charge:

> On the appointed day, one of their [US Special Forces] teams slipped in and hid well behind the lines, ready to call in air strikes, and the bomb blasts would be the signal for others to charge. When the moment came, they signaled their targets to the coalition aircraft and looked at their watches. Two minutes and 15 seconds, 10 seconds—and then,

out of nowhere, precision-guided bombs began to land on Taliban and al-Qaeda positions. The explosions were deafening, and the timing so precise that, as the soldiers described it, hundreds of Afghan horsemen literally came riding out of the smoke, coming down on the enemy in clouds of dust and flying shrapnel. A few carried RPGs. Some had as little as 10 rounds for their weapons. And they rode boldly—Americans, Afghans, towards the Taliban and al Qaeda fighters. It was the first cavalry attack of the 21st century.[31]

This stunning victory of November 5, a modern-day Kul-i-Malik in every sense, was to inspire Dostum's men to move with even greater speed and confidence. One US military analyst reported that after Bai Beche, "the dam broke," and the Uzbeks prepared to surge down the Darya Suf toward the larger Balkh Valley.[32] Momentum was now clearly on their side.

The fall of Bai Beche also seems to have unhinged the Taliban, who frantically rushed reinforcements up the Balkh Valley toward Bai Beche to halt Dostum. But this proved to be a disastrous misstep, for ODA 595's Alpha Team was monitoring their movements from the barren hills above. In their haste the Taliban played into the Green Berets' hands by leaving their hidden positions and moving out into the open. This made them easy targets for the American hunter aircraft, which divided the Balkh Valley into zones called kill boxes and began to slaughter the Taliban.

As the Taliban and al-Qaeda reinforcements rushed up the Balkh Valley from the town of Shulgerah, they were suddenly ambushed by US fighter-bombers screeching overhead. Hundreds died in the fiery carnage as the Taliban–al-Qaeda convoy was incinerated in a matter of minutes. Later witnesses to the destruction compared it to the infamous Highway of Death north of Basra where Iraqi troops were slaughtered during the 1991 Gulf War.[33] The main road up the Balkh Valley was littered with the blackened hulks of Taliban pickups and the carbonized bodies of those in them. News of the victory proved a further boon for Dostum, who continued his policy of speaking to Taliban commanders via radio and urging them to lay down their weapons and come over to his side.

As Dostum gathered momentum in the Darya Suf Valley, momentous events were taking place in the upper reaches of the neighboring Balkh Valley as well. There Dostum's Tajik ally and sometime rival, Ustad Atta, and his force of 1,500 fighters had, just days before, received their own Special Forces A-Team, Tiger 04 (ODA 534). As Dostum surged down the Darya Suf, Atta was in danger of being left behind. Not wanting to be outdone by his Uzbek rival, Atta responded by launching an attack of his own on the Taliban-occupied village of Aq Kupruk. This attack was carried out after the United States organized a joint commanders meeting with Mohaqeq, Atta, and Dostum in the village of Dehi on October 28. In this meeting the Hazaras, Tajiks, and Uzbeks all agreed to launch a joint offensive under Dostum's command.

Aq Kupruk was seen as a bridge to controlling the upper Balkh Valley. If Atta could take this town, he could stake a claim of his own to Mazar-e-Sharif and join the race northward. After a day of fighting, Atta had looked as if he were going to take Aq Kupruk. But the Taliban had merely lured him into a sense of false confidence and then counterattacked, killing scores of his men.

With the help of US-guided munitions, however, Atta and his Tajiks returned to the field and managed to defeat the Taliban by the evening of November 6. With their victory, five hundred Hazaras led by Mohammad Moheqeq began to pour down into the valley to join in the rout. The snowball effect that Dostum had always spoken of appeared to finally be gathering momentum in the valleys of the northern Hindu Kush.

With the Taliban reeling, Dostum, Atta, and Mohaqeq raced toward the town of Keshendeh, where the Balkh and Darya Suf valleys met like an arrow pointing northward toward Mazar-e-Sharif. There Dostum and his Tajik rival from the anti-Soviet jihad met and united their forces. The combined Tajik-Hazara-Uzbek force amounted to over four thousand men, and Dostum was ecstatic. As the Northern Alliance force swelled with new recruits, Dostum's dream of returning to make his pilgrimage to Mazar-e-Sharif was fast becoming a reality.

Trying to smooth over Ustad Atta's earlier resentment, Dostum congratulated him and his Tajiks and called him his brother and friend. Atta, a thirty-seven-year-old bearded mujahideen who had been a teacher, appeared to catch the spirit of the moment and joined Dostum in a rare celebration. It was now time for the allies to put aside their past differences, push the Taliban out of the Balkh Valley, and move on to Mazar-e-Sharif itself.

On the following day Dostum and Atta moved at high speeds down the Balkh Valley toward the central town of Shulgerah, which was twenty-five miles south of Mazar-e-Sharif. The valley had opened up into a plain at this stage—perfect cavalry terrain for the Uzbeks. On several occasions Dostum's men overran Taliban positions, including those bolstered by tanks and artillery.

CIA agent R.J. joined Dostum in several of his cavalry charges and offered invaluable eyewitness accounts of Uzbek horsemen in action against the Taliban. R.J.'s memories vividly bring to life Dostum's character:

General Dostum was standing in a small group of his senior officers. He was of medium height, stocky but powerful built, and was dressed in brown khaki pants, boots, and heavy black wool coat cut like a military jacket. He was wearing a turban-like dark blue head covering, with a long piece of material hanging down to serve as a scarf. He moved with a strength and confidence that commanded attention and respect. . . .

He smiled at the difficulty the Americans had in getting down [from their horses]. "Welcome, welcome my friends," he said in Dari, extending his hand to R.J. and his men. . . .

"In just a few minutes we will start the attack." Dostum motioned them toward the battlefield. . . .

As the first line of cavalry reached the infantry line, an officer in the middle of the line stood in his stirrups and raised a sword in the air. A shouted command could be heard above the firing, and the line of horsemen surged forward almost as one. Within a few steps the horses were moving at a gallop. A shudder of excitement swept through R.J. as he watched the riders bend low over the necks of their mounts, urging them on. The second line of riders reached the jump-off point, formed, corrected the line, and then broke into charge. . . .

Dostum turned his horse towards them, raising his arm and motioning in a broad sweep toward the battle. "Come, friends, let's follow the attack. We can see nothing from here." And with that he turned and kicked his horse's flanks, riding straight into the fight raging before them.[34]

R.J. and the CIA were not the only ones who came to know and respect Dostum's larger-than-life battlefield prowess.[35] As Dostum worked with the Americans to achieve their common goal, the Green Berets of ODA 595 came to intimately know the man who would later be demonized by the US press corp as a bear of a man who laughs other men to death. The Green Berets' eyewitness accounts of Dostum provide a unique historical account of this legendary Afghan figure and go a long way in humanizing him. According to after-action reports and interviews carried out with Mark Nutsch and his team:

> Over the next few weeks and months, as our relationship grew, the guy [Dostum] was phenomenal. He was working 20-hour-plus days, hardly sleeping. He was just always on the go, always talking to someone, always trying to coordinate actions of the Northern Alliance forces to make it happen. . . .
>
> Gen. Dostum was upfront and honest with me, and any member of the detachment, in any dealings that we may have had. And we were truthful and honest with him in the operations that we were going to conduct, and how we were going to go about accomplishing those objectives, like capturing Mazar-e-Sharif. We were just honest with him. And he was honest with us. . . .
>
> Somehow, we were able to find this common bond in capturing Mazar-e-Sharif, and the common bond of bringing all these different ethnic factions together to join with Gen. Dostum, and mount a coordinated attack through the Dar-e-Suff Valley and into Mazar-e-Sharif. . . .
>
> Gen. Dostum always referred to every one of my men either by first name, which is all he needed to know, or by commander, "Commander

Bill," "Commander Pete." Every one of my men was referred to as a commander, and held in the highest regard as an Afghan warrior. We're all
now part of that inner circle of the military commanders there.

So much did he trust us and respect us that he said that, if we ever
go to war in another country, that he would gladly send his men with us
to fight.[36]

For his part, Dostum could not praise his American comrades highly
enough. He claimed, "I asked for a few Americans. They brought with them
the courage of a whole Army."[37] The deep trust that Mark Nutsch and Tiger
02 came to have for Dostum and vice versa was earned in a mountain battlefield in a covert war that most Americans did not even know was happening. As the partners honed their joint skills, they began to move up the
Balkh Valley and toward Mazar-e-Sharif to achieve a victory that would
finally gain the world's attention.

While the Taliban tried to defend Shulgerah, the main town in the open
plain of the Balkh Valley, they were wiped out by a combination of Uzbek,
Tajik and Hazara cavalry charges and aerial bombardments. In one charge
the allies destroyed more than forty Taliban armored vehicles and various unarmored support vehicles.[38] The Taliban appeared to be increasingly
incapable of resisting the allies' newfound momentum, and Taliban commanders began to defect to Dostum.

Soon thereafter, Dostum had himself filmed greeting several bedraggled and shell-shocked Taliban commanders who had surrendered to his
troops. He knew that it was crucial that the Taliban understood that they
would be treated well if they surrendered, so he made a point of embracing
the Taliban prisoners of war and treating them humanely.

But not all Taliban chose to surrender. Many, especially the Kandaharis
from the south who were serving alongside the fanatical al-Qaeda fighters,
vowed to fight to the death. Dostum and his American allies were only too
happy to oblige those Taliban fighters seeking martyrdom. By this time the
Uzbeks and Americans had perfected a deadly killing triad of high-flying
aircraft, ground controllers, and horsemen. The effect was magnificent,

and Dostum moved in parallel with Atta and Mohaqeq down through the open valley toward a bottleneck at the northernmost point, the Tangi Gap. This looming chokepoint was the final obstacle the alliance would have to overcome in order to break out of the mountains. Beyond it lay the glittering prize of Mazar-e-Sharif, the key to the plains of Turkistan and perhaps Afghanistan.

The Taliban were all too aware of the importance of the Tangi Gap and placed thousands of fanatic foreign and Kandahari troops and ZSU-23-4 antiaircraft guns and BM-21 rocket launchers in dug-out defensive positions on the north side of the gorge. Anyone trying to move through the pass below them would be slaughtered. Here in the pass, fifteen miles south of Mazar, the Taliban and al-Qaeda army of the north would make their final stand defending the southern approach to the great city. As the Northern Alliance rushed northward to keep up with Dostum's frantic pace, the two sides girded themselves for the battle that could well decide the fate of Afghanistan.

The Fall of Mazar-e-Sharif

MAZAR-E-SHARIF, CAPITAL OF BALKH PROVINCE. NOVEMBER 9-10.

Staring up at the mountainsides in the cool morning haze, General Dostum conferred in Uzbek with CIA agent David Tyson. Both agreed that the Tangi Gap, which was a quarter of a mile wide, was the make-or-break point for the Northern Alliance. All of their victories thus far would be for naught if they didn't break out of the Tangi Gap and onto the plains below. Dostum predicted a slaughter of Northern Alliance troops at Tangi if the Americans didn't pave the way for them with a particularly effective bombing run. For this reason, before Dostum and his men charged the deadly gap, the Americans pounded it from the skies with B-52 strikes. Dostum watched the bombings with his binoculars and grunted as the bombs lit up the sides of the mountains.

But the battle would not be won from the skies. Someone would have to charge the Taliban positions and overrun them. Before the smoke had cleared, Dostum filled his lungs and then yelled into his radio for his men to charge. Dismounting, he led his men on foot up the hillside straight into the Taliban's weakened gunfire. The sound of mortar, tank, artillery, and RPG rounds was deafening; and were it not for the fact that Dostum was leading in person, his men might never have charged into the maelstrom.

While Dostum's charge may have seemed suicidal, he had one advantage. Whenever he and his men were blocked by tenacious Taliban resistance, the US combat controllers with him used their lasers to pinpoint the enemy positions and call in air strikes. By now the Uzbeks and the Americans had honed their skills, and Dostum's fighters knew how to calibrate their attacks with the incoming bombs. Time and again Dostum and his American allies were pinned down and appeared close to being overrun when B-52s roared overhead and rained bombs down on the Taliban. In some cases—what in military terms is called "danger close"—the Taliban were so near that the combat air controllers were almost calling bombs down on their own positions. At these moments, they were often showered with rubble and Taliban body parts from nearby bomb strikes. By all accounts the fighting was hellacious, and it took everything Dostum had to get his men to keep moving forward into the face of enemy fire.

But move they did. Some riders even managed to swim across the Balkh River under fire and circumvent the pass to launch a flank attack on the enemy. When the US bombs fell and Mohaqeq's Hazaras and Atta's Tajiks followed the Uzbek advance, imperceptibly at first, the Taliban gradually began to abandon their lines. As the sun set on the apocalyptic scene, Dostum led his men over the trenches in one last charge and took the Taliban's command and control quarters. As the soot-blackened Uzbeks broke into the enemy headquarters, Dostum had the pleasure of personally capturing a Taliban commander who, just a few weeks before, had been mocking him on the radio for not having artillery or an air force.

When the summit of the Tangi Gap fell, a loud cheer coursed through the Northern Alliance lines and down to the pass below, which was littered with the shredded bodies of horses and men. Mark Nutsch and his men could not believe that they had lived through it all, and he later said in amazement, "I survived by the grace of God." For Dostum, who had come so close to death on several occasions during the assault, it was a moment to relish. All of the frantic energy he had given to the drive down the Darya Suf and Balkh Valleys had paid off. After being bottled up in the mountains for more than three years, his triumphant followers were finally moving back down on to their beloved plains toward the prize of the north: Mazar-e-Sharif.

Staring across the brown plains as the sun set, Dostum heard forward air controller Commander Bart Decker point to a line of dots moving on the horizon. "Are those good guys or bad guys? If they're not us, I have several F-15s and F-16s on deck that can take them out."

Dostum radioed his spies in Mazar-e-Sharif to find out what was happening in the city and received word that the fall of Tangi Gap had panicked the Taliban in the town. Word had spread that Dostum had Azrael the death angel on his side and was invincible. The tide had turned against the Taliban, and Allah had given his mandate to the Uzbeks and their allies. It was time for the Taliban, who had never felt secure in Dostum's former capital, to flee the city for the safety of Kunduz in the east. Kunduz had a large Pashtun population and had served as refuge for the Taliban back in 1997 after they had been betrayed by their former ally Malik. There they could regroup and continue the battle.

But as the Taliban withdrew in a long convoy of pickup trucks along Highway 5, their headlights betrayed their movement—and Bart Decker meant to make them pay for their lack of caution. Frantically radioing to loitering US fighter-bombers, Decker gave the enemy's coordinates and told the fighter-bombers they had free reign to wreak havoc. "If it's moving on Highway 5, it's Taliban. Take 'em out—you're cleared hot!"

"Roger," came the reply. "Moving on the highway now to interdict the targeted convoy."[39]

From their mountain perch Dostum, Decker, and the members of ODA 595 watched in awe as the swooping US F-15s and F-16s annihilated the retreating Taliban convoy. As the sky lit up with explosions and the sound of bombs hitting coursed across the plains, the exhausted allies felt no pity for the fate befalling their enemies. For the American and Uzbek avengers, the memories of their countrymen jumping to their deaths out of the World Trade Centers or of Afghan women being stoned to death removed all moral qualms they may have entertained. The Taliban and their al-Qaeda allies had come to both their lands bringing death, and now they were the ones dying.

As the exhausted Uzbek and American allies collapsed for the night in trenches that had been filled with the Taliban only hours before, Dostum allowed himself a smile. Patting his American allies on the back and calling them "my friend," he pointed to the city lights in the distance and said, "Tomorrow, Mazar-e-Sharif."

On the following morning the jubilant allies fought their way through scattered Taliban resistance in the villages south of the Mazar-e-Sharif delta. But the Taliban's heart was not in the fight; they truly seemed to believe that Dostum now had the mandate to rule Mazar-e-Sharif. As the allies surged toward the city, trying to keep up with Dostum's frenetic pace, villagers poured out of their homes to greet their liberators. For the first time in years, young boys flew kites along the march route to celebrate being free of the Taliban's laws banning the practice. The American Special Forces had been given small, airdropped all-terrain vehicles known as Gators and wryly commented that "for the first time in history, US forces were going into combat on golf carts." [40]

Then, a miracle happened. With Dostum's former capital of Mazar-e-Sharif mere miles away, the skies that had been dry for so many years opened up, and a light rain fell. For the superstitious people of the north, who had suffered under a drought they blamed on the Taliban, this was seen as a sign from God. By the time the allies reached Chesme e Sayfa just south of the city, the rain had turned to a light snow, blanketing the countryside in white.

As they passed through the familiar sights of the towns south of Mazar-e-Sharif, Dostum's level of excitement rose, and the members of Tiger 02 caught his enthusiasm. In an animated voice Dostum promised the Americans that soon they would be in his former capital.

A *Time* magazine writer captured the final stages of the drive for Mazar-e-Sharif:

> In the dead of night, horses poured from the hills. They came charging down from the craggy ridges in groups of 10, their riders dressed in flowing shalwar kameez and armed with AK-47s and grenade launchers. In the Kishindi Valley below, 35 miles south of the prized northern city of Mazar-i-Sharif, the few Taliban tanks in the area not destroyed by American bombs took aim at the Northern Alliance cavalry galloping toward them. But the 600 horsemen had been ordered to charge directly into the line of fire. "If you ride fast enough, you can get to them," an Alliance spokesman later explained. "You ride straight at them. The tank will only have time to get off one or two rounds before you get there."
>
> The rebels were told to leap on top of the tanks, pull the Taliban gunners out through the open hatches and kill them. The first land battle in the century's first war began with a showdown from a distant age: fearless men on horseback against modern artillery. America's money was on the ponies.[41]

When a Taliban force bolstered by Pakistani fanatics made an unexpected defense north of Kishindi at Chesme e Sayfa in an exposed position, Dostum's forward combat controllers called in a heavy B-52 bombardment. The defenders didn't stand a chance, and Dostum rushed through the smoldering remains of the enemies' former positions to fight the last Taliban defending Mazar-e-Sharif. Along the way some of Dostum's men raced to the west and captured the symbolically important fortress of Qala-e-Jangi, Dostum's former headquarters.

Not to be outdone by his master, Commander Lal led the Uzbek cavalry clattering ahead and crossed the Pul-e-Imam Bukhri bridge to take Mazar-e-Sharif's civilian airport on the southern outskirts of the city. From there Lal and his men rode into the city's southern suburbs for the first time in over three years. Dostum was not far behind them.[42]

On the evening of November 9, 2001, Dostum and his American comrades, who had not shaved or showered in weeks, rode into the crowded streets of Mazar-e-Sharif on horseback and in captured Taliban pickup trucks. For the first time since infiltration, the scattered ODA 595 team had been reunited. The Taliban were nowhere to be found.

For the dazed Americans, still locked and loaded, the warm reception they received from the cheering townsmen was surreal. Thousands of Mazar-e-Sharif's inhabitants came out to greet their liberators and chant Dostum's name. A joyous Dostum, riding at the head of hundreds of armed Uzbeks and wearing his famous green *chapan*, pulled the turban back from his lower face and waved to the throngs on either side of the main road. The members of ODA 595 compared their joyous reception to the arrival of Allied forces in Paris after the defeat of the Nazis. Seeing the tears of joy in the inhabitants' eyes, the Americans finally understood that they were more than avengers—they were liberators.

Once in the city, the members of the Air Force close air support unit known as ODC 53 (code-named Boxer) fulfilled an important task. They symbolically buried pieces of the World Trade Center, given to them a seeming lifetime ago back in the United States, and said prayers for their countrymen who had died in the slaughter of 9/11. They had done as they promised when they swore to bury the blackened symbols of their nation's suffering in the soil where their enemy was defeated. Other pieces of the World Trade Center would be buried by Special Forces in other areas in Afghanistan where they saw success. Colonel Mulholland subsequently presented a map of these various spots to New York's police department, fire department, and port authority.[43]

As the locals began to sacrifice sheep to celebrate their liberation, Dostum turned to his American comrades and publicly hugged them. The Pasha wanted the people of the city to know that he had achieved his victory only with their help. Then, through his interpreters, he told them that he had one important promise of his own to fulfill. With a somber look on his face, Dostum left his American friends in a compound and led a group of soldiers to the blue-domed shrine of Mazar-e-Sharif.

As Dostum descended from his horse, Surkun, and strolled into the shrine, the throngs rushed in to see the great man make his historic pilgrimage. Remembering his children's tears as he left them in Ankara months earlier to wage his lonely battle with the Taliban, Dostum's mind raced back to his family. At that moment he thought of his mother, who had died in Taliban-controlled lands during his absence, and of his wife Khadija, who had died so many years before. He also thought of his best friend Yar, who had been buried in the soil many years ago after giving his life for Dostum. Unbidden, tears of grief and joy came to Dostum's eyes as he opened his hands to the heavens in Muslim fashion to pray in thanks and for the souls of those he had lost along the way to make this day possible.

Raising his wet face from his hands Dostum looked at the crowds and quietly spoke four simple words, capturing his shock at surviving his suicidal return to Afghanistan. As a cameraman filmed his sobbing face, Dostum looked into the lens and mouthed four simple words: "Thank God it's over." [44]

Aftermath

THE PLAINS OF AFGHAN TURKISTAN. NOVEMBER 2001–JULY 2003.

Word of the Northern Alliance's seizure of Mazar-e-Sharif spread across the globe after Dostum phoned CNN Turkey and triumphantly gave them the good news. In the process, many came to know the name of the Uzbek commander from Khoja Doko who had seemingly done the impossible. *Time* magazine reported, "The Taliban spent three years fighting for Mazar-i-Sharif, precisely because its capture would confirm them as masters of all Afghanistan. And that they are no longer." [45] Britain's *Independent* reported:

> The fall of the biggest city in northern Afghanistan would deliver a crucial propaganda victory to the coalition. . . . Now, at last, the coalition may show a result. Until now, the Taliban has been able to give a convincing

impression of unity and unbroken morale, but the loss of Mazar cannot be presented as anything but a disaster. Once the first crack appears in the regime's facade, things could change very fast.[46]

The cracks in the Taliban regime did not take long to appear. As Dostum had predicted, the fall of Mazar-e-Sharif brought down the Taliban's house of cards just as it had brought down Najibullah in 1992. The unexpected fall of the symbolic city finally galvanized Fahim Khan's lethargic Tajiks. As Dostum's small force marched eastward from Mazar-e-Sharif to attack the Taliban at Kunduz, Fahim's larger Tajik army began to attack Taliban lines north of Kabul. With US bombs covering their thrust, Fahim Khan and his men moved on Bagram Airfield and then surged across the Shomali Plain toward the capital.

Having heard of the loss of Mazar-e-Sharif, the Taliban did not offer much of a fight. On November 12 the Taliban, who had always been viewed in the predominately Tajik-speaking city of Kabul as an occupying force, began to withdraw to the south. On November 13, Fahim Khan's victorious troops moved into the city they had lost in 1996. In less than a week, both the capital of Afghanistan and its holiest city had fallen to the US-backed opposition. The turn of events was nothing short of miraculous.

In the mountainous heartland, the Hazaras rose up when they heard news of the fall of Mazar-e-Sharif and attacked the Taliban at Bamiyan. With the Hazaras pouring out of the mountains the dispirited Taliban withdrew, but only after burning scores of local villages. By mid-November, the Hazarajat region was free of the Taliban.

In the west Ismail Khan, the Tajik known as the Amir of Herat, joined the rout by moving out of the mountains of Ghor to retake his former capital. Once again the Taliban put up a limited fight and then withdrew.

The Northern Alliance now controlled a vast swath of land stretching from Herat through the Hazarajat to Kabul. Roughly half of Afghanistan was in their hands. This was a stunning development for a Taliban government that just a week before had been gloating that it would outlast America's ineffectual aerial bombardments. In a matter of days the stalemate in

Afghanistan had been broken, and the Taliban had been mercilessly pushed out of Northern Alliance territory.

As the stunned Americans tried to keep up with pace of events on the ground, they finally began to understand the symbolic importance that Dostum had always attached to the seizure of Mazar-e-Sharif. For those who had anticipated a long winter campaign followed by a full US invasion of sixty thousand US troops, the sudden collapse of the Taliban was a godsend. None could doubt that American lives had been saved by the unexpected fall of Mazar-e-Sharif, and for that Central Command was grateful to Dostum and the small group of American special operators riding with him, who had exceeded all expectations.

But the war in the north was still not quite finished. When Herat, Bamiyan, and Kabul fell to the Northern Alliance, a large Taliban army was trapped east of Mazar-e-Sharif at the city of Kunduz. Those Taliban who had survived the assault on Mazar-e-Sharif had fled there to make their last stand. They were closely pursued by Dostum and Atta.

As Dostum moved through the lands of Afghan Turkistan, chasing the Taliban, he was greeted by thousands of northerners who joyously held parades to welcome him. Laughing villagers covered him with flower petals as his convoy drove through their lands. The videos of Dostum's victory march and speeches typically feature him waving to crowds from the back of a Toyota pickup truck or addressing thousands in village squares and stadiums. In several of the shots, R.J., Dostum's trusted CIA friend, and members of ODA 595 and other Special Forces servicemen stand by his side in a place of honor.

But there was still work to be done. In Kunduz the Taliban remnants promised no more retreats; they and their fanatical al-Qaeda allies would fight to the death. The Americans were once again all too willing to oblige them and brought a lethal new weapon into the theater of operations, AC-130 gunships. These slow-moving propeller-driven planes had side doors that opened to reveal a bristling array of massive 40 mm Gatling machine guns and 105 mm howitzer cannons. Known as a fire-support platform in official lingo (and Puff the Magic Dragon in military slang), the AC-130 offered its pilots the perfect means to float at leisure over the enemy while firing deadly cannons directly down on them. There was nowhere to hide when a loitering AC-130 looked down on its targets. As the plane cruised over its enemies, using thermal and night-vision technology to light up humans, it rained down a hail of precision-guided shells and massive bullets. The result was a blistering barrage that seemed to have the uncanny ability to follow the enemy across the battlefield, wreaking havoc at will.

To make things more interesting, one of the AC-130s deployed to Kunduz had a navigator on board named Allison Black. When Dostum heard her voice speaking to his US Special Forces comrades, he was thrilled and called up the Taliban misogynists to let them know that the Americans had sent women to kill them. He reportedly told the Taliban, "It's the angel of death raining fire on you." [47]

As the AC-130s prowled Kunduz, mowing down suspected enemy troop concentrations in conjunction with B-52 strikes, the Taliban and al-Qaeda's resolve quickly began to collapse. Kunduz had become a tomb for the Taliban as the American *malaks* picked them off in the hundreds.

Finally, on November 24 the Taliban laid down their arms and marched out of the town in the thousands to surrender at a place in the desert called Ergenak. While the Northern Alliance Tajiks had moved from their lines in the east to join the siege, the Taliban refused to surrender to them, instead choosing to give themselves to Dostum, who had a reputation as a moderate. According to *Newsweek*, they felt "he was the least likely to seek revenge for past killings." [48]

Dostum's small army was overwhelmed by thousands of bedraggled Pakistani Taliban volunteers, local Afghan Taliban, and hardened al-Qaeda fighters. Not knowing what to do with so many prisoners of war, Dostum's outnumbered men loaded them into huge transport trucks and drove them to the west in a long convoy toward Mazar-e-Sharif. From there, the vast majority of the prisoners, Afghan Taliban, were shipped to Dostum's prison at Shiberghan, but a smaller group of several hundred foreign Ansar fighters captured near Mazar-e-Sharif and known for their zeal in combat and focus on martyrdom were taken to the fortress of Qala-e-Jangi to the west of Mazar. They seemed to have arrived rather peacefully, and Dostum talked of having the foreigners transferred to the UN to be sent home.

But there at the fortress, things went disastrously wrong, for the foreign forces still had some fight in them. Rather than surrendering, the al-Qaeda fighters planned an uprising. When one of the prisoners saw an Uzbek commander who resembled Dostum, he charged him and blew himself and the commander up with a hidden hand grenade. This incident infuriated the Uzbeks who were guarding them. Several Western journalists who were there at the time reported the scene of the bloody revolt:

STAUTH: . . . Dostum was there explaining that the foreign fighters should be handed over to the U.N.

PERRY: And he said over and over again, you know, the only way to unite Afghanistan is to play the big man and to kind of forgive. . . .

ALESSIO VINCI, CNN CORRESPONDENT: I mean we were really under the impression that this was going to be a positive story, you know. Here they are. They have surrendered. They have given themselves up as a former enemy. They were treated pretty well. They were being searched in a very nice way. They were not handcuffed. They were not, you know, they were not being, you know, mistreated at all, at all.

PELTON: The code of conduct was we're going to spare your lives because we think the war is over. You've lost. You're going to go back and everybody is going to be happy again.

VINCI: There was a genuine attempt to really make this work. . . .

VINCI: I mean the story changed when that first Taliban fighter blew himself up. Then the whole thing changed immediately. There were 400 plus Taliban prisoners and maybe 20, 30 armed guards all around them. Those [captured foreign] soldiers could have begun the uprising then at that moment and we would have been all dead right now because there was no way we could have gotten out of there alive and obviously some of them still had hand grenades. They wanted to kill Americans.

> That's what they wanted to do. They wanted to come to Afghanistan to
> kill Americans. I mean, you know, these [captive foreign] soldiers they
> have said all along, we're here to die. We're here to die. . . .
>
> PERRY: I mean they [the Northern Alliance] wanted to kill them [the pris-
> oners] in the first place but Dostum said oh, no. In the interest of
> national reconciliation, we'll let these guys go home and we'll see if
> we can all live together.[49]

Later, when the prisoners were placed in a basement in the fortress, some of them broke through a wall into a nearby arms depot, seized the weapons, and commenced an uprising. Storming out of their holding area, they gunned down their Uzbek captors. As they burst into the castle court-yard, they were surprised to see two CIA agents interrogating prisoners. The two CIA paramilitaries were Dostum's comrades-in-arms: David Tyson, the Uzbek-speaker trained at Indiana University, and Johnny Micheal Spann, the ex-Marine from Alabama. In the ensuing chaos, Spann was brutally murdered by the revolting prisoners, and Tyson barely managed to get away after gunning several of his attackers down with an AK-47.

When Dostum heard the news of the uprising and death of his Amer-ican CIA friend, he was both furious and concerned. If the hundreds of prisoners broke out of the lightly guarded fortress, they could scatter into the urban maze of nearby Mazar-e-Sharif and create chaos. This had to be prevented at all cost.

The Americans and British had recently deployed special forces in the area to replace the A-Teams fighting in Kunduz alongside Dostum and Atta. These new forces rushed to the castle and joined the Uzbek guards in trying to hold off the larger number of Taliban and al-Qaeda 055 fighters inside. The furious battle for Qala-e-Jangi was finally decided when the Americans brought in JDAMs and AC-130 Spectre gunships to bomb the fortress. The bombs landed directly on the revolting prisoners' position and annihilated them.

As the smoke cleared, the Americans and Uzbeks found a courtyard covered with the mangled bodies of al-Qaeda fighters and the horses used by the Uzbeks in the Darya Suf campaign. They also found a few bedraggled survivors in the basement of the fortress. When Dostum's men interrogated the handful of survivors, one of them, who went by the nom de guerre Abdul Hamid, surprised everyone by announcing in English that he was an American. The Uzbeks were stunned by the discovery of a young bearded jihadi volunteer from California amongst the Arab and Pakistani fanatics.

The American 055 Ansar fighter, whose real name was John Walker Lindh, was handed over to US troops, who then took him back to the United States for a trial. There the so-called American Talib made headlines as a traitor, although few knew that he had been captured along with hundreds of other al-Qaeda fighters by General Dostum's Uzbeks.

The other survivors of the Qala-e-Jangi fortress were later taken westward to the massive Soviet-built prison at Shiberghan. There they were joined by waves of prisoners being sent westward in convoys from Kunduz. In the process, an undetermined number of them died from wounds they had received in the bombardment of Kunduz or from being asphyxiated in their transport containers. Those who died en route were buried in the desert at Dasht-e-Leili just outside of Shiberghan.

Commander Lal, who was in charge of the transfer while Dostum and ODA 595 wrapped up things in the east at Kunduz, later claimed that no more than one hundred Taliban prisoners of war died on their way to Shiberghan. Lal reported, "There were many angry Uzbek soldiers who had lost loved ones to these outsiders from the south. It was war, and we were lucky there was not more bloodshed and Taliban losses considering the years of cruelty. But we had been given strict orders by General Dostum to protect the Taliban prisoners."[50]

In the joyous aftermath of the unexpected collapse of Taliban rule in the north, the deaths of an indeterminate number of Taliban, however, went unnoticed. Thousands of Taliban and al-Qaeda fighters had died in the conflict; and in light of the bad blood stemming from previous massacres in Mazar-e-Sharif, Dostum was given credit for helping keep the peace in the north. While many had predicted a bloodletting when the Northern Alliance took Mazar-e-Sharif, this never happened. Far from it. On occasion

Dostum was even reported to have walked unarmed into Pashtun villages near Mazar-e-Sharif to organize their surrender and assure their inhabitants of his protection.[51]

Soon thereafter wonderful news arrived from Kandahar. In December the Pashtun south fell when local warlords and tribesmen, led by a relatively obscure Pashtun nobleman named Hamid Karzai, rose up against the Taliban. The stunned Taliban retreated across the border into Pakistan along with bin Laden and his lieutenants or melted into the Afghan countryside to fight another day.

The US-led coalition found Karzai, who spoke fluent English, to be a perfect candidate for an interim president since he was a member of the ruling Pashtun ethnic group. Karzai was soon thereafter sworn in by a newly chosen *loya jirga* (parliament).

President Karzai subsequently chose Fahim Khan as his minister of defense in an attempt to placate the powerful Tajik component of the Northern Alliance, which had maintained control of the Afghan capital after seizing it. Dostum, who had been much more aggressive than Fahim Khan in the campaign, was relegated to the ceremonial position of deputy minister of defense. Ironically, this was the exact post that he had been given in 1992 by President Rabbani—only on this occasion instead of rejecting it, Dostum reluctantly accepted it. The new Afghan president had the backing of the powerful Americans. There was nothing that could be done to make them understand the Uzbeks' history of discrimination at the hands of Tajik- and Pashtun-dominated governments.

Dostum spent 2002 reorganizing his Jumbesh Party as a power base and positioning himself as both the defender of his downtrodden Uzbek people and as a moderate secularist in a country now dominated by mujahideen warlords. He also ran for president in the 2004 presidential elections and received 10 percent of the vote (roughly the percentage of Uzbeks and Turkmen in the country).

But his efforts to regain control of his old seat of power in Mazar-e-Sharif were thwarted once again, this time by his Tajik mujahideen rival

Ustad Atta. Atta attacked Dostum and killed several of his men, thus leading to a tank duel between the two warlords in 2002. The Americans watched in dismay as the two warlords continued to shed blood, this time against each other. President Karzai ultimately sided with Atta, making him governor of Mazar and leaving Dostum, who was less inclined to fight against his former ally, in control of the Uzbek lands to the west.

It was at this time that the Karzai government, which was trying to enforce its central authority in the provinces, joined the fray and began to subtly move against Dostum. With US support Karzai began to entice powerful Uzbek and Turkmen figures into defecting from Dostum's Jumbesh Party and joining the government. Karzai's aim was to break the power of his popular non-Pashtun rival and diminish his capacity to act independently on behalf of the Uzbeks of the north. Thus Dostum, who had always resented having his role and that of his people go unrecognized by the government of the day, continued a fight that had begun in 1992 with the overthrow of Najibullah. He sought to empower both himself and his people and achieve some modicum of Uzbek self-rule in a land that had been dominated for over a century by Pashtuns. In addition, Dostum was certainly maneuvering to maintain his own personal power.

But Dostum's new fight was to be a political rather than military battle. His mantra became, "Put away your weapons and use your vote to put Uzbeks in parliament." In the midst of this unstable climate, a shocking article entitled "Death Convoy of Afghanistan" came out in the American magazine *Newsweek*. The article called the death of the Taliban prisoners in the Uzbek convoys of November 2001 one of the "dirty secrets" of the Afghan conflict and hinted that as many as one thousand Taliban might have died. The article also provided graphic details from eyewitnesses who spoke of scores of Taliban prisoners dying from dehydration and suffocation in the shipping containers that transported them to Shiberghan prison from Kunduz. It stated that the bodies of those who died en route were then buried in the Desht-e-Leili desert to the west of Shiberghan. The article mentioned the fact that Dostum's representatives put the death toll at somewhere between 100 and 120.[52] It also quoted *National Geographic* journalist Robert Young Pelton, who was with Dostum and ODA 595 at the time of the event, who claimed that only a small number of Taliban died in the convoys. Regardless of the actual number of Taliban who died during transport, no investigation was ever launched by the United States or the United Nations into this potential massacre.

Adding to the controversy, an Irish filmmaker named Jamie Doran sensationalized the episode in an innuendo-filled documentary film entitled *Afghan Massacre: The Convoy of Death* and made the claim that three thousand Taliban may have been massacred in cold blood by Dostum *and* US Special Forces. While Doran offered no proof for his accusations, which were rejected by other reporters like Pelton who were with Dostum at the time, the accusation alone was enough to further taint Dostum's reputation. Few in the West knew anything of Dostum's career as a defender of women's rights and moderation in Mazar-e-Sharif. A hidden massacre on a scale that rivaled the deaths on 9/11 seemed plausible in a wild land like Afghanistan.

For his part, *National Geographic* photographer Robert Young Pelton, the only journalist who actually lived with Dostum and his men in the final days of the desperate campaign, had a different account based upon his unrivaled access to Dostum and direct participation in the events. According to the eyewitness account of Pelton,

> One of the curious stories to emerge from the early days of the war in Afghanistan was the "convoy of death." According to Luke Harding, Carlotta Gall, and filmmaker Jamie Doran, who was doing a documentary, there was a massacre of Taliban prisoners that was somehow being covered up. No evidence of the massacre was ever brought forward, but it remains as vividly quoted as the tank-crushing story that was retracted by Ahmed Rashid.
>
> The story was that in the last days of November 2001, General Dostum's men and—if you believe Jamie Doran—US Special Forces troops crammed Taliban prisoners who surrendered in Kunduz into shipping

containers, shot bullet holes into them, suffocated the prisoners, and then tried to hide the bodies in a well-known grave site called Desht-e-Leili.

What made this story interesting to me was that I was with the special forces team at the time and spent a significant amount of time at the prison in Shiberghan where the prisoners were being sent to. I watched them unload truck after truck [of prisoners]. [I saw them] unlock the loosely fastened doors and watched the scantily clad prisoners emerge in the frigid winter. The containers were to protect them from the bitter cold and to prevent the prisoners from simply jumping off during the long eight-to-twelve-hour journey from Ergenak (near Kunduz) to Shiberghan.

I subsequently photographed the local doctors treating the wounded prisoners along with two medics from Dostum's US Special Forces unit [ODA 595]. If there was a massacre going on the prisoners seemed to be unfazed. Those prisoners that did die suffered from disease, wounds, and the effects of being constantly bombarded and attacked for three weeks. I counted the dead and saw the doctors keeping notes of each prisoner's condition in lined notebooks. In all, of the well over three thousand prisoners I was with, about two hundred died. Some died in transit, some later at the prison.

Dostum often joked that the prisoners ate better than his soldiers did, as he paid for cooking stations, food, and supplies for the massive influx of prisoners. The irony was that during the conflict the number of Taliban killed by US and Afghan forces was never accounted for, but suddenly the very people who liberated the Afghans were considered the abusers.

The story of Talibs roasted to death and licking the sweat off each other's bodies completely ignores the subzero temperatures at the time and repeats an old story from Afghanistan's history [i.e., Malik's 1997 massacre of Taliban prisoners which Dostum reported to the UN]. The truth is there was no massacre; Dostum's goal was to bring peace to the region by sending local fighters home and the Pakistanis back to their villages—and deal with the foreigners through the UN. Most of the foreign fighters ended up in Gitmo except for some notable exceptions. One being an American Taliban I actually discovered named John Walker Lindh.[53]

But the worst damage was not done by these accusations, which were largely made by foreigners who were unfamiliar with Dostum's history as a comparative liberal. Worse damage was inadvertently done by a Pakistani journalist named Ahmed Rashid. His book, *Taliban: Militant Islam, Oil, and Fundamentalism in Central Asia*, published in 2000, was the most readily available survey of Afghan politics and history for most Westerners after 9/11, and it quickly became both a best seller and an unofficial Afghan guide book for American forces.

In his work the usually reliable Rashid relayed as fact a secondhand story of a bizarre execution that was unquestioningly accepted by Western readers. Rashid wrote of his visit to Dostum's headquarters at the Qala-e-Jangi fortress in the late 1990s and described an execution that allegedly took place while he was there:

> He wielded power ruthlessly. The first time I arrived at the fort to meet Dostum there were bloodstains and pieces of flesh in the muddy courtyard. I innocently asked the guards if a goat had been slaughtered. They told me that a man had been tied to the tracks of a Russian-made tank, which then drove around the courtyard crushing his body to mincemeat, as the garrison and Dostum watched. The Uzbeks, the roughest and toughest of all Central Asian nationalities, are noted for their love of marauding and pillaging—a hangover from their origins as a part of Genghis Khan's hordes, and Dostum was an apt leader. Over six feet tall with bulging biceps, Dostum is a bear of a man with a gruff laugh, which, some Uzbeks swear, has on occasion frightened people to death.[54]

Dostum has claimed that there were not tanks in the fortress at the time and that the soldier who told Rashid this story must have been pulling his leg. Yet with these words, Dostum's image was set in the eyes of a Western readership that was unfamiliar with his past. Dostum, the secular defender of the shrine of Mazar-e-Sharif (and his "marauding" people with him), would forever be reduced to a tank-killing caricature of a Mongol warlord who laughed men to death.

Others seized upon this secondhand story and added their own twists. The evolution of Rashid's "Dostum the tank killer" story is fascinating and demonstrates how a probable myth can become reality when rewritten over and over again. The creative retelling of the story by reporters who rarely, if ever, met Dostum later described him as "reportedly" murdering "enemy captives," "criminals," "opponents," "members of other ethnic groups," and myriad others with "tanks" (plural). One typical account of the pluralized tale of tank execution claimed, "Charged with mass murder of prisoners of war in the mid-90s by the UN [*sic;* Malik was charged in this case, because of Dostum's report of the massacre to the UN], Dostum is known to use torture and assassinations to retain power. Described by the *Chicago Sun Times* (10/21/01) as a 'cruel and cunning warlord,' he is reported to use tanks to rip apart political opponents or crush them to death."[55]

As his power base was eroded and his image as an ogre was disseminated by Western journalists who erroneously saw *all* warlords as a threat to Afghan women and secular society, Dostum naturally felt betrayed by his American allies. Having personally led countless charges against the Taliban and having fought for decades to create secular rule for his country—even when the United States was sponsoring the fundamentalist mujahideen back in the 1980s—he could not understand why the Americans and other Westerners had turned against him.

But he was worried by more than just his relationship with the Americans. Forced by the Karzai government to gradually release his Taliban prisoners at Shiberghan, Dostum warned that most of them would simply rejoin the Taliban and start burning schools, planting land mines, throwing acid in the faces of schoolgirls, and killing newly arrived coalition troops.

This prophecy came true in 2003 when Central Command refocused its energies from the unfinished campaign in Afghanistan to a new invasion known as Operation Iraqi Freedom. As the Americans launched a full-scale war in Iraq involving over 150,000 soldiers, the Taliban regrouped, reinfiltrated, and commenced a deadly guerilla war in the Pashtun south. While the conflict in Afghanistan became known in the American media as the "forgotten war" due to the focus on Iraq, the reenergized Taliban let the US-led coalition know that they, at least, had not forgotten Afghanistan.

Although Dostum offered to lead ten thousand men to fight the Taliban insurgents as he had done against the mujahideen in the 1980s, the Karzai government was loath to use a well-known Uzbek anti-jihadi *ghulam* and *gilimjan* (plunderer, literally "carpet thief") against fellow Pashtuns. Instead, the new government disarmed Dostum and his men even as it rearmed Pashtun *arbakis* (militias) in the south to fight the Taliban and al-Qaeda insurgents.

With Ustad Atta, who was declared governor of Balkh and Mazar-e-Sharif by President Karzai, working to erode Dostum's power in his former capital, and with the Uzbek general's role in the government and war relegated to the symbolic post of deputy defense minister or chief of staff of the Afghan Army, he grew increasingly frustrated. While Dostum still held *shura* councils with local Uzbek and Turkmen *aq saqals* and was clearly beloved by his own people, the Pasha found no real role for himself in the new Afghanistan he had helped make possible. On the contrary, he was demonized by the foreign press as a murderous warlord and seen as a separatist threat to the Karzai government dominated by Pashtuns and Tajiks.

Dostum, Fakir, Lal, Ahmed Khan, and other commanders bemoaned the injustice of their fate in their regular meetings at Dostum's Jumbesh compound in Mazar-e-Sharif and plotted ways to get their story out. But these weathered Uzbek warriors did not know English like the polished politician President Karzai, and they had no meaningful contacts with their former US comrades-in-arms. Mark Nutsch, R.J., Dave Tyson, Bart Decker, Matt Lienhard, and the other US Special Forces had been unceremoniously withdrawn from Afghanistan in December 2001. They were ordered to return to K2 (Karshi-Khanabad) in Uzbekistan to be personally debriefed by the secretary of defense.

But before the Americans left, they held a brief ceremony in Dostum's compound at Khoda Barq (a Russian-built village just west of Mazar-e-Sharif) where they presented Dostum and the other Uzbek, Hazara, and Tajik allied commanders with US Combat Infantry Badges.

While touched by the gifts, Dostum had been hurt by the sudden departure of the Americans, whom he considered brothers-in-arms; in addition, their exit had left him isolated in the new scheme of things. His ties with the CIA were also severed as R.J. and Dave Tyson returned to the United States escorting the remains of fellow agent Mike Spann.

It was at this time that Dostum's aide Faizullah Zaki called the Pasha from Kabul to say that a Turkish-speaking American historian had just arrived in the country seeking an interview. The American claimed to have an open mind and wanted to hear Dostum's story. Dostum considered before giving an answer. The last thing he needed was another Westerner sensationalizing him as a warlord who laughed men to death. But officials at the Turkish embassy in Kabul vouched for the American professor, who hailed from a place called Boston, Massachusetts. They claimed he might be able to help Dostum get his story out.

"*Bale*," Dostum finally responded, "OK. Send him to me. If I feel I can trust him, I will let him live with me and will tell him my story. I will treat him as a guest if I trust him.

"If not, I will send him straight back to Kabul."[56]

19

INTERVIEW WITH A WARLORD

"It will be extremely difficult to meet General Dostum after all the things that have been written about him in the foreign media. But if you do meet him, you may find out that the things the journalists have written are exaggerated."

—TUGAY TUNCER, NATO LIAISON OFFICER, TURKISH EMBASSY IN KABUL

MAZAR-E-SHARIF, KHOJA DOKO, QALA-E-JANGI, SHIBERGHAN, AND KUNDUZ. SUMMER 2003.

As the various gray-bearded *aq saqals* assembled around General Dostum prepared to depart, leaving just two commanders whom Dostum identified as Lal and Fakir on his compound's balcony, I shook off the dirt from my long journey over the Hindu Kush and took in the sight of the famous warlord. He appeared to be about fifty years old, well built, with a graying military-style crew cut; he was wearing a Western-style suit instead of a *chapan*. He also sported a mustache, which I later learned was a trademark of the pro–Communist government Jowzjani Uzbeks.

275

Dostum emanated power. When he waved his hand in dismissal, the turbaned *aq saqal* elders around him responded with deep respect. The general was clearly in charge and used to having those around him follow his orders.

When I told him that I had traveled all the way from the United States to hear his story, I could see that he was intrigued. He was used to Americans like the men from ODA 595 and the occasional journalist whom he'd met who were not intimately familiar with his or his people's background. When Lal smiled and signaled to him that he thought I was to be trusted to tell his story, he quickly warmed up to me.

Waving for the elders to leave, he gave me Turkish biscuits, sat back in his chair, and began, as he put it, to "tell me a story of Afghanistan." While he had been accused by Pashtun Communists in the Najibullah government of trying to use his powerful Jowzjani militia to carve Turkistan off from the rest of Afghanistan, he clearly saw himself as an Afghan as well as an Uzbek. It was in this Afghan context that his story unfolded.

As he began by telling me tales of his poor youth in an obscure town to the west known as Khoja Doko, I quickly realized that he was a natural storyteller. Using nuts on the table as ad hoc props, he brought to life his youthful adventures and took me back in time to a place I could hardly imagine.

"Growing up in Khoja Doko in the '60s and '70s, I thought it was the entire world. I thought everyone lived in clay houses on the edge of the desert. How little I knew of the world back then."

Dostum laughed in a contagious way as he told me of his initial scraps with village lads and his troublemaking with his childhood friend Yar. I could see that Lal and Fakir knew the stories well, and they respectfully interrupted him on occasion to remind him of certain details he had left out.

Dostum seemed to lose himself in his reminiscences, and I could see that he enjoyed talking about his life in Khoja Doko. On occasion he would move biscuits around the table to re-create childhood fights or bang his hands together to make a point. I found his infectious storytelling style to be somewhat incongruous with his image as a dreaded warlord. And in spite of the natural trepidation I felt for him, knowing he had bombarded Kabul during the civil war of the 1990s, killing hundreds, I began to warm up to him a little in return. He brought to mind a jovial Mafia don, and I realized there was a forthright quality about him. He described events such as the advent of Communism in his home village in a simplistic fashion that was lacking in sophistication and guile. He had no problem discussing his humble peasant origins, lack of education, membership in the moderate Parchami branch of the Communist Party, or his struggles to climb the social ladder in an Afghan society that considered provincial Uzbeks like him to be not much better than Shiite Hazaras.

As we talked, Dostum's aides would come and gently tap him on the shoulder from time to time to discuss various business, and I realized the Pasha was taking considerable time from his busy schedule to tell me his story. But as the sun began to set outside I knew our interview was coming to a close. I was frustrated because we had not gotten beyond his childhood years in Khoja Doko. As interesting as I found his stories of almost drowning in a river or being forced to leave school early, they did not really tell me who he was as a man.

Perhaps sensing my frustration, Dostum gave a wide grin and said, "Don't worry, *khoja*, tomorrow we'll meet again, and I'll tell you more of my story. I'll tell you how I managed to get out of Khoja Doko and into the army."

Then he abruptly left and went out into the courtyard. There I saw perhaps fifty *aq saqals* patiently sitting on chairs set up in a square around a giant armchair. Dostum sat in the chair and commenced another one of his endless *shuras*. The council meeting began with a poet reading a ballad that extolled the virtues of Dostum as a great warrior.

During the meeting, I heard a teacher from a nearby village complain to Dostum about the lack of chairs in his simple school. Could Dostum provide his students with money for chairs? Dostum patiently heard him out and then promised to have money given to him for chairs after the meeting. Another elder claimed that members of a nearby village were siphoning off water from their canals. Dostum promised to send representatives to look into the matter. And so it continued, with Dostum officiating over the time-less *shura* like some Uzbek khan of old.

I filmed the whole thing until the closing prayers began, and then, real-izing I was probably intruding, turned off my camera. As I walked away I found Commanders Lal and Fakir sipping tea on the compound balcony and asked them if I could take a picture with them. Lal seemed reluctant to do so, but Fakir made some jokes about him in Uzbek and the camera-shy com-mander finally agreed to pose for a photo. In the picture Fakir, who always seemed to be grinning, smiled from ear to ear while Lal looked more serious.

The two commanders agreed to tell me their stories when I came back on the following day, but they seemed to be both concerned about stealing the limelight from Dostum and uninterested in telling their stories to a West-erner. Theirs was the world of the Kalashnikov, not the pen. These illiterate fighting men did not have much time for foreign civilians writing stories.

Fortunately, Dostum seemed to have no such qualms and genuinely appeared to want to meet with me on the following day. That night my driver with the Bollywoodized AK-47 drove me to one of the Pasha's guest-houses outside of Mazar-e-Sharif in the village of Khoda Barq, which had been built out of prefab concrete by the Soviets. There my hosts fed me a dinner of rice pilaf, naan, and Pepsi that I ate with two Pashtun khans from the south who had come to strike a business deal with Dostum.

On the following day I was once again taken to Dostum's compound in an Uzbek-dominated neighborhood of Mazar-e-Sharif near the blue-domed tomb of Ali. Along the way my driver pointed out damage done to many of the buildings during the years of fighting. He also showed me a school known as the Sultan Rayza School where dozens of Pakistani Tali-ban holdouts had been killed by US precision-guided bombs during the taking of Mazar-e-Sharif a year and half earlier.

Soon thereafter we arrived at Dostum's nondescript walled compound. When we went through the checkpoint and entered the structure, we were met by Dostum's English-speaking major domo Ehsan Zari. He had some bad news.

"Dostum is not here. He sends his deepest apologies; he was called back to Shiberghan on urgent business. He asks for you to go there to join him as a guest in his compound there."

Thrilled to see Dostum's home base and more of Afghan Turkistan, I quickly agreed. Zari, several of Dostum's followers, and I boarded a Toyota 4Runner truck and headed out into the dusty plains west of Mazar-e-Sharif.

About an hour into the journey near a Turkmen village called Akche, the terrain become pure desert. While the plains around Mazar-e-Sharif had been watered by the Balkh River and its estuaries, there was no water to bring life to the wastelands around us. As the temperatures outside soared to over 110 degrees, our truck followed a ribbon of tarmac across the desert.

Finally the land became greener as we approached Shiberghan, which was also watered by a river coming down from the Hindu Kush. But before we entered the town, we stopped at a martyr's cemetery built on the plains outside of the city. After a brief prayer we entered the cemetery, and I found that it contained the graves of 118 of Dostum's commanders. Strangely for Afghanistan, every grave had a plastic-laminated photograph of the deceased fighter on it. This was something I had seen only in the Soviet Union, when I was in Moscow. Many of the photos showed young mustachioed Uzbeks wearing green Communist-style uniforms, and I surmised that they had died fighting during the 1980s and '90s. Other photographs were more recent and depicted the turbaned faces of *cheriks* who had died fighting against the Taliban.[1] I was told that several of the men buried in this windswept cemetery had been killed fighting the Taliban in Darya Suf. Their remains had been taken down from the mountains when the war was over in fulfillment of Dostum's promise to bury them in this spot.

Zari pointed out one faded picture in particular—Dostum's childhood friend Yar. "This man was a great warrior. Had he not given his life for the Pasha, it might be Dostum buried here, not Yar. He was Dostum's best friend. You should know that the General named his second son after Yar. His son was actually born on the very day Yar died."

I filmed the cemetery, a sad place filled with the remains of young men like Yar whose lives had been snuffed out prematurely by the perennial conflicts that had swept this land, and then returned to our truck. From there we made our way into Shiberghan, which seemed to be a rather pleasant plains town filled with bicyclists, women in burqas, shopkeepers, donkeys, and turbaned Uzbeks scurrying about their business. Once known as Little Moscow, this was the base from which Dostum began his climb to power in the 1980s.

I could tell we were in Dostum's headquarters, as billboards featuring him symbolically holding a pen instead of a weapon began to appear around town. But nothing prepared me for the sight of a large billboard featuring Dostum with words in English and Dari at the bottom of it. Sitting next to Dostum and looking at a large military map were a goatee-wearing Commander Mark Nutsch and another member of Tiger 02. Below the blond-haired, blue-eyed Americans the billboard stated in Uzbek and English: THANK YOU TO THE AMERICAN MILITARY FOR LIBERATING AFGHANISTAN FROM TERRORISM.

The message was astounding considering the fact that in the south the Taliban insurgents were killing anyone who collaborated with the "American infidel occupiers." It spoke volumes about the level of pro-American sentiment in this Uzbek town. What had once been called Little Moscow might now be called Little Washington.

From the site of the billboard we drove past a soccer field that had been used as a place of public execution by the Taliban during their three years of occupation. My driver told me that the Taliban had taken local women there to be shot in the head for adultery and for teaching girls.

Our discussion ended when we arrived at Dostum's Soviet-built Jumbesh Party compound. This high-walled concrete structure with a couple of guard towers on it served as Dostum's local headquarters. We entered the inner courtyard through a small entrance and found a two-storied building in the center. This served as a reception house for guests; on another wall of the compound was a guesthouse where I was given a room. I was told that Dostum would come see me later in the evening.

To pass the time, I wandered around the compound and found to my shock that it had an air-conditioned hall with something that I thought did not exist in Afghanistan: a swimming pool. Mesmerized, I walked into the hall and found two Uzbeks playing ping-pong. The combination of air-conditioning, swimming pool, and ping-pong players seemed to transport me off the hot plains of Afghan Turkistan to someplace more Western.

Seeing my look of shock, one of the ping-pong players smiled and invited me to join him for a game. I realized he was a younger version of Dostum, complete with the mustache and bulk. I instantly understood that he was the general's younger brother Abdul Kadir.

After telling me his personal story, he invited me for a walk in the compound's large courtyard, which was filled with pomegranate trees. In the center of the courtyard stood a ten-foot concrete statue of a pomegranate plant. As a historian of Central Asia, I knew that the pomegranate was an ancient sign of authority and had been mounted on scepters in the land since the dawn of history. Pointing to the statue, Abdul Kadir asked me if I knew what it was. When I replied that it was a pomegranate, he appeared to be happy. Then he told me, "Did you know that an American reporter came here last year and stayed as our guest for a day? When he returned to America he accused my brother of being an opium warlord. He claimed that he had built a concrete statue of an *opium* poppy plant in his 'palace'! This is how he paid back our hospitality."

We went back to the house in the center of the compound, and he gave me a copy of the offending article from *Harper's* magazine, which read, "In the center of the compound is Dostum's residence. Beyond is a garden with long rows of rose bushes and fruit trees, a small mosque in one corner, and a large fountain, also made in concrete, in the shape of an opium poppy. A giant concrete poppy fountain."[2]

I could see that the article angered Abdul Kadir, and I was intrigued to hear that Dostum actually had someone monitoring the English-language press for articles about him. But this article paled in comparison to one he gave me from the *Washington Times* in which a journalist claimed to have heard someone being "skinned alive" three hundred yards away in Dostum's compound the previous year.[3] Abdul Kadir explained that the journalist had visited the compound soon after Dostum populated its garden with peacocks. Hearing the peacocks the reporter had succumbed to the urge to sensationalize the story. The reporter had made it more exciting by describing the peacock's human-like calls as sounding like someone "being skinned alive" (and this, presumably, within earshot of an investigative American journalist). There were still a few peacocks left roaming the courtyard; having heard their cries, I was inclined to believe Abdul Kadir's account.

I came to see why Dostum distrusted the Western media and why he felt betrayed by his American allies, who seemed to have put all of their eggs in the Karzai basket. When he arrived that evening for our interview I promised him I would not embellish my story the way the journalists had. While I understood Dostum had the urge to spin his stories to make himself look good and knew Dostum had committed some unquestionably atrocious acts (most notably his role in the 1993 attack on Kabul alongside Hekmatyar), it did not take an abundance of common sense to realize some of the more outlandish stories about him were fraudulent.

That evening Dostum met me again and took me further into his story. He told me of his fights with other village lads and his fame as a *kurash* wrestler. When he was done I asked him if I could visit Khoja Doko, his home village, and see the setting of his childhood exploits. While warning me that there was not much to see, he said he would be delighted to have one of his drivers take me there.

But on the following day the Pasha was nowhere to be found. I was told he had gone south to settle a dispute between Pashtun and Uzbek villagers who had bad blood between them stemming from the Taliban occupation. I had a guest waiting for me, however. He introduced himself as Mohammad Omar and told me he was General Dostum's older stepbrother. He had a kind, weather-beaten face, and I noticed that he was barefoot and wearing a peasant farmer's clothes. He told me that, unlike his younger brother, Abdul Kadir, he had had nothing to do with the Pasha's career. Eschewing all advantages that might come to him through his famous general brother, he had remained a simple farmer in Khoja Doko. He appeared to be very gentle, and as we drove out into the desert toward the village, he constantly attended to my needs.

After about a forty-five-minute drive he pointed to a two-humped hill with a village at its base on the right side of the road and announced that we had arrived. Driving into Khoja Doko in a wave of dust, I noticed parched melon fields surrounding the village and barefoot children riding donkeys on the road. Once in the village Mohammad Omar took me to his child-hood home. Nothing, however, could have prepared me for its primitive state. The clay-walled, domed home had dirt floors, no lighting or toilets, and appeared to be better suited for animals than humans. I found it hard to imagine an entire family living in the simple hut.

From his former house, Mohammad Omar took me up the hill of Khoja Doko. We walked past a graveyard, and he showed me the graves of several village aq saqal elders who had been hung by the Taliban when they con-quered the village in 1997 following Malik's betrayal. He told me that he and several other villagers had hidden in a cavelike well on the side of the hill until the Taliban's killing frenzy had spent itself.

When we arrived on the top of the hill, we found a simple school with-out heating or desks, with posters on the walls warning the children not to play with suspicious-looking objects. These included landmines, rocket-propelled grenade rounds, and mortars. Walking outside, I could see why the teachers had felt compelled to hang the warnings. The hillside was lit-tered with the casings of thousands of AK-47 and machine gun bullets that testified to previous battles fought from this strategic position. An anti-aircraft gun with trenches dug around it stood just outside the door of the school. Mohammad Omar told me that the gun had been used against the Taliban in 1997 and 1998 but that the Taliban had overrun the hill anyway. Dostum had barely managed to escape in a helicopter on the first occasion.

Walking down the hill we visited the local police station where in his youth Dostum had been dragged for beating several older kids with a stick.

The local police showed me whips and chains that the Taliban police had used on the locals during their occupation. They told me that their village had suffered more than most for being the home of the Taliban's archenemy. But other than being the home of the Pasha, there did not seem to be much else of interest in the village.

When we were done with our tour Mohammad Omar took me out to his field, and there we shared melons in the shade of his *kepe* (a thatched, yurt-like hut) built to provide him with shelter from the heat. He told me that as a boy Dostum had been impetuous, and it was a miracle he had lived as long as he had. In some ways the military had given him the perfect means to channel his combative energies and break away from the poverty of his home village.

But for all of his success, Dostum still looked up to Mohammad Omar and came to visit him on occasion to seek advice. On one of those visits, Mohammad Omar had given him a green *chapan* as a gift. It was this *chapan* that the Pasha had worn into battle and sworn not to remove until the Taliban were expelled from the land.

As the sun set on Khoja Doko I thanked Mohammad Omar for being my guide and left him at his simple home before my driver took me back to the larger town of Shiberghan. That night I reflected on one name from Dostum's childhood that had been conspicuously missing in my discussions with him and his family members: his first wife, Khadija. Other than the passing hints that they had shared something most Afghan marriages did not have—passion—and that she had died early, the subject had been off-limits.

On the following day as Dostum's convoy drove into the compound, I decided to broach the subject. I did so over a meal that did not include Dostum consuming a dozen chickens or bottles of vodka, just rice pilaf and naan. When I brought up the subject of his wife, Dostum blanched and looked away. Clearly I had broken a local taboo. In Afghan culture it was unheard of to ask about another man's wife.

Dostum acted as if I had not mentioned her name and instead talked about his work in the natural gas and oil fields in his youth. He also talked about the Kizil Ayak Sheikh and the village of the same name. On that day I was taken to the village of Kizil Ayak and met some of the local Uzbek and Turkmen wrestlers whom Dostum had fought there in his youth. One of them, Nebi Pahlawan, joked about Dostum and claimed that Dostum had bitten him during one of their matches. He told me to tell Dostum what he had said when I next saw him.

That evening when I returned to Shiberghan and asked Dostum about his wrestling experiences in the town, he laughed and said that it was actually Nebi who had bitten him, not the other way around.

I then asked the general to tell me about the Darya Suf campaign, but he told me to be patient; first he would tell me of his rise from a simple foot soldier to a general who had the power to overthrow President Najibullah. On the following day when Dostum met with me, he showed me pictures from a scrapbook. They featured images of a smiling younger version of him sporting a dark black mustache and a green Communist government uniform.

"Back then, when I fought for the government against the rebels, I really thought we were fighting for the future of Afghanistan," he said. "We could not understand why the USA, a land where women were free, would support the fundamentalist mujahideen. I'd never met an American before, but I felt that they would cease their support for the mujahideen if they only knew what we were trying to build under the Communists. We were increasing literacy, building schools and clinics, freeing women, fighting the mullahs. The same things the Americans want for Afghanistan today. By Afghan standards many of the Americans would have been 'Communists,' since they stood for these same things we did. But the Americans were obsessed with beating the Soviets; they did not care about the impact of their proxy war on the Afghan people. We were all pawns in their war with the Soviets. When the mujahideen took control of the country and forced women into their burqas, we paid the price for the Americans' victory."

I found Dostum's views of the war to be diametrically opposed to my own. As a college student in the 1980s, I had idolized Massoud and his Soviet-killing rebels. Like most Americans at the time, I had overlooked the mujahideen's fundamentalist tendencies and focused on their role as freedom fighters. Listening to Dostum I came to see the war against the Soviets not in black-and-white terms but in gray hues. It was in this gray zone that Dostum, a moderate Parchami "Communist," had clearly operated. I also read between the lines and realized that Dostum had certainly fought as an opportunist who used the war to increase his own power, regardless of the noble motives he attributed to himself.

"When the mujahideen conquered Kabul, the first thing they did was start forcing women out of jobs and schools. But in the north here I kept the universities and schools open to women. You should see one of my schools tomorrow."

The following day I was driven to a girls' school named for Khadija that was sponsored by Dostum—most classrooms had a picture of him none-too-subtly hung on the walls. When I entered the school I was shocked to see hundreds of unveiled high school–age girls shyly posing for pictures and learning English, sewing, and computer skills. After seeing women and girls merely as burqa-clad wraiths with no faces, it was wonderful to meet these girls without veils on. Several of the girls told me stories about life under the Taliban, and one girl broke into tears as she recalled the killing of her father by the Taliban's dreaded Committee for the Promotion of Virtue and Prevention of Vice. The girls told me that they had been forced out of school for three years by the Taliban; many of them were only now catching up on classes that had been disrupted years earlier.

But not all education had been disrupted. The girls told me of one brave woman who had continued to teach them in an underground home school during the Taliban occupation. This teacher had risked her life to continue to teach them basic math, literature, and the sciences. If I wanted to meet a real hero, I had to meet Meryem Ayubi. I was told that she now ran an orphanage for war orphans that was also funded and run by General Dostum. So on the following day, we drove out to meet this courageous woman.

Like the schoolgirls, Meryem had nothing but praise for Dostum and told me that he had funded her orphanage since the early 1990s. Lining up dozens of adorable orphans, she had them sing a song thanking Dostum and another song welcoming me to the school. Looking at the smiling children, I saw them as the ultimate victims of the fighting between men that had shattered their lives and taken away their parents. There was little glory in the suffering that had been inflicted on them or in the misery of countless widows who had lost their husbands fighting under Dostum or anyone else.

But Meryem clearly saw Dostum as a protector rather than a warlord with blood on his hands. "On the day the Pasha arrived to liberate us from the Taliban in 2001, thousands of Shiberghan's women lined the road to cheer for him," she told me. "When we travel to his compound to get funding for our schools and orphanages, he treats us as equals, not as inferior women. He is unique for Afghanistan's leaders. If he is a warlord, then he is the only pro–women's rights warlord in the country, maybe in the world!" she proclaimed. She may have been exaggerating to keep the support of the local warlord, but I had no doubt her overall sentiments were real.

That evening I saw several women who were local politicians meeting Dostum at his compound. Like Meryem Ayubi they were unveiled. I wondered why this aspect of Dostum's character had never been discussed by the reporters who had highlighted the more unsavory aspects of his personality. While it was obvious that Dostum was giving me a tour designed to impress me, the girls and women I saw that day had expressed genuine gratitude toward the Pasha.

On the following day Dostum finally began to talk about his wars with the Taliban. He admitted that when the Taliban first appeared on the scene he had not seen them as a threat to his well-defended realm.

"When they first appeared in the south and began fighting against the southern mujahideen," he said, "it did not bother me that much. It was just one group of fundamentalists fighting another. I never thought they would attempt to conquer the whole country. Massoud and Rabbani thought the same thing; everyone underestimated them. Their arrival on the scene allowed me to patch things up with Massoud, who was actually quite reasonable. I had always resented him for not giving me the respect I and my men deserved. When the Taliban came, he and President Rabbani finally treated us with respect. They treated us as allies."

I asked Dostum when he had first begun to understand how fanatical the Taliban were.

He responded, "It was not until they defeated Ismail Khan and took Herat that I began to hear stories of their religious brutality and their violence toward non-Pashtuns. They really were something new to Afghanistan. They were totally uncompromising, whereas the mujahideen were always willing to compromise and make deals in the Afghan fashion. The Taliban believed that God ordained everything they did. They stood for everything I hated, and it's not surprising that they labeled me an infidel."

Dostum paused to stare at me and then abruptly offered a most unexpected suggestion. "You must meet the Taliban yourself to understand their blind belief in their mission. I'll have Ehsan take you to the prison where I have thousands of Taliban prisoners of war being housed. President Karzai wants me to release them immediately, but I've warned him they will only cause trouble. You must see them yourself to understand."

With that, he ushered me out to one of his SUVs and had me driven to his fortresslike prison on the outskirts of Shiberghan. When we got there I was confronted by a medieval-style, high-walled prison with giant iron gates. Filming as I went, I was led through the creaking iron doors and taken to the prison's infirmary. There I saw my first Taliban. They stared at me with blank looks on their faces, although it was obvious from my clothes, blue eyes, and sandy-brown hair that I was a Western infidel.

From there we went to the prison's kitchen, where several prisoners were stirring gruel in large, steaming vats. The scene looked like something out of a movie set in the Middle Ages. But the real shock took place when we walked into a courtyard with several cellblocks leading into it. The blocks were labeled "Afghanistan Block" and "Pakistan Block." My guard took me to the Pakistan Block, where I saw several bearded Taliban, including one who looked to be in his sixties, staring out at me through the prison bars.

Behind them, squeezed into a long block, were hundreds more of their comrades. I realized that, when the other blocks were included, I was standing in the presence of thousands of Taliban prisoners of war. It was slightly unnerving being in the midst of so many of the enemy. My hackles involuntarily rose as I met the prisoners' blank stares. I realized that some of these prisoners may have been involved in the uprising at Qala-e-Jangi that had led to the death of CIA agent Micheal Spann.

To cover my fears I pulled out my camera and took several pictures of the Taliban prisoners. Then my Uzbek guards unceremoniously dragged several of them out into the courtyard and let me interview them via Zari, who spoke both Pashtho and Urdu, the main language of Pakistan.

The interviews were fascinating. I encountered everything from unapologetic hatred for America and everything it stands for to one Taliban prisoner who condemned 9/11 and bin Laden. The prisoners spoke with horror of what it had been like to be bombed by the US air force during the 2001 campaign. One prisoner described in particularly graphic terms how frightening it had been to be hunted at night by AC-130 gunships at Kunduz: he believed the Americans had unleashed demons on them.

Several of the Taliban I interviewed had also fought at Darya Suf and spoke in fearful terms about the shock of being overwhelmed by Dostum's Uzbek cavalry. Many of them appeared to have symptoms of post-traumatic stress disorder and seemed to have a hard time grasping their tragic fate. I gradually began to feel sorry for many of the prisoners, who appeared to have joined the Taliban jihad out of a misguided urge to protect their faith from infidels. Many expressed regret at having volunteered to come to Afghanistan to wage war against fellow Muslims from the Northern Alliance.

When I asked the prisoners if they were aware of any large-scale massacres of hundreds, if not thousands, of their comrades on the convoys from Kunduz to Shiberghan, they denied any knowledge of such an event. They did, however, freely recount stories of extreme brutality at the hands of their captors, and the discomforts of the convoys and life in prison. Most spoke openly, and several condemned Dostum as a "bad Muslim" for fighting against them alongside the United States. I found their candor to be surprising considering they were being held in a medieval-style prison in the back of nowhere by a supposedly merciless and bloodthirsty warlord.

Zari seemed to be unconcerned by their comments and merely said, "You see, I told you they were fanatics. Can you believe they ruled over our lands for over three years! Your 9/11 was nothing by comparison; imagine if they had conquered New York instead of just attacking it once."

On the following day Dostum introduced me to a famous comrade-in-arms named Ahmed Khan. The general told me that he would be busy for a few days but that Ahmed Khan would take me with him to his compound in the eastern province of Samangan and entertain me. Once again I was driven across the northern desert, this time to the town of Aibek, the capital of Samangan Province. Ahmed Khan was the local Uzbek warlord who ran things in Aibek much as Dostum did in the west.

When I arrived, Ahmed Khan warmly greeted me and told me his story. As his name indicated, he was a khan, a member of the wealthy landowning elite. In 1978 when the Communists launched their land redistribution program, his father lost considerable land. In response, the elder Khan had led the local Uzbek villagers into the hills of southern Samangan to wage jihad.

Ahmed Khan had been too young to follow his father at the time but had smuggled food up to him and his men. Later, when his father was killed by the Soviets, his oldest brother had taken over as head of the mujahideen band, but he too had been killed. Ahmed Khan, who had by then proven himself as a fighter, was chosen to lead their band. He fought the Soviets until they withdrew, but his fighters then came under pressure from Massoud in the east. Pressured by Tajik mujahideen, Ahmed Khan had gone over to Dostum with his men like many other Uzbek mujahideen had done at the time.

Since then he had been a loyal ally of Dostum and had stayed in Afghanistan to fight the Taliban from the mountains when the Pasha fled to Turkey. He and his men had gathered in the mountains at Balkhab to meet Dostum when he returned in April 2001. From there Ahmed Khan led his men in fighting out of the Darya Suf and helped Dostum and Lal take Mazar-e-Sharif.

After the war Ahmed Khan became a member of parliament and broke with Dostum for a while before rejoining him. He later accused Dostum of trying to have him killed in retaliation for breaking with him, and I sensed that it would be unhealthy to be on the powerful warlord's bad side.

Having given me his life story, Ahmed Khan took me to some ancient Buddhist ruins in the hills above his city. Standing on the ruins of the Throne of Rustem, he pointed into the deserts and hills to the west and told me that it was there the Taliban had been defeated in November 2001. He then offered to have his nephew, Hikmet, who had fought in the campaign, drive me into the hills to show me the terrain between Mazar-e-Sharif and the Tangi Gap where Dostum and his *cheriks* had fought.

On the following day we drove westward into the sand dune–like hills for hours, stopping occasionally at a nomadic Uzbek encampment of yurts to meet locals. Finally we arrived at a clay-walled fort on a hill facing the Tangi Gap. Carefully avoiding land mines that Dostum's men had planted around the fort walls, Hikmet pointed to the southwest. On the horizon we could see a wall of mountains with a narrow pass in the middle.

"We fought our way out of the mountains with the help of the Americans and their bombs," Hikmet explained. "The explosions were incredible. US bombs, Taliban multirocket launcher rounds, whinnying horses, screaming men. Nothing can convey to you what it was like at the Battle of Tangi Gap. Dostum led from the front, and the Americans moved like locusts around the battlefield, calling to their bombers. Like Dostum told us, it was a battle of the ages. Our children and grandchildren will know this story, and now you will share it with your own people."

Now that I had heard the story of the campaign from both the Taliban prisoners and Ahmed Khan and his men, it was time to travel back to Shiberghan to get the story from Dostum himself. Along the way we decided to stop by the famous Shrine of Ali in Mazar-e-Sharif. After several hours we arrived at the mosque, which glimmered blue in the hundred degree–plus

heat. I noticed women in white burqas gliding across the marble courtyard surrounding the sacred spot and worshippers removing their shoes to
pray in the mosque. Although I was not a Muslim, my secular Uzbek hosts
assured me I could visit the mosque with them if I kept a low profile. Following them with some trepidation, I removed my shoes, walked across the
hot courtyard with burning feet, and entered the cool sanctuary.

As I left the glaring sunlight and entered the dark confines of the
mosque, my eyes tried to adjust to the gloom. The first thing I noticed was
a cauldron-shaped holy relic on the right with pilgrims crawling around it.
This was the famous Dik-i Ali, the Drum of Ali, which Sufi Muslims far and
wide believe has magical powers. Devotees circled around the drum-shaped
cauldron on their knees to gain Ali's protection. Their murmuring and
chanting echoed throughout the mosque, and I sensed they were invok-
ing the aid of ancient powers that were far older than either the Prophet
Muhammad or his son-in-law Ali.

But as I attempted to follow my turbaned Uzbek friends deeper into the
confines of the shrine, I was abruptly halted by a bearded mullah who sensed
that I was not a Muslim. He angrily demanded that I recite the fatiha, the
opening verse of the Koran, to prove that I was a believer. I stumbled over
the fatiha and recited the first part—*Bismillahi rahmani rahim Al hamdu lil-
lahi rabbil alamin* ("In the name of Allah, the most gracious, the most mer-
ciful. All praises to Allah, Lord of the Universe")—but then forgot the rest.

Sensing my discomfort, my Uzbek hosts whispered for me to put some
money in the alms bowl the mullah had before him, so I quickly did as I
was told. The mullah seemed to be mollified by my offerings and incomplete
fatiha and waved me in. With a pounding heart, I entered the holy of holies
of the shrine, the tomb of Ali, the most sacred place in Afghanistan. I followed the counterclockwise movement of believers who moved around the
tomb chanting prayers. Then I made my way back out into the glaring light
to continue my journey, awed by the ancient shrine.

As we drove westward, my companions asked me if I wanted to make
a visit to the famous fortress of Qala-e-Jangi. I was told that Dostum had

some business there and would briefly meet us. It was in this nineteenth-century Wauberian fortress built by the Iron Amir, Abdur Rahman, that the Taliban had risen up and killed CIA agent Micheal Spann. I was excited to see the site of both an al-Qaeda last stand and the capture of John Lindh, the American Talib, and promptly said yes.

Half an hour later, the massive fortress appeared on the left side of the road. We were waved into the castle and met the Uzbek fort commander, who gave us a guided tour. The tour started out with a visit to Dostum's plush living quarters, following which we made our rounds of the walls. Along the way we stood in craters made by US precision-guided bombs dropped during the suppression of the November 2001 Taliban prisoner uprising. Then we made our way down to the epicenter of the uprising, a structure in the central courtyard known as the Pink House, which had housed the prisoners.

Along the way we met Dostum and then passed a five-foot-tall marble obelisk with an engraving on the side in Uzbek, Dari, and English. I was amazed to see that it was a marker thanking the hero Micheal Spann for his sacrifice in freeing the United States and Afghanistan from terrorism. I was touched to see that Dostum had built a memorial to the brave CIA officer who had died so far from his homeland, fighting against those who had attacked the United States on 9/11. I asked if many other foreigners had seen his memorial to his American friend, and he responded in the negative; I was among the first Western "tourists" to see it.

Leaving the lonely memorial to Spann, we parted ways with Dostum and made our way to the Pink House itself. I was told that the Taliban prisoners of war had been placed in the basement below the building after one of them had blown himself up trying to kill a man he thought was Dostum. From there, they had burrowed their way into a nearby ammunition depot and charged out with guns blazing. But their rebellion had been suppressed by US aerial bombardments, and the survivors had fled back to the cellar with their guns. There Commander Lal and his men had attacked them by shooting into ventilation shafts and eventually diverting a freezing cold rivulet from a nearby stream into the basement. Finally the remaining Taliban, including John Walker Lindh, had surrendered.

Excited to see the actual scene of the battle, I made my way down a metal staircase to the basement but was overwhelmed by the smell. Peering into the gloom below, I saw spent RPG rounds, bullet and artillery casings, tattered clothes, and other telltale signs of slaughter. My guides told me there were still live rounds and dead bodies down in the darkness so I chose not to descend into the charnel pit. I shivered as I imagined the horrors that had taken place in this spot just a year and half earlier and then made my way back up into the daylight.

From Qala-e-Jangi we drove back to Shiberghan. The next day I pressed Dostum to tell me more about the November 2001 Darya Suf campaign. While there had been some reports in the press about American heroics in the campaign, Dostum and his men had been relegated to the role of mere native backdrops to American heroism. I wanted to know more about the Uzbek perspective on the campaign. Dostum again praised his American comrades, whom he always referred to as his *dosts* (friends) and *jasurs* (brave men), and then agreed to discuss the campaign. But first he wanted to show me something that he thought was an important starting point to understanding the campaign: his horses.

We drove to a clay-walled stable near Dostum's actual home, and there he showed me the secret to his men's success in the war. The first horse he pointed out was his white stallion, Surkun, the one he had ridden in the mountains. He told me that Surkun had been trained to run for cover when he heard the sound of Taliban MiGs hunting the *cheriks* from the sky. On more than one occasion Surkun had saved his life, and I could see that Dostum valued his four-legged comrade. From Surkun, Dostum took us to several other horses. He explained that they had been ridden by the Green Berets of ODA 595. He showed me one horse named Saman (meaning "yellow") that had been ridden by "Mark Commander" and told me he was keeping the horse for the day that his American master Captain Nutsch returned.

Dostum explained to me that the horses were the secret of the Uzbeks' success. They could go places the Taliban pickups could not, and they got his soldiers across contested terrain in battle quicker than on foot. They also gave his men a feeling of momentum that helped them emerge victorious from several key battles. He bemoaned the fact that so many horses had been killed in the Qala-e-Jangi uprising. "They survived the fighting in the hills and were heroes, but they did not survive the American bombs and Taliban gunfire at the fortress."

From the stables Dostum took me to his house, where he proudly showed me a certificate given to him by an American Green Beret A-Team; the document made him an honorary member for his role in fighting the terrorists in Operation Enduring Freedom. He also showed me a Sig pistol given to him as a gift by Central Command leader General Tommy Franks after the campaign had ended. He seemed to genuinely prize these tokens of American appreciation, and I could see that he was proud of his ties to America.

I asked Dostum to see his famous green *chapan* and was disappointed to hear that he had given it to one of the Americans as a gift. Somewhere in America, the silk riding jacket worn by General Dostum in his mountain campaign now resides in someone's closet as a souvenir of the 2001 war.[4]

Having shown me his prizes, Dostum sat down with me on his porch and told me the entire story of the incredible November 2001 charge down the Darya Suf and Balkh valleys to Mazar-e-Sharif. He began by telling me how lonely the campaign was before the Americans came. "To tell you the truth, when I left my family in Turkey and returned to the mountains to fight the Taliban in April of 2001, I did not know if I would ever see them again. It was the hardest decision of my life. My family called it a suicide mission and begged me not to go back to Afghanistan. They were crying terribly, but I had to do it. Too many of my men were dying in the mountains without me; they needed me."

I asked him what he felt when he heard about the attacks on America on 9/11, and he paused before responding.

"I never thought the Americans could be attacked that way—they seemed so modern, so rich. But the evil in my country did not know borders, and it came to America. I knew when I heard the news of the attacks that the Americans would be coming. I knew I would want revenge if they'd done the same thing to my country, so surely the powerful Americans would.

"When Commander Mark and his soldiers arrived, they quickly grew to trust us. Americans are like that, they quickly become friends. We were never friends with the Russians; they never trusted us, and we didn't trust them. But the Americans were different. They believed in what they were doing. The Russians didn't. For that, we all admired them. They were courageous and had a sense of mission that inspired my own men.

"All the Americans, including the ones from the CIA, fought well. They were my friends. Of course the greatest gift my American friends brought us was bombs. The precision of their bombs was something I had never seen before. My men believed it was almost magic, and I encouraged them in this belief. I let them know that the Americans were like angels. My men truly believed they were going to do as our ancestors had done and overcome the larger enemy with the help of our own killer angels. History would repeat itself!

"Once we got our momentum, I worked hard to keep it going. It was crucial that we not stop. If we had stopped, the Taliban might have regained the momentum, and we could have all been killed. Our victory was not inevitable; we could have all been wiped out on more than one occasion. That's what makes our seizure of Mazar-e-Sharif so extraordinary. There were so many more of the enemy than us. And we were divided. Ustad Atta was more interested in getting an edge on me than defeating the common enemy. The Americans did not speak our language. The al-Qaeda fighters were determined to fight to the death. We were very low on ammunition. So many things were against us. We needed a miracle, and that's what we got. It was far from inevitable, as some people suggest in hindsight."

As Dostum described the brutal warfare that saw his small force of Americans, Uzbeks, Turkmen, Hazaras, and Tajiks push down the Balkh Valley toward the prize of Mazar-e-Sharif, his eyes lit up. I could see that he was losing himself in the story, and several times my translator had to ask him to slow down so he could translate. While Dostum often began his stories in simple Turkish so I could understand, when he got excited he invariably switched into Uzbek.

As he relayed his account, he asked one of his servants to bring me something to help him tell the story. The servant quickly came back with a photo album, and there they were: Dostum, R.J., Micheal Spann, Mark Nutsch, Bart Decker, ODA 595, Lal, Fakir, and Ahmed Khan, all caught in action by an unknown Uzbek combat photographer. The pictures were extraordinary. Images of Americans in tan camo uniforms, Dostum with CIA agent Micheal Spann the day before his death, Dostum on horseback in his green *chapan* with a red Turkmen carpet behind him. There were even pictures of Dostum meeting with Massoud when he first returned in April 2001 to fight the Taliban. The photos were an extraordinary historical record of one of the most important military campaigns in modern history.

Dostum waved to his servant, and he brought in some black leather saddles that the Pasha told me had been airdropped for the Americans who did not like the Uzbek's small wooden saddles. He also showed me a beautiful red Turkmen carpet that he had slept on every night while fighting in the mountains. I noticed that it still had sand in it, and I could imagine the general wrapping himself in it at night to keep out the mountain cold.

Dostum told me what it had been like to finally arrive in his former capital of Mazar-e-Sharif after so many years in exile: "It was a miracle, *khoja*, a real miracle. Just like the ancient battles. We were two thousand men fighting against fifty thousand, yet *we* went on the offensive. My men firmly believed we would win just like our ancestors did against their enemies. That was our secret—we believed we could do it.

"I will always be grateful to Commander Mark and the other American 'angels' for helping us make it possible. The day I walked into the Shrine of Ali and finally said my prayers was one of the greatest days of my life."

Several nights later I told Dostum that my time in the realm of the Uzbeks of Turkistan had run out and I had to return home. Dostum seemed to be disappointed to have me go. I could tell that in many ways it had been cathartic for him to be able to tell his side of the story to someone from the same land that had sent reporters who seemed bent on destroying his reputation. I was perhaps the first foreigner he had told his whole story to, and I could tell that he wanted me to get it straight, even if it was one that was designed to make him look good.

For my part I had to admit that for all my earlier skepticism, I had come to see Dostum in a less negative light. While I knew I could take a lot of what the general said with a grain of salt—he was trying to rehabilitate his image as a man who was part warlord, part opportunist, part mercenary— the gist of his story rung true. There was no doubt that he was a genuine hero to his own oppressed people, and I felt it was my mission to share that aspect of his identity with my people.

Before I left his house, Dostum told me he had one more thing to show me. He got up abruptly and sighed as if he were doing something he didn't want to do. He led me out to his truck, where his loyal bodyguard Akram and several other guards awaited him. I heard Dostum tell him to take us to the house, and we drove into Shiberghan. We suddenly stopped at a rather average-looking structure, and Dostum and his bodyguards got out. Dostum breathed deeply and told me that this was the house he had lived in with his wife Khadija back in the 1980s and early 1990s. With tears in his eyes, Dostum told me the story of how he first met the woman he would marry. After their marriage they had lived here and had children. It was here, he told me, that Khadija had died in an accident with a rifle.

I was stunned by the story and wanted to investigate it further, but realized I had already probed too far into territory that few Afghan men discuss. The historian in me wanted to track down the maids who had been with Khadija at the time of her death to see if they could corroborate Dostum's account. But I knew this was simply impossible in a land where women could not talk to strange men, especially about such a sensitive topic that had happened many years earlier. While my mind instantly created alternative scenarios to explain Khadija's tragic death—could it have been suicide? murder?—I was left with just one account of her demise, Dostum's.

With that, Dostum suddenly turned away and re-entered the SUV. I could tell the visit had been difficult for him, but I felt it was crucial that I know this final secret of Dostum's pain. Perhaps the loss explained as much about the man as any talk of moderate Parchami Communism, Najibullah's betrayal, Uzbek repression at the hands of Pashtun Taliban, or distaste for the excesses of jihadism. I now felt I finally understood the man who was an enigma to so many.

On the following afternoon I prepared to say good-bye to the Pasha. Just before my truck arrived to take me back to Kabul, Dostum's convoy arrived in a cloud of dust. Dostum emerged wearing a *shalwar kameez* over which he wore a Western-style blazer, his uniform of choice. By his side were two teenagers, whom he introduced as his sons, Batur and Yar.

Having introduced his sons, Dostum smiled and waved for one his followers to fetch something. He told me he had some gifts for me. Not knowing what to expect, I was surprised when the servant emerged from the truck with a beautiful, handwoven red Turkmen carpet. I instantly recognized it. It was the carpet that Dostum had always had rolled behind his saddle in the pictures I'd seen of him fighting on horseback in the mountains.

"Pasha, I can't accept such a gift," I told him, but he only smiled and waved for another servant to bring me another gift.

The other servant emerged with a photo album. When I opened it up, I realized it was the album of Dostum's mountain campaign that I had been shown the night before. I was at a loss for words, and Dostum seemed to take great pleasure in having flummoxed me. All of his guards beamed with smiles as I sputtered and tried to tell him that I could not possibly accept such valuable gifts.

Patting me on the shoulder, Dostum called me his friend and thanked me for having come so far to tell his story to my countrymen. "When you are done writing your book, you can return to Afghanistan and give me my pictures back. I trust you, *khoja*. Now have a safe trip back to your world and don't forget the world you saw here."

We shook hands, and I boarded my awaiting truck for the long trek back over the plains and mountains to Kabul. My last image of Dostum was of him waving to me from the compound courtyard with his hand on his son Batur's shoulder. As I drove away I realized I had perhaps witnessed the twilight of Dostum's career as a warlord. There seemed to be no room for men like him in a centralizing, modernizing Afghanistan that was now being run by a class of technocrats and recently returned expatriates who had never fought for their country. They were the future of the Uzbeks, not this man whose life had been spent fighting.

On my final night I had asked Dostum about his seeming irrelevance in the new scheme of things, and he had given me a sad smile. "Perhaps that is for the best, *khoja*. It's time for a new generation who don't have blood on their hands to build our nation. Perhaps it is fitting that I am my people's last warlord. That would make me very happy indeed. That is my wish for my people."

I was not sure if I believed him, since I knew he was still actively maneuvering to keep his power in the north. Those who crossed him still did so at their own risk. And if the Taliban ever did come back, I was sure he would use his old networks to once again lead his people against them. While it might have been the twilight of his career, it was not yet over.

Looking back in my rearview mirror, I could see that Dostum was gone. I silently prayed that for his sake and the sake of his people, his wish, if true, might come to pass.

EPILOGUE

I N DECEMBER 2001 Mark Nutsch and Tiger 02 were called home from
their deployment to Afghanistan. Afterward they were personally
greeted by Secretary Rumsfeld and feted as heroes. Their extraordinary
light-footprint campaign is credited by military historians with enabling
the disunited and outgunned Northern Alliance to take down the Taliban
in a matter of weeks. Soon after returning to America, Nutsch and the other
team members began a *Flags of Our Fathers*–style tour of major US military
facilities, speaking on their unparalleled successes against such great odds.
Upon returning home, Nutsch also had the joy of meeting his newborn
daughter, Kaija, whom his wife Amy had delivered in Kansas while he was
fighting in the Hindu Kush with Dostum.

In 2002 the Kansas State Legislature publicly honored Captain Mark
Nutsch, the head of Tiger 02, in a ceremony held in the capital. During the
ceremony, Nutsch modestly claimed that he was "no hero." Mark would
later return to Afghanistan with several other ex–Special Forces to help run
a charity for Afghan children known as Afghan Care Today. There he was
warmly greeted by his old comrades from the Darya Suf campaign, including Dostum, Mohaqeq, and Ustad Atta. To this day Nutsch is outspoken in
his praise of the unsung Uzbeks, Tajiks, and Hazaras who fought alongside
his small team of Green Berets in October and November 2001.

In 2003 Bill Bennett, army sergeant first class, one of the twelve members of ODA 595/Tiger 02 and leader of Charlie Team, died of wounds he received when his unit executed a raid on enemy forces in Ramadi, Iraq.[1]

In 2003 Master Sergeant Bart Decker retired from the air force's elite Twenty-Third Special Tactics Squadron based at Hurlburt Field, Florida. He and his wife and daughters now live near their former base in the Florida panhandle. A blown-up version of the famous picture of Bart riding on horseback with Uzbek riders in the background, which Secretary Rumsfeld showed to the media in 2001, now hangs in the Smithsonian's American History Museum.

After his initial deployment to Afghanistan in 2001, Air Force Staff Sergeant Matt Lienhard took up an assignment with the Twenty-Fourth Special Tactics Squadron at Fort Bragg, North Carolina. Upon successful completion of his operator's training course he was assigned to a tactical team there. After that he participated in the 2003 invasion of Iraq and ultimately completed a remarkable five combat tours in Iraq and five in Afghanistan. He spent those deployments attached to both the army and navy special operations teams, where he conducted dozens of direct action and reconnaissance missions. Having survived this extensive combat experience he became the noncommissioned officer in charge of joint air force combat control and para-rescue team known as USAF Special Tactics Team. He is married to his wife, Nikki, and has a two-year-old daughter named Jesse.

In 2004 Dostum's number two, Commander Lal, died of a massive heart attack that many claimed was a result of the years of stress from fighting in the mountains. Dostum went into mourning for a year and refused to let his daughter Rahila marry until the mourning period was over. Lal is now buried in the martyrs' cemetery in Shiberghan, near Dostum's childhood friend and former comrade Yar.

In 2005 Dostum survived a close brush with death when an al-Qaeda suicide bomber blew himself up near the general during a public prayer ceremony at a soccer stadium in Shiberghan.[2] His younger brother, Abdul

Kadir, who was wearing a thick green *chapan* jacket given to him by his older brother Mohammad, absorbed much of the bomb's shrapnel. The attempted assassination, a failed reprise of the killing of Massoud, was said to be punishment for Dostum's key role in assisting the US in Operation Enduring Freedom. Ironically, the bombing came at a time when many voices in America and the West were trying to have Dostum arrested as a "war criminal" for killing too many Taliban in the desperate 2001 campaign.

Later in 2005 I returned to Afghanistan with my new wife, Feyza, and introduced her to Dostum. The first thing I did was give Dostum back his photos, having made copies of them in America. Dostum treated us like royalty for over a month and let us live in his compound in Shiberghan. During this time, Feyza, who is from Istanbul, Turkey, befriended Dostum and his daughters and traveled with me from the Panjshir Valley in the east to Khoja Doko in the west and to Bamiyan in the south with the son of the Kizil Ayak Sheikh, Seracettin Mahdum.

In 2006 the CIA built an exhibit at its headquarters in Langley, Virginia, to showcase the role of CIA Special Activity Division agents in the Darya Suf campaign. It features a mannequin of agent David Tyson wearing a local *chapan*. The exhibit highlights the extraordinary role of the Agency in the campaign but makes little reference to the equally important role of Dostum and the Uzbeks. David Tyson still works for the CIA in Muslim Eurasia. His comrade R.J., aka "Baba Jan," has retired to New Mexico, and the slain agent Micheal Spann, the first US combat fatality in the war on terror, was given a CIA Intelligence Star and a hero's burial in Arlington National Cemetery in 2001.

In 2008 President Karzai exiled Dostum as a *jang salar* (warlord) to Turkey, where he lived with his wife and children in Ankara. Dostum and seventy of his followers were accused of kidnapping and beating a rival Turkmen political leader who had betrayed him and was working to undermine his support in the north in favor of Karzai. The Turkmen leader was freed only after government troops surrounded Dostum's compound in Kabul and forced a defiant Dostum to release him.[3]

Dostum's Uzbek people nonetheless submitted numerous petitions to the Karzai government asking that their defender be returned to help them fight Taliban insurgents who had begun infiltrating their lands from Kunduz and Faryab. They also promised to vote en masse for President Karzai's rival, a Tajik former aid for Massoud, Dr. Abdullah Abdullah, in the August 2009 elections if Dostum was not allowed to return.

On August 16, 2009, Karzai allowed Dostum to return to a hero's welcome as thousands of his followers greeted him at Kabul International Airport. As part of the deal, Dostum convinced his people to vote for Karzai. Dostum's reputation as Afghanistan's most resilient warlord was once again established, and he is now living in Shiberghan, Mazar-e-Sharif, and Kabul, where he has compounds. He has repeatedly asked the Karzai government for permission to fight his Taliban enemies. Thus far the government has rejected his request to create a militia to fight the increasingly bold Taliban insurgents in the Kunduz area. That may change as the Taliban increase their strength following the American/NATO withdrawal and when Karzai is replaced.

In August 2012, Ahmed Khan, Dostum's loyal commander and ex-mujahideen, was killed in a suicide bombing in Aibek held during the wedding of his daughter. The bomber was said to be a Taliban terrorist punishing the warlord for fighting the Taliban in the 2001 campaign.[4]

In October 2012 a three-ton, eighteen-foot bronze statue of a horse-mounted Green Beret entitled *De Oppresso Liber* (the Green Beret motto: "Free the oppressed"), created by sculptor Douwe Blumberg to honor the A-Teams of Afghanistan, was placed in the shadow of One World Trade Center, the new skyscraper rising up to replace the destroyed World Trade Center towers. Lieutenant General John Mulholland, the former colonel who directed the overall A-Team insertions into Afghanistan in October 2001, Mark Nutsch, and several other Green Beret "horse soldiers" reunited there for the dedication.

In January 2013 the Green Berets reestablished their severed contact with Dostum and sent a twelve-man team to liaise with him in Shiberghan and make contingency plans for a post-US withdrawal resurgence of the Taliban on the plains of Turkistan. Dostum joyfully celebrated the return of his American *"dosts"* by staging a public *buzkashi* game that the special forces participated in. Before leaving, the Americans were all given gifts of ceremonial green *chapans* to wear as a sign of honor. The CIA also reestablished contact with Dostum and are reassessing his role in a post-2014 Afghanistan that will likely see a rise in Taliban power once the American-led coalition withdraws its troops.

Today the dusty red Turkmen roll-up carpet that Dostum used in the Darya Suf campaign sits in my study in Boston. Whenever I see it, I am reminded of the Uzbek warlord across the world who befriended me and the American avengers who came to his country to fight the common enemy.

ACKNOWLEDGMENTS

FIRST AND FOREMOST I would like to thank my intrepid wife, Feyza, who married me with the understanding that I would one day take her to Paris. Instead I ended up taking her not once but twice to the war zone in Afghanistan. There she put up with the intense heat, blowing sand, travel alongside armed men, greasy food that we ate with our hands, endless off-road journeys, ever-present danger, and never-present toilets. It was a real boon having her by my side as we traveled the mountains and deserts of Afghanistan in 2005 and 2007, and I could not have researched and written this book without her strong moral support and constant encouragement.

Thanks are also due to my parents, Donna and Gareth. It was they who first encouraged my interest in the nomadic peoples of Central Asia in high school and supported my lifelong fascination with the descendants of Genghis Khan in every way imaginable. The time spent in Wales and other lands in Europe that they took me on when I was growing up also built my confidence to travel and explore on my own as I got older. While many Americans are afraid to travel the world, I was taught to see it as a place I could "conquer." As always they proofed this work and offered me excellent advice on how to write this story.

I also owe a huge debt of gratitude to General Abdul Rashid Dostum, the subject of this book. Dostum took me in when I came into his realm out of the blue, prying into his life. I found Dostum to be a generous host and wonderful storyteller, and a gentleman when I introduced him to my wife on our second trip. Dostum took considerable time from his responsibilities to meet with me and patiently tell me his remarkable story. If that was not enough, he also gave me his personal photos to embellish this volume. I could not have written this book without Dostum's proactive support, so I offer a huge *rahmat* to him.

I would also like to thank General Dostum's younger brother Abdul Kadir Dostum. Abdul Kadir proved to be a wonderful guide and storyteller in his own right. Abdul Kadir literally gave me the coat off his back, gifting me the green riding *chapan* (covered with his blood and bomb soot from a previous terrorist attack) that had been given to him by his older brother.

I also owe a tremendous debt of gratitude to Captain Mark Nutsch. Nutsch, the head of the Green Beret team that fought on horseback alongside Dostum in 2001, was an excellent eyewitness to that extraordinary campaign. His eye for detail and remarkable memory of the war were crucial to bringing the mountain campaign to life. Nutsch's recollections were surpassed only by his modesty and his genuine desire to share the credit for the campaign with the Uzbeks who fought alongside him and his men. I am grateful to Nutsch for his bravery in the 2001 mountain operations and rest better at night knowing there are men like him out there defending the rest of us.

The same holds true for Master Sergeant Bart Decker of the United States Air Force. Like Nutsch, I found Decker, who called in precision-guided bombs on the Taliban in advance of Dostum's cavalry charges, to be both self-effacing and a natural military historian. Having seen the famous photo of Decker riding on horseback in the mountains of Afghanistan that was declassified for the media by Secretary of Defense Donald Rumsfeld, it was a thrill to meet the man himself. I could not have told this story without Decker's eyewitness accounts. Decker was also kind enough to provide me with his personal photos from the war, some of the only American pictures of the extraordinary Darya Suf campaign.

This book benefited tremendously from the crucial eyewitness accounts of the Darya Suf campaign provided by Air Force combat controller Matt Lienhard. I would like to thank him for tracking me down and sharing these invaluable stories of the fight in the Hindu Kush. I was awed not only by Lienhard's remarkable account of the battle but by the fact that he would go on to partake in four more combat tours in Afghanistan and five in Iraq. America truly owes a great debt of gratitude to men like Lienhard who have repeatedly risked so much for the rest of us.

Thanks also to the Turkmen leader Seracettin Mahdum, who acted as my guide, fixer, and translator during my second trip to visit Dostum in 2005. From helping me get into the Shrine of Ali in Mazar to taking me across the Hindu Kush to the Panjshir Valley, Seracettin's assistance was invaluable. It was a real honor and privilege to work with the son of the Kizil Ayak Sheikh, one of Afghanistan's most famous holy men and head of that country's Turkmen community.

I would also like to say thanks to Ehsan Zari and Faizullah Zeki, who acted as guides and translators during my first visit to Dostum, and to Meryem Ayubi, who bravely ran an orphanage during all the years of fighting and shared her stories with me. She deserves to have a book written about her in her own right. I would also like to thank the Smith Richardson Foundation for funding my second trip to visit Dostum.

Teshekur to Tugay Tuncer of NATO and the Turkish diplomatic corps, who acted not only as a model of what an *elchibay* (gentleman diplomat) should be but also housed me in Kabul when I first arrived and arranged my initial contacts with Dostum's people. I would also like to thank Yavuz Selim and his family in Ankara, Turkey, for their hospitality and for helping me plan my second trip to Afghanistan. And I must not forget to thank my parents-in-law, Feruzan and Kemal Altindag, who provided me with a quiet summer home in which to write this book in Cesme on the Aegean coast of Turkey.

My Scottish American friend with the improbable name of Forbes McIntosh sat me down over a beer at the union at the University of Wisconsin in Madison and first suggested that I write this book, so I owe him thanks as well. I am also grateful to Andy Anderson, former Green Beret colonel, for first linking me up with the elusive Mark Nutsch, for whom I had been searching for years in hopes of interviewing him.

I would also like to thank my colleagues and chairmen Mark Santow and Len Travers for creating a wonderful work environment at the University of Massachusetts–Dartmouth that allowed me to write this book. I also owe a huge debt of gratitude to my indispensible and brilliant secretary Sue Foley, who played a vital role in this and all my other academic projects. And thanks to Brian Merrill and Tim Paicopolos for proofing this work and my former *khoja* (professor) Uli Schamiloglu for teaching me about the Turkic-Mongol nomads of Central Asia at Indiana University and the University of Wisconsin. Thanks also to my former advisor Kemal Karpat, the legendary Turkish historian. In addition, this book could not have been published had my literary agents, Faye Swetky and D. J. Herda, and my talented editor, Lisa Reardon, not believed in it and worked to improve it. Last I would like to offer my thanks to my former student Matt Chatigny for developing the YouTube documentary on Dostum titled *Realm of the Warlord.*

Any mistakes or blunders found in this book are my own and in no way reflect on all the good people above who have aided, inspired, and assisted me in this project. For further photos, articles, and videos on Dostum and Afghanistan, see brianglynwilliams.com.

NOTES

CHAPTER 1: THE WARLORD OF MAZAR

1. Tom Cooper, "Afghanistan without the Soviets," Part 3, *Air Combat Information Journal* (October 29, 2003).

2. The Taliban were far from being a group of tribal thugs. They had a small air force, the best artillery in Afghanistan, and approximately 100 tanks and 250 armored fighting vehicles. For an analysis of the Taliban army's fighting strength, see "The Taliban's Military Strength Prior to Hostilities," *Jane's Intelligence Review*, www.janes.com/defence/news/misc/jwa011008_2_n.shtml.

3. Romesh Ratnesar, "The Afghan Way of War," *Time*, November 11, 2001.

4. "Northern Alliance Takes Key City," *ABC Radio*, November 10, 2001, www.abc.net.au/am/stories/s413342.htm.

5. "Northern Alliance Takes Mazar e Sharif," *Fox News*, November 9, 2001, www.foxnews.com/story/0,2933,38385,00.html.

6. The pictures Rumsfeld showed of a US Air Force combat controller named Bart Decker can be found at www.defenselink.mil/photos/newsphoto.aspx?newsphotoid=3741.

7. Unlike the US-led invasion of Iraq, which was covered by hundreds of embedded reporters, there was little coverage from the inaccessible battlefields of Afghanistan.

8. Jim Garamone (American Forces Press Service), "Wolfowitz Shares Special Forces' Afghanistan Dispatches," November 15, 2001, www.defenselink.mil/news/newsarticle.aspx?id=44448.

9. For his part, Dostum was publicly grateful to the Americans and claimed, "We owe very much to the American forces. Without their air power, we couldn't have

defeated terrorism the way we did." "More Important than a Position in the Government Is Keeping the Peace: A Q&A with Afghan Deputy Defense Minister Abdul Rashid Dostum," *Eurasianet*, April 24, 2002.

10. Tommy Franks, *American Soldier* (New York: Regan Books, 2005), 235.

11. "Rumsfeld Calls Afghanistan Model of Success of Iraq," Defense Department Report no. 680 (August 9, 2002).

12. Sara Carter, "Big Fish among the Afghan Warlords," *Washington Times*, October 12, 2008.

13. Major Isaac Peltier, *Surrogate Warfare: The Role of US Army Special Forces* (Fort Leavenworth: School of Advanced Military Studies, n.d.), 3.

14. Sara Carter, "Big Fish."

15. Andrew Bushell, "Uzbek Warlord Remains Enigma to Outside World; Gen. Dostum, Challenger to Karzai Is Cunning, Barbaric," *Washington Times*, February 23, 2002.

16. Scott Carrier, "Over There: Afghanistan after the Fall," *Harper's,* April 2002, http://hearingvoices.com/webwork/carrier/afghan/istan3.html.

17. Jamie Doran, "Afghan Massacre: The Convoy of Death," *Information Clearinghouse*, www.informationclearinghouse.info/article3267.htm.

18. Ahmed Rashid, *Taliban: Militant Islam, Oil and Fundamentalism in Central Asia* (New Haven: Yale University Press, 2000), 56.

19. Scott Carrier, "Over There," *The Best American Travel Writing* (New York: Houghton Mifflin, 2003): 101.

20. Andrew Bushell, "Uzbek Warlord Remains Enigma."

21. Mike Ingram, "Why Britain Should be Indicted for War Crimes: The SAS Role in the Qala-i-Janghi Massacre," *World Socialist Web Site*, December 10, 2001, www.wsws.org/articles/2001/dec2001/sas-d10.shtml.

CHAPTER 2: HOW TO MEET A WARLORD

1. For the small number of US special forces involved in the "invasion" of Afghanistan, see Martin Ewans, *Conflict in Afghanistan* (New York: Routledge, 2005): 166–67.

CHAPTER 3: THE APPROACHING STORM

1. "How the Stern New Rulers of Afghanistan Took Hold," *New York Times*, December 31, 1996.

CHAPTER 4: RAIDERS

1. "Document 17 from [Excised] to DIA Washington D.C., 'IIR [Excised] Pakistan Involvement in Afghanistan,' November 7, 1996, Confidential, 2 pp. [Excised]," *National Security Archive*, www.gwu.edu/~nsarchiv/NSAEBB/NSAEBB227/index .htm#17.

2. For an analysis of the Taliban army, see "The Taliban's Military Strength Prior to Hostilities," *Jane's World Armies*, October 8, 2001, www.janes.com/defence/news /misc/jwa011008_2_n.shtml.

3. Human Rights Watch, "Pakistan's Support of the Taliban," *Human Rights Watch*, July 2001, www.hrw.org/reports/2001/afghan2/Afghan0701-02.htm#P410_114894.

4. Author's interview with Commander Hikmet in Aibek, northern Afghanistan, July 2005.

5. Human Rights Watch, "Afghanistan. Ethnically Motivated Abuses against Civilians," *Human Rights Watch*, October 2001.

CHAPTER 5: LAST LINE OF DEFENSE

1. Jonathan Mahler, *The Challenge: Hamdan vs. Rumsfeld and the Fight over Presidential Power* (New York; Farrar, Straus and Giroux, 2008), 82.

2. Steve Coll, "Flawed Ally Was America's Best Hope," *Washington Post*, February 23, 2004.

3. "Document 31. Defense Intelligence Agency, Cable, 'IIR [Excised]/The Assassination of Massoud Related to 11 September 2001 Attack,' November 21, 2001, Secret," *National Security Archive*. (See pages 4–5.)

4. Ahmed Rashid, *Descent into Chaos* (New York: Penguin, 2008), 62.

5. Based on the author's interviews with Massoud's friends and commanders in Jangalak, Panjshir Valley, 2005.

6. Bijan Omrani and Matthew Leeming, *Afghanistan: A Companion and Guide* (New York: Odyssey Books and Guides, 2005), 220–21.

7. "Document 29. Defense Intelligence Agency, Cable, 'IIR [Excised]/Veteran Afghanistan Traveler's Analysis of al-Qaeda and Taliban Military, Political and Cultural Landscape and its Weaknesses,' October 2, 2001, Secret, 7 pp.," *National Security Archive*, www.gwu.edu/~nsarchiv/NSAEBB/NSAEBB97/index .htm#doc5http://www.gwu.edu/~nsarchiv/NSAEBB/NSAEBB97/index.htm#doc5. (See pages 4–6.)

8. Jon Lee Anderson, *The Lion's Grave: Dispatches from Afghanistan* (New York: Grove Press, 2002), 193.

9. Richard Mackenzie, "The Succession: The Price of Neglecting Afghanistan," *New Republic* 219, no. 11–12 (September 14, 1998).

10. This account was conveyed to me in the village of Jangalak in Panjshir Valley, Afghanistan, by one of Massoud's bodyguards in August of 2005.

11. This account of the dangerous day of September 11 comes from my interviews with Massoud's childhood friends and companions who were with him at the time of his death. (Interviews were conducted in Jangalak, Panjshir Valley, in 2005).

12. "How Much Did Afghan Leader Know?," *CNN*, November 6, 2003.

13. Jonathan Mahler, "Hamdan: Guantánamo's Mystery Man," *Time*, July 21, 2008.

14. Steve Coll, "Flawed Ally Was Hunt's Best Hope," *Washington Post*, February 23, 2004.

15. "Afghan Opposition Leader's Fate Unclear," *BBC*, September 10, 2001.

16. "Before September 11th: The Secret History," *Time*, August 12, 2002.

17. "Afghan Opposition Leaders' Fate Unclear," *BBC*.

CHAPTER 6: THE EVIL COMES TO AMERICA

1. This previously undisclosed information was conveyed to me on December 7, 2007, while I was working as an expert witness in the Military Commissions hearing for Salim Hamdan in Guantánamo Bay, Cuba.

2. Ed Vulliamy, "The March to the Brink of Battle," *Observer*, September 23, 2001, and Luke Harding and Rory McCarthy, "War-Weary Afghans Flee in Fear," *Observer*, September 16, 2001.

3. Richard Clarke, *Against All Enemies: Inside America's War on Terror* (New York: Free Press, 2004), 23.

4. Bob Woodward and Dan Baltz, "Combating Terrorism: 'It Starts Today,'" *Washington Post*, February 1, 2002.

5. "Bring Me the Head of Bin Laden," *BBC*, May 4, 2005.

CHAPTER 7: SEARCH FOR A PLAN

1. Donald Rumsfeld, *Known and Unknown: A Memoir* (New York: Sentinel, 2011), 372.

2. Sid Jacobson and Ernie Colón, *After 9/11: America's War on Terror (2001–)* (New York: Hill and Wang, 2008), 14.

3. George Tenet, *At the Center of the Storm: My Years at the CIA* (New York: HarperCollins, 2007), 176.

4. Ibid., 186.

5. See the actual suggestion made by Richard Clarke in the recently declassified memo: "A Comprehensive Strategy to Fight Al-Qaeda?," *National Security Archive*, www.gwu.edu/~nsarchiv/NSAEBB/NSAEBB147/index.htm.

6. Hy Rothstein, *Afghanistan and the Troubled Future of Unconventional Warfare* (Annapolis: Naval Institute Press, 2006), 176.

7. Ibid., 127.

8. Maureen Dowd, "The Ballad of Bushie and Flashy," *New York Times*, January 20, 2007.

9. Romesh Ratnesar, "Into the Fray," *Time*, October 29, 2001.

10. This quote was given to me by Dostum during an interview in his compound in Shiberghan, Afghanistan, in August of 2005.

11. Ahmed Rashid, "Taliban in Key Defeat as Rebels Turn to the King," *Telegraph* (UK), September 25, 2001.

12. Tenet, *At the Center of the Storm*, 207.

13. Robin Wright, "In from the Cold and Able to Take the Heat," *Washington Post*, September 12, 2005.

14. Henry Crumpton, *The Art of Intelligence* (New York; Penguin Press, 2012), 178.

15. Ibid., 181.

16. Kathy Gannon, *I Is for Infidel: From Holy War to Holy Terror—18 Years in Afghanistan* (New York: Public Affairs, 2005), 114.

CHAPTER 8: KHOJA DOKO VILLAGE, 1954

1. G. Whitney Azoy, *Buzkashi: Game and Power in Afghanistan* (Prospect Heights, IL: Waveland Press, 2003), 11.

2. J. L. Lee, *The Ancient Supremacy: Bukhara, Afghanistan and the Battle for Balkh, 1731–1901* (Leiden, Netherlands: EJ Brill, 1996), 241.

3. For the only available account of the atrocities surrounding the Pashtuns' conquest of the lands of the Uzbeks in English, see Lee, *Ancient Supremacy*, 543–69.

4. This fortress was built in the Vauban style. Sébastien Le Prestre de Vauban was a seventeenth-century French military engineer whose fortifications revolutionized defensive warfare in Europe.

CHAPTER 9: THE FIRST BATTLES

1. In an interview with Turkish author Yavuz Selim, Dostum claimed, "When I was young, I had unhealthy contacts with the quarrelsome groups [in the village]. I was closer to the poor families' youngsters. We understood each other better." Yavuz Selim, *Dostum ve Afganistan*, 55.

CHAPTER 10: THE SOLDIER

1. This story was conveyed to me more than once by General Dostum and his brothers; it seems to have had a strong impact on them at the time.

2. From Dostum's recollection of the event, as conveyed to the author.

CHAPTER 11: THE TRAITOR

1. Dostum and his brothers recounted the speech; I have reproduced it here as best I could considering the differences in opinion and the amount of time that had passed since the event.

2. "Pahlawan" is a nickname that means strong man, hero, or wrestler.

3. This account was conveyed to me in an interview held in Gandamack Hotel, Kabul, in July of 2005, with English war correspondent Peter Jouvenal, who reported on these events.

4. Dostum's relations with the Russians do not appear to have been close. On one occasion, he and his men clashed with Russian soldiers who had needlessly killed mujahideen who were close to surrendering.

CHAPTER 12: KHADIJA

1. Phillip Corwin, *Doomed in Afghanistan: A UN Officer's Memoirs of the Fall of Kabul and Najibullah's Failed Escape, 1992* (New Brunswick: Rutgers University Press, 2003), 138.

2. This is perhaps one of the most famous stories of Dostum. I heard it from Dostum and several of his comrades.

CHAPTER 13: CONSPIRACIES

1. Marc Sageman, *Understanding Terror Networks* (Pittsburgh: University of Pennsylvania Press, 2004), 58–59.

2. Massoud was clearly interested in unifying the northern peoples against Pashtun dominance at this stage and was ahead of Dostum, who came around to the idea later. Husain Haqqani, *Pakistan: Between Mosque and Military* (New York: Carnegie Endowment for International Peace, 2005), 227.

3. For more on Najibullah's campaign to disarm Dostum's commanders, see Selim, *Dostum ve Afghanistan*, 130–38.

4. Terence White, who was in Kabul at the time, claims that Dostum's decision to revolt came when Najibullah "unwisely chose to sack his strongest supporter, Abdul Rashid Dostum." Terence White, *Hot Steel: From Soviet-Era Afghanistan*

to Post-9/11 (New York: Penguin, 2006), 81. Similarly, Barnett Rubin writes, "He [Najibullah] tried to extend the control of Pashtun military officers who were loyal to him over the northern militias by shifting key Pashtun generals into positions of command. . . . The attempt to strengthen the monitoring of the northern militias by Pashtun commanders provoked the revolt." Barnett Rubin, *The Search for Peace in Afghanistan* (New Haven: Yale University Press, 1995), 131.

5. Dostum claimed, "Uzbeks and Turkmen in the north of Afghanistan will not allow the situation where Pashtuns will be in charge of everything as in the days of old." Kh. Khasimbekov, *Uzbeki Severnogo Afganistana* [*The Uzbeks of Northern Afghanistan*] (Moscow: Russian Academy of Science, 1994), 38.

6. Selim, *Dostum ve Afghanistan*, 137.

7. Barnett Rubin, *The Fragmentation of Afghanistan* (New Haven: Yale University Press, 1995), 160.

8. Ibid., 270.

9. Ibid., 268.

10. Selim, *Dostum ve Afghanistan*, 138–39.

11. Rubin, *Fragmentation of Afghanistan*, 220.

CHAPTER 14: THE WARLORD

1. Rubin, *Fragmentation of Afghanistan*, 271–72.

2. Several sources in Kabul told me this famous phrase.

3. White, *Hot Steel*, 81.

4. Dostum told me this on more than one occasion and seemed to be hurt by the lack of recognition he received for his role in taking Kabul.

5. The provinces controlled by Dostum in whole or in part were Baghlan, Kunduz, Balkh, Samangan, Sar-e-Pol, Jowzjan, and Faryab. Tom Cooper confirms the fact that Dostum transferred Massoud's troops into the capital on his Antonov transport planes. Tom Cooper, "Afghanistan: 1979–2001," Part 3, *Air Combat Information Group Journal*, www.acig.org/artman/publish/article_339.shtml.

6. Tim Weiner, "The Commander: Rebel with Long Career of Picking Fights (and Sides)," *New York Times*, November 10, 2001.

7. Cooper, "Afghanistan: 1979–2001."

8. Antonio Giustozzi, *Empires of Mud: Wars and Warlords in Afghanistan* (New York: Columbia University Press, 2009), 106. Giustozzi claims that the Tajik-dominated Rabbani government "discriminated" against Dostum's alliance of northern mujahideen and ex-Communists known as the Harkat i Shamal (the Movement of the North).

9. M. Hassan Kakar, *Afghanistan: The Soviet Invasion and the Afghan Response, 1979–1982* (Berkeley: University of California Press, 1989), 289. Cooper, "Afghanistan: 1979–2001."

10. Ibid.

11. Amin Saikal, *Modern Afghanistan: A History of Struggle and Survival* (London: IB Tauris, 2006), 215.

12. Ibid., 216.

13. Human Rights Watch, *Blood-Stained Hands: Past Atrocities in Kabul and the Legacy of Impunity* (New York: Human Rights Watch, 2005), 96.

14. John Griffiths, *Afghanistan: A History of Conflict* (London: Andre Deutsch, 2001), 221.

CHAPTER 15: THE COUP

1. Kakar, *Afghanistan*, 289.

2. White, *Hot Steel*, 91.

3. Amin Saikal, *Modern Afghanistan: A History of Struggle and Survival* (London: IB Tauris, 2006), 216.

4. Rauf Beg, *Adi, Afghanistan'di. Talibanlarin Eline Nasil Dustu?* [*Its Name was Afghanistan. How Did It Fall into the Taliban's Hands?*], (Istanbul: Turan Kultur Vakfi, 2001), 158–59.

5. Amin Saikal, "The Rabbani Government, 1992–1996" in *Fundamentalism Reborn? Afghanistan and the Taliban*, ed. Williams Maley (London: Hurst and Co., 2001), 33.

6. Ibid.

7. Chris Stephen, "Fighters to Repay Taliban Cruelty," *Observer*, October 21, 2001.

8. *Izvestiia*, May 26, 1994.

9. Tom Cole, "The Texture of Time," *Lemar-Aftaab Afghan Magazine*, October–December 1998, www.afghanmagazine.com/oct98/articles/mazararticle/index.html.

10. Basharat Peer, "Exiled Residents of Mazar-e-Sharif Overjoyed," *Rediff.com*, November 12, 2001, www.rediff.com/us/2001/nov/12ny4.htm.

11. John Burns, "Afghan Fights Islamic Tide: As a Savior or Conqueror?," *New York Times*, October 14, 1996.

12. David Loyn, *Butcher and Bolt* (London: Hutchinson, 2008), 256.

13. Weiner, "The Commander."

14. Phillip Corwin, *Doomed in Afghanistan: A UN Officer's Memoirs of the Fall of Kabul and Najibullah's Failed Escape, 1992* (New Brunswick: Rutgers University Press, 2003), 194.

15. Rashid, *Taliban*, 50.

16. Michael Griffin, *Reap the Whirlwind: The Taliban Movement in Afghanistan* (London: Pluto Press, 2001), 49.

17. "The Afghan Arabs," Part 3, *Asharq Alaswat,* July 10, 2005, www.asharqalawsat .com/english/news.asp?section=3&id=744.

18. Ibid.

19. Angelo Rasanayagam, *Afghanistan: A Modern History* (New York: I. B. Tauris, 2005), 153.

20. Kamal Matinuddin, *The Taliban Phenomenon: Afghanistan 1994–1997* (Oxford: Oxford University Press, 1999), 95.

21. Lyon, *Butcher and Bolt*, 256.

22. ABC-TV, "Dostum the Kingmaker–Afghanistan," October 22, 1996, www.youtube .com/watch?v=xkHdrZ4C1TM.

23. Alan Johnston, "An Encounter with General Dostum," *BBC News*, October 26, 2001.

24. Selim, *Dostum ve Afganistan*, 124.

CHAPTER 16: MALIK

1. While the word originally meant "wrestler," many mujahdieen commanders adopted the name, and it came to signify a hero.

2. Antonio Giustozzi, "Respectable Warlords?: The Transition from War of All against All to Peaceful Competition in Afghanistan" (working paper, Crisis States Research Centre, London School of Economics and Political Science, London, UK, 2003), 9.

3. Mary Smith, *Before the Taliban: Living with War, Hoping for Peace* (London: Inyx, 2001), 188. Roy Gutman, *How We Missed the Story: Osama Bin Laden, the Taliban and the Hijacking of Afghanistan* (Washington, DC: United States Institute of Peace, 2008), 103.

4. Beg, *Adi, Afghanistan'di*, 279.

5. Griffin, *Reap the Whirlwind*.

6. Gutman, *How We Missed the Story*, 104.

7. Griffin, *Reap the Whirlwind*, 97.

8. Rashid, *Taliban*, 57.

9. Beg, *Adi, Afghanistan'di*, 306.

10. Ibid.

11. Selim, *Dostum ve Afganistan*, 206.

12. Ibid., 208.

13. Gutman, *How We Missed the Story*, 104.

14. Selim, *Dostum ve Afganistan*, 212.

15. Beg, *Adi, Afghanistan'di*, 313.

16. Griffin, *Reap the Whirlwind*, 99.

17. Ibid.

18. Gutman, *How We Missed the Story*, 106–7.

19. Beg, *Adi, Afghanistan'di*, 316.

20. "U.N. Tells How Taliban Were Killed by the 100's," *New York Times*, December 17, 1997.

21. Rashid, *Taliban*, 62.

22. Selim, *Dostum ve Afganistan*, 225.

23. Gutman, *How We Missed the Story*, 116–17.

24. "Afghanistan Reports of Mass Graves of Taleban Militia," *Amnesty International*, November 1, 1997.

25. Bureau of Democracy, Human Rights, and Labor, US Department of State, "Afghanistan Country Report on Human Rights Practices for 1997," *US Department of State*, March 11, 2008, http://www.state.gov/j/drl/rls/hrrpt/2007/100611.htm.

26. Selim, *Dostum ve Afganistan*, 225. Rashid, *Taliban*, 70.

27. Selim, *Dostum ve Afganistan*, 237.

28. Michael Sheridan, "No Mercy. Men, Women and Children Were Murdered in Their Homes as Taliban Gunmen Took Over Mazar e Sharif," *Sunday Times*, November 1, 1998.

29. Sheridan, "No Mercy."

30. Selim, *Dostum ve Afganistan*, 242.

31. This story was told to me by both Lal Muhammad and Dostum; I have tried to capture Dostum's words based on their retelling.

CHAPTER 17: THE AMERICANS

1. Michael Smith, *Killer Elite* (London: St. Martin's, 2008), 221.

2. Gary Schroen, *First In: An Insider's Account of How the CIA Spearheaded the War on Terror in Afghanistan* (New York: Ballantine Books, 2005), 98, 183.

3. Robin Moore, *The Hunt for Bin Laden* (New York: Random House, 2003), 133.

4. Schroen, *First In*, 182.

5. This account comes from my discussions with Dostum and from Henry Crumpton, "Intelligence and Homeland Defense," in *Transforming US Intelligence*, ed. Jennifer Sims, et al. (Washington, DC: Georgetown University Press, 2005), 170.

6. Dave Tyson's cover was later blown. A picture of him with a beard can be found at www.americanspecialops.com/cia-special-operations.

7. "Bring Me the Head of Bin Laden," *BBC*, May 4, 2005.

8. Two of the Green Berets sent in spoke Arabic and Russian, but not the local languages.

9. Moore, *Hunt for Bin Laden*, 65. *Frontline*, "Interview. US Special Forces ODA 595," *Public Broadcasting Service*, http://www.pbs.org/wgbh/pages/frontline/shows/campaign/interviews/595.html.

10. *Frontline*, "Interview. US Special Forces."

11. Ibid.

12. Robert Young Pelton, "The Legend of Heavy D and the Boys," in *American Soldier Stories of Special Forces from Iraq to Afghanistan*, ed. Nate Hardcastle (New York: Thunder's Mouth Press, 2002), 2.

13. Bob Woodward, *Bush at War* (New York: Simon and Schuster, 2002), 274.

14. *Frontline*, "Interview. US Special Forces."

15. Charles Briscoe, et al., *Weapon of Choice: ARSOF in Afghanistan* (Fort Leavenworth, KS: US Army Publications, 2003), 123.

16. Dick Camp, *Boots on the Ground* (Minneapolis: Zenith Press, 2011), 131.

17. Richard Stewart, *Special Forces in Afghanistan. Oct. 01-Mar. 02* (Carlisle Barracks, PA: Command and General Staff College, 2002), 196. (Available online at www-cgsc.army.mil/carl/download/csipubs/armed_dipl/armed_2.pdf.)

18. "Monument Honors Horse Soldiers Who Fought in Afghanistan," *CNN*, October 6, 2011.

19. Briscoe, *Weapon of Choice*, 125. *Frontline*, "Interview. US Special Forces."

20. Briscoe, *Weapon of Choice*, 127.

21. Interview with Captain Mark Nutsch in Boston, November 2011.

CHAPTER 18: THE OFFENSIVE BEGINS

1. Camp, *Boots on the Ground*, 139.

2. The previous paragraphs come from e-mails sent to the author by Captain Mark Nutsch describing the campaign.

3. Interview with Master Sergeant Bart Decker at Twenty-Third Special Tactics Squadron headquarters, Hurlburt Field, Florida, in December of 2008.

4. Stephen Biddle, *Afghanistan and the Future of Warfare: Implications for Army and Defense Policy* (Carlisle Barracks, PA: Strategic Studies Institute, 2002), 10.

5. Author interview with Mark Nutsch, Boston, November 2011.

6. Garamone, "Wolfowitz Shares."

7. Moore, *Hunt for Bin Laden*, 70.

8. E-mail sent to the author by Mark Nutsch, May 2012.

9. Camp, *Boots on the Ground*, 134.

10. Woodward, *Bush at War*, 291.

11. Ibid., 292.

12. Rumsfeld, *Known and Unknown*, 396.

13. Schroen, *First In*, 251, 268.

14. Ibid., 228.

15. Actually one air controller was sent in on the night of October 30–31, to be followed by his team on November 2.

16. Schroen, *First In*, 311.

17. Author interview with Bart Decker, Hurlburt Field, Florida.

18. Benjamin Lambeth, *Air Power Against Terror: America's Conduct of Operation Enduring Freedom* (Santa Monica: Rand, 2005), 127.

19. Communication with Bart Decker.

20. Moore, *Hunt for Bin Laden*, 77–78.

21. Wil Hylton, "Mazar i Sharif," *Esquire*, August 1, 2002.

22. After-action report from ODC 53 provided to the author by Bart Decker.

23. Hylton, "Mazar i Sharif."

24. Communication from Matt Lienhard to the author, March 2013.

25. The pictures Rumsfeld showed of Bart Decker can be found at www.defenselink.mil/photos/newsphoto.aspx?newsphotoid=3741. Another closeup of Bart Decker can be found here: www.sgtmacsbar.com/Stories/SuperWarrior/SuperWarrior.html.

26. Stephen Biddle, *Afghanistan and the Future of Warfare: Implications for Army and Defense Policy* (Carlisle Barracks, PA: Strategic Studies Institute, 2002), 38–39.

27. Schroen, *First In*, 336.

28. "Monument Honors US 'Horse Soldiers' Who Invaded Afghanistan," *CNN*, October 6, 2011.

29. Moore, *Hunt for Bin Laden*, 76–77.

30. Woodward, *Bush at War*, 252.

31. "Secretary Rumsfeld Speaks on '21st Century Transformation' of US Armed Forces" (speech given at Fort McNair, Washington, D.C., Thursday, January 31, 2002), *US Department of Defense*, www.defenselink.mil/speeches/speech.aspx?speechid=183.

32. Biddle, *Afghanistan and the Future*, 18.

33. Ibid., 34.

34. Schroen, *First In*, 249–55.

35. Dostum's bravery in battle was undisputed. Antonio Giustozzi, for example, wrote, "Dostum's martial reputation was established by 1992. As the Commander of the 53rd Div. he was known as a brave and decisive military leader who never gave up the opportunity for a fight and who would take the battlefield with his troops, rather than observing the battle from some remote position, as most generals would have done. . . . Fighters, and in particular Afghans, tend to like this type of military leader, who shares with them at least some of the dangers of a battlefield. Many of his fighters even tattooed his name on their chest and forearms in an expression of identification with him." Giustozzi, *Empires of Mud*, 108.

36. *Frontline*, "Interview. US Special Forces."

37. "Legislature Honors Kansas Warrior," *Topeka Capital-Journal*, April 12, 2002.

38. Stewart, *Special Forces in Afghanistan*, 196.

39. This story was conveyed to me by Bart Decker during our interview in Hurlburt Field, Florida.

40. Author interview with Captain Mark Nutsch, Boston, November 2011.

41. Romesh Ratnesar, "The Afghan Way of War," *Time*, November 11, 2001.

42. In our interviews, Dostum grumbled that Atta had broken their agreement and entered Mazar-e-Sharif first in an attempt to claim it for himself.

43. Interview with Captain Mark Nutsch, Boston, November 2011.

44. The video of this scene, with a smiling crowd surrounding Dostum as he enters the mosque and prays, can be found at youtube.com under Dostum. Found at http://www.youtube.com/dostum2008.

45. Tony Karon, "Rebels: Mazar-i-Sharif Is Ours," *Time*, November 9, 2001.

46. Raymond Whitaker, "Fall of Strategic City Would Alter Course of Conflict War on Terrorism," *Independent* (UK), November 10, 2001.

47. Patrick Winn, "A Small Cadre of Women Prove their Mettle in Combat," *Air Force Times*, January 13, 2008.

48. Babak Dehghanpisheh, John Barry, and Roy Gutman, "The Afghan Convoy of Death," *Newsweek*, August 26, 2002.

49. "CNN Presents: 'House of War. The Uprising in Mazar e Sharif,'" *CNN*, August 3, 2002, http://transcripts.cnn.com/TRANSCRIPTS/0208/03/cp.00.html.

50. Author interview with Commander Lal, Mazar-e-Sharif, August 2003.

51. Pelton, "The Legend of Heavy D," 2.

52. Dehghanpisheh, et al., "Afghan Convoy of Death."

53. Communication from Robert Young Pelton to the author, March 2013.

54. Rashid, *Taliban*, 56.

55. Peter Phillips, "Corporate Media Ignores Hypocrisy on War Crimes," *Project Censored,* May 2, 2010, www.projectcensored.org/top-stories/articles/corporate-media-ignores-us-hypocrisy-on-war-crimes. For a more detailed comparison of the "Dostum the tank killer" stories, see Brian Glyn Williams, "Writing the Dostum name: Field Research with an Uzbek Warlord in Afghan Turkistan," *Central Eurasian Studies Review* 6, no. 1/2 (Fall 2007) Under "Publications" at www.brianglynwilliams.com.

56. This story was told to me by Faizullah Zaki when I later met him again in Shiberghan in 2005.

CHAPTER 19: INTERVIEW WITH A WARLORD

1. The photographs and the rather ad hoc graves have since been replaced by more permanent stone graves.

2. Carrier, "Over There."

3. Bushell, "Uzbek Warlord Remains Enigma." The article states: "This contrasts with screams from his compound that can be heard more than 300 yards away. One of Gen. Dostum's soldiers explains: 'Mohammed was caught doing something he shouldn't have, and now they are skinning him alive.'"

4. In 2005, I was similarly given the green *chapan* belonging to Abdul Kadir Dostum that had been given to him by his older brother Mohammad Omar at the same time he gave Dostum his *chapan*. The one I was given had blood and blackened burn holes in it, which came from an al-Qaeda suicide bombing that almost killed Dostum and Abdul Kadir in 2004.

EPILOGUE

1. A website devoted to Bill Bennett can be found here: www.fallenheroesmemorial.com/oif/profiles/bennettwilliamm.html.

2. For riveting footage of the suicide attack, see "Afghan Warlord Rashid Dostum Narrowly Escaped a Suicide Attack," *Internet Archive*, http://archive.org/details/AfghanWarlordRashidDostumNarrowlyEscapedASuicideAttack.

3. "Warlord Under Seige after Kidnap and Torture of Former Ally," *Independent*, March 11, 2008.

4. Brian Glyn Willliams, "Post Mortem Analysis of Afghanistan's Second Most Powerful Uzbek Warlord, Ahmed Khan 'Samangani,'" *Terrorism Monitor*, August 6, 2012.

INDEX

ML a/13